ROSWELL

Your Travel Guide to the UFO Capital of the World!

Lynn Michelsohn

On ne sait jamais . . .
One never knows . . .
— Antoine de Saint-Exupéry

Cleanan Press, Inc.
Roswell, New Mexico

**Roswell,
Your Travel Guide to the UFO Capital of the World!**
by Lynn Michelsohn

Copyright © 2008 by Lynn Michelsohn

Published by Cleanan Press, Inc. 200 West First Street, Roswell, NM 88203 USA

ISBN (10) 0-9771614-7-1
ISBN (13) 978-0-9771614-7-8

First Edition
1.0

Illustrations by Moses Michelsohn.
Cover photograph, "Roswell Street Lamp," by Aaron Michelsohn.
"UFO Breakdown" by J. Shannon Webster, copyright © 1996, used with permission.

REQUEST TO TRAVELERS
Help us make this guidebook the Best in the Universe! Please mail or email your corrections, additions, suggestions, and comments to the addresses for Roswell at

www.cleananpress.com

where you will also find travel updates and more information about
Roswell, The UFO Capital of the World!

Welcome to Roswell!

Most tourists come here because of the UFOs. They didn't come at all before 1997, the 50th Anniversary of the famous UFO Crash, so we're still learning how to be a tourist destination. In the process, we're discovering that we have some pretty interesting sights (or sites) in addition to our alien connection: sites related to ancient religions of the Americas, the taming of the Wild West, and the birth of modern rocketry, just to name a few. While our role hasn't usually been as spectacular in these other activities as it was in the 1947 UFO Crash, learning something about our heritage through "little" events helps us deepen our understanding of our world. Besides, it's fun!

Lynn Michelsohn
2008

Acknowledgments

Much of the information in this guidebook comes from publications listed in Appendix A, especially from the many interesting books and articles by Elvis Fleming and the Historical Society for Southeast New Mexico, the fascinating photo compilations of Linda Stockley Weiler, and the detailed history of NMMI by William Gibbs and Eugene Jackman. Several out-of-print books available in the Roswell Public Library also provided information.

Roswell City Historian Elvis Fleming helped track down information and tirelessly corrected errors in many parts of the manuscript. When sources conflicted, his opinion usually prevailed. English teacher and local historian Valarie Grant led a delightful tour of South Park Cemetery. Novelist Alice Duncan shared her mother's memories of early Roswell and assisted greatly in many ways with the manuscript. Court interpreter Rachel Garcia served as Spanish language consultant and also provided information about eerie events. Jalene Clausen, Grant Reigelman, and Abdullah Feroze helped sample local cuisine.

Many others have kindly provided information: Colonel Jerry Klopfer, Leslie Ellison, Adam Camp, and Jesse Eckel about NMMI; Sergeants Navarette and Gonzales about the National Guard; Elaine Mayfield, Renee Roach, Ivan Hall and Doris Calloway about City government, activities, and facilities; Michael Trujillo, Danielle Irvin, and Alice Terrell about specific businesses; Sherry Bixler about wildlife; Kandy Irvin and Maribel Sigala about nightlife; Walter Haut about events of 1947; Travis Dunlap about the NM DOT; John LeMay (at www.mystrangenewmexico.com) about alien ghosts; Dusty Huckabee about historical figures and landmarks; Judy Armstrong and Donna Oracion about ENMU-R; Richard Lucero about the Roswell Police Department; John and Mary Capps about events and celebrities; Bobby Villegas about Hispanic Roswell; and Julie Shuster about the UFO Museum. Numerous other Roswell folks have added bits and pieces to the story.

Table of Contents

Introduction

Chapter I. Roswell

What is the Real Roswell?

— A town of 50,000 (we keep claiming in spite of what the Census Bureau says).

— Anglos (meaning Caucasians) with Southern manners, conservative ideas, and a hint of Western individualism.

— Hispanics who are mostly just a few generations removed from Mexico, unlike those northern New Mexicans whose ancestors arrived from Spain in the 1600s.

— A scattering of African-Americans, Asians, and maybe an occasional Navajo or Mescalero Apache, but more likely a one-sixteenth Cherokee who drifted west from Oklahoma.

— A sprinkling of "arty" types, some UFO nuts, an occasional real cowboy, and a good chunk of Midwestern retirees who enjoy the low cost of living while playing golf all winter.

— An economy based on ranching and farming, oil and gas, and now tourism; plus enough medical, educational, professional, and business people to keep the place going, as the closest real city is two hundred miles in any direction.

In some ways Roswell hasn't changed much since Sheriff Pat Garrett kept— or didn't keep—the peace. Someone said, "They call it the Land of Mañana, but that really overstates the pace of life here." You won't find much excitement in Roswell, except of course when it rains and there's water in the rivers—although it's usually deeper in the streets—or when all those UFO folks arrive every year in early July for the Festival.

Anyway, Roswell is a good place to raise a family: wholesome and safe, except for the occasional tornado or drive-by shooting. Roswell calls itself "the Pearl of the Pecos" and a pretty smart fellow named Will Rogers once called it "the prettiest little town in the West."

Roswell isn't on the way to anywhere, except maybe Carlsbad Caverns if you're driving south from the Mother Road—what's left of Route 66—or if you're headed west from Texas to the skiing or horse racing in Ruidoso. You really have to want to be here to get here!

Roswell is a small (some say "backward") town in the middle of nowhere. It isn't a resort destination. If you can accept Roswell for what it is, you will be pleased with your stay, and maybe even learn a few things. Enjoy this outpost in the Land of Enchantment: seek out Roswell's little pleasures, track down its footnotes to history, discover its quirks—like whatever happened here in July 1947.

The Setting

Geology and Geography

Rocks underlying Southeastern New Mexico are mostly sedimentary: limestone, sandstone, and shale laid down in a shallow sea that covered this part of the state during the Permian Period ending 245 million years ago, just before dinosaurs ruled the Jurassic Period. The layers of rock here are not perfectly horizontal however, but gradually slope upward forming the Sacramento Mountains starting 50 miles (80 km) or so west of Roswell.

Limestone layers in the underlying rocks contain large amounts of gypsum that dissolves out to turn the ground water alkali and create fissures and caverns beneath the surface. Rain falling on the eastern slopes of the Sacramento Mountains seeps into these Swiss-cheese-like limestone layers—that are often sandwiched between less porous layers of sandstone and shale—and gradually seeps down the slope until it reaches the Roswell area. In 1890 the discovery that wells drilled down about 250 feet (75 m) hit this water source led to an agricultural boom around Roswell.

Those less porous layers of Permian sandstone and shale also create another, and even more important, phenomenon in Southeastern New Mexico. Oil rising from lower layers of rock gets trapped when it hits the less porous layers, thus forming underground pools of petroleum waiting to be tapped by oil wells: the Permian Basin Oilfield—the "Oil Patch."

During more recent times—geologically speaking—molten lava pushed up through the sedimentary layers along fault lines, or cracks in the rock, to create features such as the 11,973' (3,650 m) dormant volcano Sierra Blanca Peak, the 10,083' (3,073 m) laccolith Capitan Mountain, and the lava flow that blankets the surface in the Valley of Fires 90 miles (145 km) west of Roswell.

The Pecos ("PAY-cuss") River just east of Roswell has cut down through the sedimentary rock layers to create the Pecos Valley. The Pecos River and its tributaries, including the Hondo River, have also partially filled this valley with sand and gravel carried down from eroding hills and mountains farther upstream.

Therefore, Roswell sits in the Pecos Valley on a sand and gravel flood plain that rests on underlying layers of sedimentary rock, mainly limestone. To the west rise the volcanic peaks. To the east rise layers of sedimentary rock not eroded away by the Pecos River—the Llano Estacado ("YAH-no es-tah-CAH-doh," which means "staked plains," and nobody knows what that means), also called the High Plains, where you can "look farther and see less" than any other spot on earth. The Pecos Valley surrounding Roswell appears to be low, flat country, but at 3,600' (1,100 m) we are still higher than many mountain tops elsewhere in the United States.

Today the Pecos River flows three miles east of town while its main tributary, the Hondo (meaning "deep") River, flows—when it flows—through the middle of town, as does a smaller tributary, the North Spring River. Other smaller tributaries, including the Berrendo River just north of town and the South Spring River just south of town, flow only during heavy rains. Water from artesian springs once filled these small streams but heavy irrigation from wells tapping the aquifer has dried them up. Although the Hondo River originates in the Sacramento Mountains where it is fed regularly by rainfall and snowmelt, so much water is diverted for irrigation along the way that it that it rarely flows either. The Pecos River does flow year round. It starts as a sparkling, splashing trout stream in the mountains up near Santa Fe but with much of its water also diverted for irrigation, it lazes along through red mud bars here in the clay, limestone, and gypsum of the Permian Basin.

Climate

A character in a Zane Gray western novel once described this part of New Mexico as "terrible in summer and harder in winter." Summers are HOT—but it's a dry heat. Low humidity and thin air at high altitude mean that temperatures drop rapidly after sundown, often into the 70s (20s C) at night even after the most scorching summer day. Winters are usually mild, with some days rising into the 70s (20s C) even in December and January, although freezing temperatures are common at night, and several brief snowfalls—or an occasional blizzard—can be expected.

The 10-12 inches (about 30 cm) of rain we get each year here on the northern edge of the Chihuahuan Desert comes mostly during evening thunderstorms in the "monsoon" season of July and August. It is not unusual for three months to elapse between showers.

Plants

High gypsum and salt content in the soil of Southeastern New Mexico, coupled with low rainfall, discourages growth of all but the most hardy vegetation. In the 1860s Trailblazer Charles Goodnight called the Pecos Valley the most desolate country he had ever explored, although the river abounded in fish and the banks in rattlesnakes—and quicksand.

Clumps of gramma grass cover the plains so this doesn't look much like a desert, but if an area is green, it is irrigated. We don't have sagebrush—it's too hot and dry here. Prickly pear cactus with yellow flowers and purplish fruit, cholla ("CHOY-yah") cactus with purplish flowers and yellow fruit, agave ("a-GAH-vay")—also called Century Plant—and sotol ("SO-tall") are common. Scrubby bushes dotting the plains are mainly mesquite and creosote—an interesting desert plant that poisons off competitors. Wildflowers blanket fields briefly when there's a wet spring. Small trees and bushes grow along stream banks but usually if you see a tree it's because someone planted it and waters it regularly. Two introduced species have become pests: tamarisk or salt cedar along water, and tumbleweed or Russian thistle in fields.

In town, green lawns with abundant flowers, especially roses, and large trees—all heavily watered—give Roswell a Midwestern look.

Animals

Most animals in Southeastern New Mexico are adapted to its hot, dry summers and cold, dry winters.

Although insects are plentiful, none are particularly notable—at least to us non-entomologists. Hundreds of species of dragonflies and damselflies do inhabit wet areas and, amazingly, mosquitoes occasionally become a nuisance after rainy spells. Scorpions and tarantulas make occasional appearances.

Waters are warm so most people fish for bass or catfish, although Bottomless Lakes are stocked with trout during the winter. Rattlesnakes and horned toads are popularly known but numerous other small reptiles and even some amphibians make their homes here.

A good selection of central and western birds lives here year round, winters here, or migrates through. Sparrows, doves, and grackles are common in town. Cranes, geese, and ducks winter here, feeding in fields, resting on ponds, and flying in between. Hummingbirds, bluebirds, kites, orioles, swallows, terns, hawks, and many others nest here. Vultures and warblers migrate through. Roadrunners and Burrowing Owls are always fun to spot, usually in open areas.

Jackrabbits and ground squirrels are also plentiful in open areas and pronghorn "antelope" (not really an antelope but the only member of an ungulate family unique to North America) aren't difficult to find. A few deer and foxes hide in the brush and road-killed skunks are common. Badgers, raccoons, porcupines, coyotes, bats, and maybe bobcats or mountain lions live here but are rarely seen. Ancestors of the tree squirrels living in town were supposedly imported from "back east" by Pecos Valley developer J.J. Hagerman.

Roswell History

Pre-History

Ten to twenty thousand years ago ancient peoples including Sandia ("san-DEE-ah") Man, Clovis Man, and Folsom Man—all named after the New Mexico locations where their artifacts were first discovered—roamed the plains of eastern New Mexico hunting ice-age mammals.

By 100 AD their semi-nomadic descendents were cultivating crops of corn, then beans, squash, and cotton: a skill that spread north from central Mexico along with pottery making, weaving, and religious beliefs.

By 900 AD, the Jornada Mogollon ("hor-NA-da moggy-YAWN") people lived in small villages of pit houses and adobe structures throughout Southeastern New Mexico. In addition to small-scale farming, the Mogollon depended on the abundant bison in the fertile Pecos Valley for food and clothing materials. Beginning in the 1400s nomadic bands of Apaches and Navajos, then Comanches, moving into the Southwest from the Northern Plains replaced the Mogollon.

The Rule of Spain and Mexico

Spaniards Alvar Nunez Cabeza de Vaca in 1536, Francisco Coronado in 1540, and Antonio de Espejo in 1583 led the first European explorers into the Pecos Valley. All were just passing through. In 1590 Gaspar Castano de Sosa led an unauthorized group of 170 potential settlers up the Pecos River from Mexico to near Taos in Northern New Mexico, but he was promptly arrested for his efforts. (Easterners please note: all of this took place long before anyone ever heard of Jamestown or Plymouth Rock.)

The Roswell area was pretty much ignored by Europeans and Native Americans, other than roving bands of Apaches and Comanches, for the rest of Spain's rule of our region (until 1821) and throughout Mexican sovereignty (1821-1848).

Early Settlers in the American Era

The Roswell area and most of New Mexico became an American Territory in 1850 as a result of the 1848 Mexican War.

During the 1850s groups of Mexican farmers began to migrate north into this new area of the United States looking for better economic opportunities—sound familiar?

About 1865 a group of Hispanics already living in Northern New Mexico moved south and established a settlement 15 miles (24 km) west of today's Roswell on the Hondo River, a tributary of the Pecos River. They named their village—among other things—Plaza de Missouri, not because they were Missourians but because some had worked as freighters on the Santa Fe Trail, which originated in Missouri, and they thought this name would give their town "class."

Another group moving north from Mexico settled 15 miles (24 km) down the Hondo River at the site of the present-day Roswell neighborhood of Chihuahuita ("chee-hwah-HWEE-tah"). They evidently had fewer aspirations than their upstream neighbors and simply called their settlement Rio Hondo.

A third group of Hispanics settled a few miles to the northeast of Rio Hondo on another small tributary of the Pecos, and similarly called their settlement and river, El Berrendo ("beh-REN-doh"), which means "the mottled one," referring to the abundant herds of pronghorn in the area.

Plaza de Missouri initially flourished by raising crops to supply Fort Stanton to the west, but as upstream farmers and ranchers diverted more and more water from the Hondo River for irrigation, their agriculture suffered. Settlers had abandoned the town by 1872.

El Berrendo also flourished until raids by renegade cowboys during the Lincoln County War routed out all of the settlers in 1878.

Rio Hondo managed to persist, but underwent substantial changes.

Cattlemen and Cowboys

After the Civil War, Manifest Destiny and the Homestead Act brought Americans westward in droves, where they rapidly overwhelmed Hispanic culture in Southeastern New Mexico.

In 1866 Charles Goodnight and Oliver Loving brought their herd of Texas longhorns westward to the Pecos River at a point 200 miles (320 km) south of Roswell. From there they drove their cattle up the Pecos River through the Roswell area to Fort Sumner, 85 miles (135 km) to the north, and sold most of the herd to the United States Army to feed the (eventually) 9,000 Navajos and Apaches held in captivity at nearby Bosque Redondo ("BOS-kay reh-DON-doh"). Oliver Loving continued on northward another 450 miles (725 km) to Denver with the rest of the herd. Their Goodnight-Loving Trail became the standard route for cattle drives from southern Texas and New Mexico to markets farther north in New Mexico and in Colorado and Wyoming.

The following year, 1867, Texas cattleman John Chisum began driving his own cattle up the Goodnight-Loving Trail, acquiring land along the way in Southeastern New Mexico. He also drove herds from the Roswell area up the Hondo River to Fort Stanton, or on westward through the Organ Mountain Gap and across the plains of southern New Mexico to Arizona. This route became known as the Chisum Trail—not to be confused with the "Come a ti-yi-yippy-yippy-yay"

Chisholm Trail in Texas.

The Anglo town of Roswell got its start as a camping spot on the Goodnight-Loving Trail about that same time. Abundant water and grass where the Hondo River flowed into the Pecos River satisfied the herds. An adobe building appeared that housed a trading post and other activities designed to satisfy the hard-living cowpunchers. Professional gambler Van Smith purchased this building from the original owner in 1869, added additional structures, and called the settlement "Roswell" after his father, Roswell Smith, establishing a Post Office here in 1873.

Anglo settlers, most with ties to the Old South, rapidly came to dominate Southeastern New Mexico, making it distinctly different from the rest of the Hispanic-dominated Territory and giving rise to its nickname, "Little Texas." In 1875 Chisum moved his headquarters to South Spring River Ranch, four miles (6 km) southeast of "downtown" Roswell. First John Chisum, then Captain Joseph Lea ("LEE"), then other settlers, established vast cattle empires throughout the area. Cattle ranching dominated Southeastern New Mexico from 1870 through 1900. The Lincoln County War from about 1878 to about 1881, fought between two rival factions each trying to establish economic dominance, took its toll here but made Billy the Kid and our Sheriff Pat Garrett famous.

Artesian Water, Agriculture, and the County Seat

After the discovery of artesian water in Roswell in 1890, agriculture grew in importance and Roswell's population boomed. Now that abundant water was available for irrigation, cotton and alfalfa farming began to develop, along with vast apple orchards. When the railroad arrived in 1894 it brought even more new settlers, as well as "lungers"—TB patients looking for a therapeutic climate. The railroad also allowed export of agricultural and ranching products. About this time cattle ranching declined here because of drought, overproduction, and the end of the open range, but sheep ranching and the wool industry grew.

As the county seat of newly formed Chaves County—carved out of Lincoln County in 1889—Roswell attracted lawyers as well as bankers and merchants. Settlers also moved here because of its educational opportunities: good public schools, then the New Mexico Military Institute and much later, Eastern New Mexico University—Roswell. Roswell rapidly became the agricultural, commercial, political, and cultural center of Southeastern New Mexico.

The Oil Patch

Wildcat oil drilling moved west from Texas into New Mexico in the 1920s. Early wells produced signs of oil, but not until 1924 did wildcatters bring in their first gusher near Artesia, 40 miles (65 km) south of Roswell. Over the next few years it became clear that eastern New Mexico was an important part of the Oil Patch—the Permian Basin Oilfield that underlies eastern New Mexico and western Texas. Roswell developed as a business center for oil field exploration and production companies, and as a place for roughnecks and roustabouts, like cattle punchers before them, to spend their hard-earned money.

The Military

The Great Depression interrupted steady growth in Roswell during the 1930s as it did everywhere else, but the economic boom resumed with World War

II, helped by the establishment of Roswell Army Air Field just south of town in 1941. The RAAF trained pilots and bombardiers throughout World War II. After the Air Force became independent from the Army in 1947, the RAAF became Walker Air Force Base, an important Strategic Air Command location.

From Struggling Little Town to the Hub of Southeastern New Mexico

Roswell lost one-third of its population when Walker Air Force Base closed in 1967. Economic recovery was slow, but an initiative to promote Roswell's warm climate and low cost of living to retirees aided growth. The facilities of the former Air Force base were developed as the Roswell Industrial Air Center, attracting light manufacturing and businesses related to air transportation.

Fruit orchards had declined in the 1930s after a severe freeze but agriculture remained strong. Important crops in Roswell today include cotton, alfalfa, chile, and in recent years, pecans. Dairy farming has grown hugely over the last 20 years.

Tourism, based primarily on Roswell's status as the world's premier UFO site, increased steadily after publicity surrounding the 1997 Fiftieth Anniversary celebration of the Roswell UFO Crash. Talk of an alien-themed amusement park and resort complex promises even greater growth.

Roswell moves into the Twenty-First Century promoting itself as the Hub of Southeastern New Mexico. Its historical enterprises of ranching and farming, oil and gas, business and commerce, education, and medical care continue strong today, while tourism is rapidly becoming a major economic force.

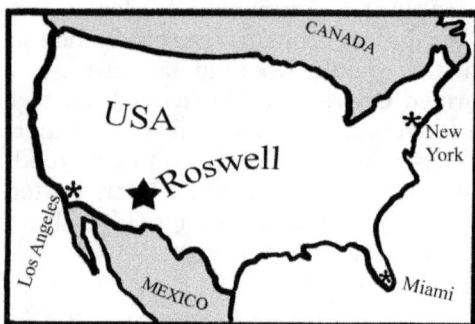

Getting to Roswell
(If you don't have your own UFO)

Roswell is more or less "Two Hundred Miles (320 km) from Anywhere," that is, from Albuquerque, Santa Fe, Las Cruces, El Paso, Lubbock, Midland, Odessa, and Amarillo.

By Air

Three daily one-and-one-half-hour flights on American Eagle Airlines jets connect us with Dallas-Ft. Worth. Flights are expensive, occasionally canceled, and often bumpy in summer heat, but are certainly the quickest and easiest way to get to Roswell from the east. Roswell lost its air connection to Albuquerque at the end of 2007—but is currently looking for a carrier to resume flights. Airport: 1 Jerry Smith Circle. 347-5703.

By Train
You can't get here by train unless you're adept at hopping a freight. The closest Amtrak stations are in Albuquerque 200 miles (320 km) to the northwest and in El Paso 200 miles (320 km) to the south.

By Bus
You can get here by bus, but it's painful. One or two buses a day arrive from Albuquerque (4 hours), Amarillo (5 hours), or El Paso (5 hours). Bus Station: 1100 North Virginia Avenue. 623-0947. www.greyhound.com

By Car
Car travel is easy, just long. Gas up, bring water and snacks, and "use the facilities" before you leave as there are few gas stations, convenience stores, or restrooms along the way. Roads are good four-lanes or fairly good two-lanes from all directions, with little traffic. Frequent gaps in cell phone service occur but friendly folks will stop to help if you have car trouble.

Note: Tourists driving down to Roswell from I-40 like to stop at the Mesa Rest Area 60 miles (100 km) north of Roswell to have their pictures taken in front of the "Watch For Rattlesnakes" sign. While you're there, check out *El Jefe*. You can't miss him. As his name implies, he's the biggest thing around.

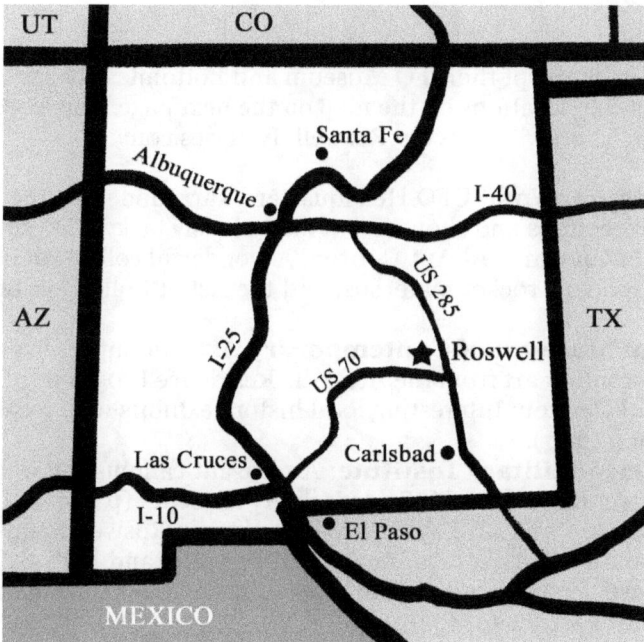

New Mexico

Getting around Roswell

Finding your way around Roswell is easy, as most streets conform to a square N-S-E-W grid. The main street is called Main Street and runs North-South. The major East-West Street is 2nd Street. Free city maps are available at the Visitor's Center in the Civic Center at 912 North Main Street, at the Chamber of Commerce at 131 West 2nd Street, and in the telephone directory.

Pecos Trails Transit System buses run frequently along Main Street during the day and evening from the Mall at the north end of town to the Airport Terminal at its south end, with numerous stops along the way. Feeder buses also run east and west from Main Street, but that gets more complicated. Schedules and route information are available at the Pecos Trails bus station, 505 North Main Street, 624-6766, www.roswell-nm.gov. Buses run M-F 6-10, Sat 7-10, Sun 10:30-6:30, holidays variable.

Hertz (347-2211) and Avis (347-2500) car rental agencies operate from the airport. Enterprise (622-4866) is located in town. Rental cars are also available from the Ford (623-3673) and Toyota (637-3933) dealerships.

There are sometimes taxis in Roswell that can be summoned by telephone, but service is spotty: Sunshine Cab Company, 910-3400; T-N-T Taxi, 627-4777.

Some, but not many, motels offer shuttle service to and from the airport.

Roswell's flat landscape makes for easy biking but you will have to bring your own bicycle as rentals are not available.

Highlights of Roswell

All are FREE except the UFO Museum and Bottomless Lakes State Park.
Numbers refer to locations on the map on the next page. For more information
see www.RoswellMysteries.com

1) UFO Museum: World UFO Headquarters, surrounded by the **UFO District** with alien street lamps and shops full of marvelously tacky UFO souvenirs (p 58).
2) Roswell Museum and Art Center: A wonderful collection of Southwestern Art, Robert Goddard rocket materials, and the Aston Collection of Western Artifacts (p 35).
3) Anderson Museum of Contemporary Art: An impressive and fun collection of contemporary art from the Artist-in-Residence Program (p 118).
4) Historical Center: Interesting local history exhibits with local books for sale in the Gift Shop (p 77).
5) New Mexico Military Institute: A pleasant campus for walking, with distinctive architecture and the McBride Military Museum (p 80).
6) Spring River Park and Zoo: The best place in Roswell to take kids! A small collection of native and exotic animals, a playground and kid's fishing pond, and antique carousel and miniature train rides for a small fee during the summer and on fall and spring weekends (p 99).
Spring River Recreation Trail: Five miles (8 km) of paved pathway for hiking and biking follow the Spring River through the heart of Roswell (p 92).

Bitter Lake National Wildlife Refuge: Nature trails, an eight-mile (13 km) nature drive, and excellent year-round birding with thousands of Snow Geese and Sandhill Cranes from November to March (p 121).

Bottomless Lakes State Park: Water-filled sinkholes with camping, hiking, and fishing—plus swimming, paddleboats, and nature programs during the summer (p 129).

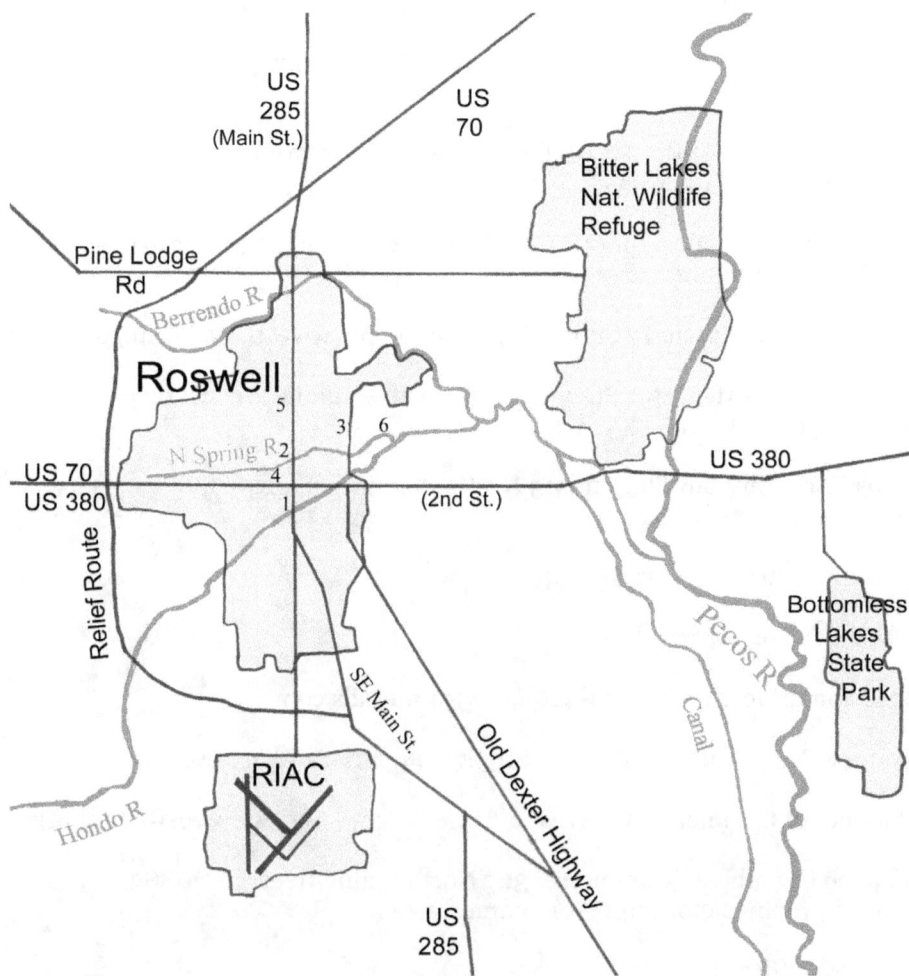

The Roswell Area

Useful Services

Emergency Services (Police, Fire, Ambulance): 911

Roswell City Police Department: 128 West 2nd Street, 624-6770, www.roswellnmpolice.com

Chaves County Sheriff's Department: 1 St. Mary's Place, 624-6500, www.co.chaves.nm.us

Eastern New Mexico Medical Center: 405 West Country Club Road, 622-8170, www.enmmc.com

Roswell Regional Hospital: 117 East 19th Street, 627-7000, www.roswellregional.com

Counseling Associates, Inc. Mental Health Center (and 24-hour Crisis Line): 500 North Main Street, 623-1480

Airport Terminal: 1 Jerry Smith Circle, 347-5703, www.roswell-nm.gov

Greyhound/TNM&O Bus Station: 1100 North Virginia Avenue, 623-0471, www.greyhound.com

Pecos Trails City Bus Station: 515 North Main Street, 624-6766, www.roswell-nm.gov

Sunshine Cab Company: 910-3400

T-N-T Taxi: 627-4777

Road conditions: 1-800-432-4269, www.nmroads.com

Visitor's Center: 912 North Main Street, 624-7704, www.roswellcc.com

Chamber of Commerce: 131 West 2nd Street, 623-5695, www.roswellnm.org

Hispano Chamber of Commerce: 327 North Main Street, 624-0889, www.roswellhispanochamberofcommerce.com

U.S. Post Office
    Main Office: 415 North Pennsylvania Avenue, 623-9868
    Walker Branch: 5904 South Main Street, 347-2262

Roswell Public Library: 301 North Pennsylvania Avenue, 622-7101, www.roswellpubliclibrary.org

Restaurants open 24 hours a day
>Denny's: 2200 North Main Street, 622-9960
>IHOP: 2304 North Main Street, 625-6767

Telephone Area Code: 575 (Santa Fe, Albuquerque, and northwest New Mexico are 505)

Roswell Zip Codes: 88201 (2nd Street and north)
>88202 (Post Office boxes)
>88203 (south of 2nd Street)

Accommodations

Roswell has the usual inexpensive and middle-range national motel chains. There are also several independent motels, bed and breakfast inns, RV parks, and campgrounds. Rooms are usually available without advanced reservations, except during special events like the UFO Festival, Eastern New Mexico State Fair, NMMI special weekends, and sports tournaments. Visitors usually rate motels affiliated with national chains more highly than independent motels in Roswell, but you may want to check out some recent reviews at travel websites such as www.travel.yahoo.com or www.tripadvisor.com.

Motel Chains (see national chains' websites)
>Best Western El Rancho Palacio Motel, 2205 North Main Street,
>>622-2721
>
>Best Western Sally Port Inn and Suites, 2000 North Main Street,
>>622-6430
>
>Budget Inn, 2101 North Main Street, 623-6050
>Comfort Inn, 3595 North Main Street, 623-4567
>Day's Inn, 1310 North Main Street, 623-5021
>Fairfield Inn and Suites, 1201 North Main Street, 624-1300
>Hampton Inn and Suites, 3607 North Main Street, 623-5151
>Holiday Inn Express, 2300 North Main Street, 627-9900
>La Quinta Inn, 200 East 19th Street, 622-8000
>Motel 6, 3307 North Main Street, 625-6666
>National 9 Inn, 2001 North Main Street, 622-0110
>Ramada Inn, 2803 West 2nd Street, 623-9440
>Super 8 Motel, 3575 North Main Street, 622-8886

Independent Motels
>Belmont Motel, 2100 West 2nd Street, 623-5622
>Crane Motel, 1212 West 2nd Street, 623-1293
>Frontier Motel, 3010 North Main Street, 622-1400
>Leisure Inn, 2700 West 2nd Street, 622-2575
>Mayo Lodge, 1716 West 2nd Street, 622-0210
>Western Inn, 2331 North Main Street, 623-9425

Other Accommodations
> Country Club Bed & Breakfast, 400 East Country Club Road,
>   624-1794
> Cozy Cowboy Cottage Rentals, 624-3258, www.cozycowboy.com

RV Parks
> Red Barn RV Park, 2806 East 2nd Street, 623-4897
> Town and Country RV Park, 331 West Brasher Road, 624-1833,
>   www.townandcountryrvpark.com
> Thunderbird Mobile Home Park, 907 North Atkinson Avenue, 622-6771
> Trailer Village Campgrounds, 1706 East 2nd Street, 623-6040

Camping
> Bottomless Lakes State Park, 624-6058

Dining

"No shoes, No shirt, No service" is about as strict as the dress code gets in Roswell. Some people wear dressy casual to upscale restaurants in the evening—you might even see a sport coat or a suit—but you will feel comfortable in casual clothing, excluding bathing suits, anywhere any time.

Although some restaurants are pricier than others, the bill generally depends more on what you order—steak versus chicken versus a bean burrito—than on where you eat. Reservations are rarely needed, except at pricier places for lunch or dinner on Fridays or Saturdays, during special events, or for large groups. A few restaurants have liquor licenses and bars. More have beer and wine licenses. Bringing your own alcohol is frowned upon. Smoking is not permitted in restaurants, bars, or any other public building in New Mexico.

There are basically four types of restaurants in Roswell. "Gourmet" is not one of them:

1)   National chains: These are the same everywhere, except for the UFO-shaped McDonald's downtown. Most are in the Mall area at the north end of town, with some fast-food places on South Main Street near Hobbs Street. What's missing? Dunkin' Donuts and Krispy Kreme!

3)   Nicer, pricier restaurants: Tourists prefer these, but don't expect anything fancy. Locals enjoy them on special occasions. All serve liquor.
>   Tia Juana's Mexican Grill and Cantina, p 115
>   Pasta Café, p 35
>   Cattle Baron Steak and Seafood Restaurant, p35
>   Pepper's Grill and Bar, p 41

4)   Where the "locals" eat: These restaurants have good food and "local color." Some serve liquor. Many have beer and wine. Most are Mexican restaurants serving a combination of Mexican and New Mexican food, but also serve basic American food like burgers and fries.

Downtown area:

Farley's Fun, Food, and Pub (American), p 35

Los Amigos (Mexican), p 35

Martin's Capitol Café (Mexican), p 49

Billy Ray's Restaurant and Lounge (American), p 51

La Posta (Mexican), p 67

El Toro Bravo (Mexican), p 60

Two other interesting places downtown are:

Pecos Flavors Winery (New Mexico wines, beers, snacks), p 50

Not of This World (Espresso bar and Internet Café), p 52

Some others a little farther out:

North:

J.D.'s Patio and Grille, p 115

Mi Cabana (Mexican, 2nd location), p 115

Hunan (Chinese), p 115

China King Super Buffet (Chinese), p 115

Hungry American (BBQ), p 115

Price's Truck Stop Café (American), p 116

East:

Margarita's (Chinese and Mexican), p 123

Cowboy Café (American), p 123

South:

Portofino Italian Restaurant (Italian), p 132

Mi Cabana (Mexican), p 127

Popo's Mexican Restaurant (Mexican), p 128

La Hacienda Mexican Restaurant (Mexican), p 137

Rosario's Mexican Restaurant (Mexican) p 131

Cattleman's Steak House (steak), p 134

Ooy's Express (Thai), p 137

West:

Kwan Den Chinese Restaurant (Chinese), p 140

Red Onion Restaurant (Mexican), p 141

Chew's West Restaurant (Chinese), p 141

RIAC:

Phillip's Kountry Kettle (Cajun and American), p 106

Anita's (Mexican), p 106

Burrito Express (burritos), p 106

Food is also available at limited times in the airport snack bar, currently the Frappucino Grill (p 112) and ENMU-R Campus Union (p 110).

5) Take-out or order-at-the-counter:

Downtown:

Fat's Burritos, p 38

What's Cooking, p 39

Tinnie Mercantile Store and Deli, p 76

Munchies Pizza and Subs, p 68

Burritos and More, p 68

North:
  Burrito Express, p 118
  Cecilio's, p 120
South:
  The Snazzy Pig BBQ Joint, p 13
Bakeries:
  Mama Tucker's Donut and Cake Shop, p 115
  El Toro Bravo Bakery, p 60
  Pan Dulce Bakery, p 105

Vegetarian Roswell

Although no strictly vegetarian restaurants have yet landed in Roswell, it's easy to find non-meat dishes at most places. Salad bars, or just Big Salads, are plentiful; the huge salad bar at the Cattle Baron is especially inviting. Chinese and Thai restaurants usually have meatless entrees while Mexican restaurants offer many cheese-based or bean-based dishes. Sometimes beans or chile (especially the green) may be flavored with meat or meat broth; ask if you want to know.

Vegans will have a harder time in Roswell, but are probably used to ferreting out edibles. There is always the fall-back selection—a bean burrito.

Activities and Entertainment

Movies Theaters: Galaxy 8 Cinema, 623-1010

Skateboarding: Cielo Grande, p 143

Bowling: Town and Country Entertainment Center, 623-7627

Gyms: Check the Yellow Pages under "Health Clubs"

Swimming:
  NMMI Godfrey Athletic Center, 624-8286
  Cahoon Park Pool (summer), 624-6764
  ENMU-R Pool (summer) 624-7000

Pool Tables:
  Farley's Fun, Food and Pub, 627-1100
  Town and Country Lounge, 623-7627
  Rookies Sports Bar, 622-6430

Video and Arcade Games:
  Peter Piper Pizza, 622-3474
  Cici's Pizza, 625-2424
  Rookie's Sports Bar, 622-6430

Paddle Boating: Bottomless Lakes State Park (summer), 624-6058

Fishing:
> Bottomless Lakes State Park, 624-6058
> Bitter Lake National Wildlife Refuge, 622-6755
> Pecos River, p 125
> Spring River Park and Zoo (under 12 only), 624-6760

Golf:
> NMMI Golf Course, 622-6033
> Spring River Golf Course, 622-9506

Tennis:
> Cahoon Park, 624-6720
> NMMI Godfrey Athletic Center, 624-8286

Walking:
> Cielo Grande (track), p 135
> NMMI Sports Complex (track), p 90
> Spring River Recreation Trail, p 92
> Hondo River Recreation Trail, p 101
> South Main Street Commuter Trail, p 135

Drag Racing: Area 51 Dragway (summer), p 113

High School and NMMI sporting events:
> RISD Athletic Department, 627-2514
> NMMI, 622-6250

Classical Music: Roswell Symphony Orchestra. Five concerts and three chamber concerts a year, 623-6882

Theater: Roswell Community Little Theater. Five productions a year, 622-1982

Other Events: Check the newspaper, Visitor's Center (624-7704), or Chamber of Commerce (623-5695)

Nightlife

Up Your Alley Bar, 3905 Southeast Main Street, 623-7627
> This place becomes packed, and sometimes rowdy, on weekends when DJs play a variety of music.

Billy Ray's Restaurant and Lounge, 118 East 3rd Street, 627-0997
> Live bands playing Tejano, country, or rock music on Fridays; Saturday night Karaoke; and occasional comedy nights attract regular patrons.

Boot Scooters, 4404 Southeast Main Street, 622-9618
Crowds gather here for Karaoke on Tuesdays, and on Tejano Night every Thursday to dance to live Tex-Mex bands. Other nights DJs play a mix of Tejano, country, and rock.

Bud's Lounge and Package Store, 3017 North Main Street, 623-0636
Folks come here Saturday nights for live country music or DJs playing a variety of music on Wednesday and Friday nights.

Farley's Fun, Food, and Pub, 1315 North Main Street, 627-1100
Pool tables attract patrons to this lively "pub," as do live bands on the patio Saturday evenings in the summer.

Not of This World, 209 North Main Street, 627-0077
On Friday nights this Espresso bar and Internet café becomes a "non-alcoholic Christian dance club" for teens and young adults.

Pepper's Grill and Bar, 600 North Main Street, 623-1700
Summer often finds folks dancing to live music on the patio on Friday nights or at the Party on the Patio with DJs, prizes, and drink specials on Wednesday evenings. Monday night football is popular in the fall.

Rookies Sports Bar, 2000 North Main Street, 622-6430
Occasional comedians, regular pool tournaments, karaoke on Thursday nights, and live bands on Saturday nights enliven this sports bar.

Roswell with Children

Few attractions in Roswell are designed specifically for children, but many can interest and delight properly guided youngsters—and most are FREE.
Key: P = Preschool ages, E = Elementary school ages, T = Teens.

Outdoor Activities:

Playground equipment (swings, jungle gyms, etc.): P, E, T. Cahoon Park (p 94), Poe Corn Park (p 105), Enchanted Lands Park (p 92), Melendez Park (p 128), plus a few other small parks scattered throughout Roswell.

Spring River Park and Zoo (p 99): P, E, T. The best place in Roswell to take kids! Fishing Pond (under 12, bring your own rod, tackle, and bait), picnic tables, grills, playground equipment, animals; ride the miniature train and the antique carousel in summer and on spring and fall weekends; feed the geese (bring bread or wild bird seed) in winter.

Cielo Grande (p 143): P, E, T. Play structure, soccer fields, walking track, small skateboard park, Unity Center with pool tables for teens.

NMMI (p 80): P, E, T. Spacious lawns, walkways, plazas, statues, interesting architecture, small rock garden, Godfrey Athletic Center (pool, gyms, tennis and racquetball), Golf Course, occasional parades, Military Museum of sorts, information for prospective students.

South Park Cemetery (p 134): P, E, T. Follow the walking tour brochure to find interesting gravestones.

Pioneer Plaza (p 46): P, E, T. Benches for sitting, Chisum statue—notice the Jinglebob earmarks (on the steer, not Chisum).

Spring River Recreation Trail (p 92): P, E, T. Hike a small portion or the whole trail (but then you need to get back to where you started).

Swimming: P, E, T. Cahoon Park (p 94), ENMU-R (p 110), and Bottomless Lakes (p 129) in summer; NMMI Godfrey Athletic Center (p 87) year-round.

Tennis: E, T. Free courts in Cahoon Park (p 95), and at NMMI (p 87) for a fee.

Golf: E, T. NMMI Golf Course (p 90), Spring River Golf Course (p 94). Student rates at both courses.

Drag Racing (p 113): E, T. Friday and Saturday evenings during the summer.

High School or NMMI Sports (p 21): E, T. Visitors are always welcome. Phone for schedules.

Bottomless Lakes State Park (p 129): P, E, T. Hiking, fishing (bring your own equipment); swimming, paddle boats, and nature programs in summer.

Bitter Lake National Wildlife Refuge (p 121): P, E, T. Birds (especially in winter), nature walking trail and driving tour, occasional Ranger-led tours, fishing and hunting in season (bring your own equipment).

Festivals, Parades: P, E, T. Most festivals have family-friendly events. The Visitor's Center has information.

Indoor Activities:

UFO Museum (pp 30, 58): E, T. UFO and Sci-Fi enthusiasts will enjoy it, the older ones more than the younger ones. All ages will love the Gift Shop!

Souvenir Shops (p 31): E, T. Always a hit! Give the kids their own money and let them comparison shop between stores—these are close enough to walk back and forth. The Spacewalk at Roswell Space Center (p 53) and Hangar 84 at Alien Zone II (p 60) are fun.

Civic Center Mural (p 38): E, T. A game of I Spy keeps children occupied while adults gather information at the Visitor's Center, and helps identify sights to look for in Roswell.

Roswell Museum and Art Center (p 35): E, T. Jimenez' fiberglass sculptures, other kid-friendly art, interesting Western artifacts, a Robert Goddard video, a spacesuit and a moon rock, Capitan Mountain in Peter Hurd's paintings, a small activities room (behind the Western exhibit), and another Gift Shop.

Goddard Planetarium (p 37): E, T. Occasional planetarium shows, especially during the UFO Festival.

Anderson Museum of Contemporary Art (p 118): E, T. Some wild and wacky art—the school of golf bag fish is a favorite.

Historical Center (p 77): E, T. Kids especially like the old-fashioned kitchen, and the varied exhibits upstairs (Little League World Champions, toys, Mariachi music).

Petroleum Building (p 67): E, T. The view from the 8th floor is most interesting if you have already visited some of the places you can spot from the balcony (WARNING: Hold on to your children!). If your kids need to burn off some excess energy, let them walk up. Before you go up, stop in **Munchies** to order the Pizza Special. It will be ready when you come down.

Roswell Public Library (p 72): P, E, T. A delightful children's area, story time and crafts sessions for the little ones on Wednesdays and Saturdays (call for times), free Internet.

Roswell Livestock Auction (p 117): P, E, T. Have you ever seen a live cattle auction? An exciting glimpse of the real West! Mondays beginning at 9:00 a.m.

Roswell Livestock and Farm Supply (p 123): P, E, T. Shop for a cowboy hat, then go across the street to the **Cowboy Café** for a green chile cheeseburger and a slice of pie.

Peter Piper Pizza (2611 North main Street): P, E, T. Video and arcade games are a hit with all ages—as is the pizza.

Bowling (p 131): E, T. Family friendly, especially during the daytime.

Movies (p 115): P, E, T. Eight screens, behind the Mall.

Not of This World (p 52): T. A gathering spot for teens in the evening, a "Christian dance club" on Friday nights.

Little Theater, Concerts: E, T. The Visitor's Center has schedules of upcoming events.

Dangers

Crimes such as robbery and assault are rare, but common sense says avoid lonely spots, especially at night or when alone. Lock your car and keep valuables out of plain sight. Carrying concealed firearms is allowed with a permit.

If it snows while you're in Roswell, as it does a couple of times a year, stay off the roads. It will probably melt by noon. Nobody knows how to drive in snow and ice here.

Rattlesnakes are a real danger outside of town, but are rarely seen in town. If bitten, remain calm (right!). Go immediately to the emergency room at Eastern NM Medical Center (405 West Country Club Road) or Roswell Regional Hospital (117 East 19th Street), or call 911 for an ambulance.

Bees, wasps, and ants are painful, just like anywhere else. Tarantulas shouldn't bother you unless you harass them. You might get stung by a scorpion, especially inside in a dark corner. It hurts like a bee sting, but is not dangerous unless you have an allergic reaction.

Although Plague—yes, *that* Plague—is endemic in Northern New Mexico, it rarely gets this far south. We have not had problems with Hantavirus or Lyme Disease so far. Our first death from West Nile Virus occurred in 2007.

The summer sun is HOT and will dehydrate you quickly. Drink lots of water. Wear a hat. Never go hiking without **plenty** of water—at least a gallon a day per person.

At 3,600' (1,100 m) the altitude shouldn't bother you unless you are from sea level or in very poor shape. Then, take it easy. Wear sunscreen as you will burn faster here than at lower altitudes.

Tornadoes occur occasionally. Take cover in a low, protected area if outside, or in the sturdiest room away from windows inside. Do not stand upright outside in a thunderstorm, especially while holding a golf club.

Chapter II. On the Trail of the 1947 Roswell UFO Crash

I am convinced that UFOs exist because I have seen one.
— President Jimmy Carter

The Events

These are some of the stories that have been told. Numerous additions, contradictions, refutations, revisions, and denials have surfaced since 1947. Stop in at the UFO Museum to see which have been most recently supported or debunked —or whether new ones have appeared.

Public interest in UFOs peaked during the summer of 1947. Although World War II was over, Cold War tensions were escalating and sightings of strange objects in the sky grabbed headlines around the country. In early July radar operators around New Mexico began reporting strange objects on their screens and unusual malfunctions in their equipment.

~

Several people saw a crashed saucer containing dead aliens on the Plains of San Augustin near Magdalena, New Mexico, 200 miles (320 km) west of Roswell in July 1947.

~

In early July 1947 Roswell Army Air Field workers were sent to a desolate rocky site about 25 miles (40 km) north of Roswell, now owned by the Corn family, where they found a crashed saucer-shaped aircraft and dead aliens. They were ordered to close off the area, gather up all the debris and bodies, and return it all to the Army Air Field in Roswell.

~

In early July 1947 Glenn Dennis, a mortician at Ballard Funeral Home, received two telephone calls from the RAAF Mortuary Officer. In his first call the officer asked Dennis if the funeral home stocked child-sized caskets that could be hermetically sealed. During the second call he asked about preparing and preserving tissue. Both times he indicated that his questions were just routine, for future reference.

Later that same day, Dennis received a call to transport an injured airman to the RAAF, as Ballard's also operated the town ambulance. When he delivered the airman to the RAAF hospital he noticed strange debris inside another ambulance parked beside the entrance. As he entered the building, Dennis encountered a nurse he knew, Naomi Selff, who looked shaken. She told him to leave quickly, and two other military men reinforced the command, even threatening him.

The next morning Dennis and Nurse Selff met for coffee at the RAAF Officer's Club where she told him that she had assisted in autopsies on three small gray bodies. She sketched a picture on a napkin of the creatures with large heads, large slanted eyes, and four fingers on each hand, adding that the bodies had smelled so bad that they were eventually moved from the hospital to Hangar 84 out by the airstrip. A few days later Nurse Selff was transferred and later word came that she had died in an airplane crash.

~

On the evening of July 3, 1947, as Roswell hardware store owner Dan Wilmot and his wife Grace sat on their front porch hoping for a cool breeze, a huge saucer-shaped object zoomed overhead flying in a northwesterly direction. The Wilmots ran into their yard and watched the glowing saucer for 40 to 50 seconds until it disappeared in the direction of Six-Mile Hill west of town.

~

Trucker Jim Ragsdale took a lady friend to Boy Scout Mountain, 45 miles (70 km) west of Roswell, for an amorous encounter on the evening of July 4, 1947. There they saw a strange object fly over, and then saw the flash from an explosion behind a hill. When they went to investigate, rough terrain kept them from getting close but at a distance they spotted wreckage of a disk-shaped object and alien bodies. They left when they saw military vehicles approaching.

~

Mother Superior Mary Bernadette and Sister Capistrano of the Catholic nursing order Sisters of the Sorrowful Mother saw what appeared to be an explosion in the sky to the north of Roswell as they were looking out a third-floor window of St. Mary's Hospital late on the evening of July 4, 1947.

~

When cowboy W.W. "Mack" Brazel (cousin of Wayne Brazel, the man acquitted of murdering Sheriff Pat Garrett in 1908), foreman of the Foster Ranch near Corona, 75 miles (120 km) north of Roswell, rode out to check on his sheep the morning after a particularly violent storm in early summer 1947, he and young neighbor Dee Proctor found a wide swath of strange debris spread across the prairie. Brazel collected several pieces of odd material that he later showed the parents of his young friend. They urged him to report his find to the authorities.

On Sunday, July 6, Brazel drove into Roswell bringing his story and some of the debris to Sheriff George Wilcox in his office next to the jail at the back of the Chaves County Courthouse. The sheriff was not particularly interested, but did telephone the Roswell Army Air Field in case this indicated a crashed airplane. He was put in touch with RAAF Intelligence Officer Major Jesse Marcel who agreed to come into town to talk to Brazel.

After Major Marcel interviewed Mack Brazel at the Sheriff's Office he reported back to his commanding officer, Colonel William "Butch" Blanchard, who sent him and another officer out to the debris field with Brazel to investigate. They arrived late in the day, spent Sunday night on the Foster ranch, then Major Marcel and the other officer spent Monday, July 7 gathering up pieces of the strange foil and material inscribed with odd symbols. Major Marcel returned home late Monday evening where he showed the debris to his wife and son.

~

While Mack Brazel had been waiting for Major Marcel in Sheriff Wilcox's office that Sunday afternoon, Roswell Radio Station KGFL reporter Frank Joyce had called the Sheriff's Office on a routine newsgathering mission. Sheriff Wilcox let him speak to Brazel. Monday morning when Joyce told Radio Station KGFL owner Walt Whitmore, Sr. about Brazel, Whitmore drove to the Foster Ranch, picked up Brazel, and brought him back to his house in Roswell. There he recorded an interview with Brazel who then spent Monday night at Whitmore's house.

~

On Tuesday morning July 8, Major Marcel returned to the RAAF and showed the strange material he had found to Colonel Blanchard. The colonel immediately ordered out a force of men to cordon off the debris area, pick up everything they could find, and return it to the RAAF where they would store it all under guard in Hangar 84 along the airstrip. Colonel Blanchard sent Major Marcel to Fort Worth Army Air Field, along with some of the debris, to see General Roger Ramey, head of the Eighth Air Force. He also ordered Lt. Walter Haut, RAAF Information Officer, to distribute a press release about the crash.

At lunchtime on Tuesday, July 8, Lt. Haut delivered copies of his press release about the crashed flying saucer to the two town radio stations, KGFL and KSWS, and then to the two town newspapers, the *Roswell Morning Dispatch*, a morning paper, and the *Roswell Daily Record*, an evening paper.

As soon as Reporter Frank Joyce at KGFL read Lt. Haut's press release he put the story on the United Press wire. The news flashed around the world Tuesday afternoon and was even picked up by the London *Times*.

At KSWS, Station Manager George Walsh put the crashed-saucer story on the Associated Press wire while station owner John McBoyle called KOAT, their sister station in Albuquerque, and asked them to send the story to their affiliated ABC and Mutual Radio Networks. However when KOAT teletype operator Lydia Sleppy started her transmission to the networks, the FBI interrupted it with orders to kill the story.

When Walt Whitmore contacted the RAAF Tuesday afternoon for more information about the crash, the military appeared at Whitmore's home to pick up Brazel and the recording of his interview. That same afternoon Whitmore received telephone calls from an FCC representative and from New Mexico Senator Dennis Chavez' office telling him not to run the flying saucer story, saying that it was a matter of national security and the radio station would lose its license if he did not cooperate.

Later that Tuesday afternoon Colonel Blanchard rescinded the flying saucer story and sent men to the radio and newspaper offices to retrieve the press releases, but it was too late to suppress the excitement. The headline in the *Roswell Daily Record* for Tuesday evening July 8 read, "RAAF Captures Flying Saucer on Ranch in Roswell Region."

~

Wednesday, July 9, the day after the *Roswell Daily Record* printed its famous headline, General Ramey, Commander of the Eighth Air Force, released information to the press in Fort Worth that the debris recovered near Roswell had come from the crash of a weather balloon. This led to the *Roswell Daily Record*'s headline for July 9, "General Ramey Empties Roswell Saucer."

~

Several days later, the military escorted Mack Brazel to the offices of the *Roswell Daily Record* for an interview in which he changed his story, claiming to have found debris from a weather balloon on June 14. Brazel then went to see Frank Joyce at KGFL, again accompanied by military escort, and repeated his story that the debris had come from a weather balloon. However, at the end of that interview, when mention was made of "little green men" Brazel muttered angrily, "They weren't green!"

By the second week of July 1947 the materials from Hangar 84, now described as debris from a crashed weather balloon, had been flown to Wright-Patterson Air Force Base in Ohio. The excitement in Roswell was over. Everyone involved, from military personnel to civilians, was ordered not to discuss the incident further. And they didn't—not until thirty years later.

~

In 1980, after reviewing available records and interviewing as many of the participants as they could find, Charles Berlitz and William Moore published *The Roswell Incident*, describing the events of that July in 1947. They concluded that something not-of-this-earth had crashed northwest of Roswell and that the government had worked hard to cover up the facts. Initially their book attracted little attention outside of UFO circles, even in Roswell, until a 1989 episode of the TV show *Unsolved Mysteries* featured the 1947 Roswell Crash. Interest began to grow.

Walter Haut, Glenn Dennis, and Roswell realtor Max Littell founded the UFO Museum in 1991. Kevin Randle and Donald Schmitt published *UFO Crash at Roswell* that same year while Stanton Friedman and Don Berliner published *Crash at Corona* the next year. The TV movie *Roswell* aired in 1994 and more books about the incident began to appear, including teen novels about aliens attending Roswell High School. The 1947 Roswell UFO Crash had taken off!

Publicity surrounding the 1997 UFO Festival on the 50th Anniversary of the Crash attracted worldwide attention. Since then the number of books, movies, TV shows, websites, blogs, and controversies has continued to grow, until today "Roswell" is one of the best known names around the globe—and who knows where else? As the marker at the Corn Ranch Crash Site reads:

> *We don't know who they were.*
> *We don't know why they came.*
> *We only know they changed our view of the universe.*

The Locations

Some of the Reported Crash Sites:
> **Corn Ranch**: This site is 25 miles (40 km) north of Roswell, pp 26, 117.
> **Foster Ranch**: Mack Brazel's debris field is near Corona, 75 miles (120 km) northwest of Roswell, p 27.
> **Boy Scout Mountain**: The "Ragsdale Site" is 45 miles (70 km) west of Roswell, pp 27, 144.
> **Plains of San Augustin**: This most distant site is 200 miles (320 km) west of Roswell, p 26.

Sheriff Wilcox's Office (Chaves County Courthouse): The section of the Courthouse containing the Chaves County Jail and Sheriff's Office was demolished in 1996, p 43. The current Chaves County Sheriff's Office is in the Chaves County Administrative Center, p 133.

Roswell Daily Record Offices (Pioneer Plaza): Currently the *Roswell Daily Record* offices are at 2301 North Main Street. The building housing the 1947 offices was demolished in 1997 along with the rest of the buildings in the Pioneer Block to create Pioneer Plaza, p 48.

Roswell Morning Dispatch Offices (UFO Museum): This building has become the UFO Museum Gift Shop, p 59.

Radio Station KGFL (Elegante Hair Salon): Roswell's first radio station went off the air in 1974, p 65.

Radio Station KSWS (Schlotsky's Deli): After several changes, KSWS became today's KOBR-TV, pp 44, 64.

Hangar 84: Currently vacant but impressive, this building is large enough to hold several mysteries, p 113.

Ballard Funeral Home: The funeral home that employed Glenn Dennis is still in operation at its same 1947 location, p 133.

RAAF Hospital (New Mexico Rehabilitation Center): The current brick facility on this site replaced the frame RAAF Hospital building that was the scene of the alien autopsy, p 108.

RAAF Officer's Club (ENMU-R Campus Union): You can have lunch on the spot where Nurse Selff drew aliens, p 110.

Whitmore house: The house where Mack Brazel gave the interview that was never broadcast is still here but is no longer in the Whitmore family, p 137.

Roswell High School: The popular books and TV series about alien teens were set here, p 137.

UFO Museum: "The Truth is Here," p 58.

The Museum

As interest in the 1947 UFO Crash grew throughout the 1980s, Walter Haut (1922-2005), the former RAAF Information Officer who wrote the 1947 press release about the crashed saucer, and Glenn Dennis (1925-2004), the mortician who had been consulted by the RAAF about small coffins and preserving tissue, began focusing their energy on creating a museum devoted to UFO information and research.

In the early 1990s Haut and Dennis, looking for a home for the UFO Museum, enlisted Roswell realtor Max Littell (1916-2001) in the project. They incorporated as a non-profit educational organization in 1991 and in 1992 opened their first museum—mainly a collection of newspaper clippings—in one of the buildings later demolished to create Pioneer Plaza. The new UFO Museum quickly established itself as an important force in UFO circles, and as Roswell's first major tourist attraction.

In 1997 the Museum moved to its current, and much larger, location and almost immediately began planning for future expansion. At one point, a site several miles west of town was considered but local businesses objected strongly to losing their downtown tourist draw. The Museum decided to remain in the downtown area and acquired land at the site of the former Holsum Bakery (723 North Main Street). In spite of the 2007 groundbreaking for the "multi-million-dollar state-of-the-art" museum (Question: just what constitutes "state of the art" for a UFO museum?) funds are still being sought, so the museum will likely remain in its current location for a few more years, much to the relief of nearby businesses.

Today the International UFO Museum and Research Center in Roswell, housing the world's premier research library on UFO and alien-related subjects, is the focal point for both serious researchers and popular UFO enthusiasts the world over. Would you like to chat with the daughter of Museum founder Walter Haut? She's the current Museum Director, Julie Shuster.

The Festival

Since 1996 the UFO Museum or the Roswell Chamber of Commerce has sponsored an annual UFO Festival around the time of the Crash—usually the July 4th weekend. In 2007 the City assumed sponsorship of the Festival, which features everything from serious presentations by researchers and authors to frivolous fun for the whole family. The Fiftieth Anniversary Festival in 1997 and the Sixtieth in 2007 have stirred up the most excitement so far, but celebrations typically include events such as UFO speakers, celebrity appearances, the Alien Chase, concerts, carnivals, trade shows, panel discussions, food booths, air shows, costume contests, parades, film festivals, book signings, sports competitions, and *lots* of media attention. The four-day UFO Festival brings out two types of UFO enthusiasts in abundance—those who devote serious study to alien-oriented questions, and those who think the whole thing is a hoot and the most fun to hit Roswell since the last cattle drive. For more information about all of the fun visit www.UFOfestivalRoswell.com or www.roswellufomuseum.com.

The Souvenirs

Souvenir Shops

Most stores in Roswell can scare up an alien or UFO souvenir if pressed. These that specialize in other-worldly merchandise are all in the Downtown area, except for Wal-Mart:

UFO Museum Gift Shop, p 59
Alien Corner, p 58
Roswell Landing, p 52
Planet Roswell, p 55
Alien Zone, p 54
Alien Zone II, p 60
Roswell Space Center, p 53
Starchild, p 60
Wal-Mart Super Center, 115

For Your Memory or Memory Card

Formal Photos Ops
UFO Museum, p 58
Alien Zone "Area 51," p 54
Exhibits
UFO Museum, p 58
Alien Zone II "Hangar 84," p 60
Roswell Space Center "Spacewalk," p 53

Outdoor Murals and other Art Works that feature Aliens or Space
    UFO Museum Mural, p 59
    McDonald's Space Mural, p 38
    Roswell Space Center Mural—and garbage cans, p 53
    Copy Rite Building Mural, p 66
    Art Museum Annex Mural, p 37
    Goddard High School Space Mural, p 119
    Adult Center Carving, p 96
    Wal-Mart Super Center Windows, p 115
    Alien Street Lamps, p 52
    Roswell High School (no aliens, just the sign), p 137
Flying Saucers
    McDonald's Restaurant, p 38
    UFO Museum façade, p 58
    Starchild façade, p 60
    Corner of South Monroe and East Hobbs Streets
    Corner of South Elm and East Alameda Streets, p 104
    Corner of South Georgia and West McGaffey Streets
        west of the Relief Route

Available During the UFO Festival Only

Souvenir Booths at the Civic Center and UFO Museum
Crash Site Tours
UFO Haunted House
Goddard Planetarium Space Show
Roswell Community Little Theater UFO Production
For other activities, ask at the UFO Museum or Visitor's Center

The Song
(To be sung in a New Mexico drawl, accompanied by guitar)

UFO BREAKDOWN
J. Shannon Webster

In 1947 when the craft went down
There was hurryin' & scurryin' all over town.
They brought in pieces of the thing at risk
& they brought in the pilots of the flying disk.
    The nurse walked in and she said, "My stars!
    What you got on the table is a man from Mars!"
The Air Force gathered up the evidence &
Locked it all away behind a great big fence.
They flew it all out on the very next day,
But I swear I overheard a G-man say,
    "Someone in Roswell knows (they know)
    what happened to the UFOs!"

The local newspaper covered all the crimes
And it got picked up by the London *Times*.
They rounded up the rancher who had broke the news
& corralled him for an interview.
 He said, "That's the dumbest thing that I never seen.
 Oh, and by the way ... they ain't green!"
Without a saucer and without a corpse,
People just went on back to work of course.
Everybody went on their merry own way,
But every now and then you'd hear a local say,
 "Someone in Roswell knows (they know)
 what happened to the UFOs!"

Ever since the UFO came that day there've been
Things that couldn't be explained in some other way:
Edsels, rap music, Shamu the Whale,
Pet Rocks, body-piercing, Zima, Dan Quayle,
 Rush Limbaugh, bell-bottoms, Michael Jackson's nose,
 Pot-bellied pigs and TV talk shows,
Studio wrestling, Coke without caffeine,
Madonna, Grenada & bucking machines.
Try to get the files on the flying disk &
The GAO will tell you that they don't exist.
 Someone in Washington knows (they know)
 What happened to the UFOs!

I was riding the swing late one night
When there came upon me a blinding light.
I wasn't worried or afraid of course,
But it was all that I could do to sit my horse.
 I can take the flashing lights, I don't mind the rattle,
 But it kinda makes me nervous what they do to the cattle!
Now on solitary nights 'neath a prairie moon,
I get that sense that I ain't alone,
But I feel a little better 'bout the human race,
Knowing there's a back-up in outer space.
 Someone in Andromeda knows (they know)
 What happened to the UFOs!

Touring Roswell

Chapter III. Main Street Downtown

The heart of Roswell's original business district lay between two rivers: the Spring River on the north and the Hondo River on the south. After NMMI relocated north of town in 1898, the area from the Spring River up to its location at the top of North Hill gradually began to develop, as did areas along the town's southern edge. This guidebook considers Main Street Downtown to be that section of Roswell's Main Street beginning at NMMI in the 1400 block of North Main Street, continuing southward downhill and on across the Spring River, past the Courthouse, through the UFO District, past the UFO Museum, and ending at the Hondo River Recreation Trail along the Hondo River in the 400 block of South Main Street. Today's downtown business district as well as most historic sites and UFO-related attractions are here.

Downtown Shopping

Visitors sometimes call Roswell's UFO-themed downtown area "tacky." Others love its unique aura, as Main Street from the Courthouse to the UFO Museum and several adjacent side streets are lined with souvenir shops selling everything you could ever want related to aliens and UFOs. Each souvenir seems tackier than the next, but that's part of the fun. Other shops along here sell antiques and collectibles, quilting and scrapbooking supplies, music and musical instruments, office and teacher supplies, art, jewelry, wine, gifts, clothing, and flowers, making this the most concentrated shopping area in Roswell—except for the Mall.

Downtown Parking

The Civic Center parking lot (entrance from the 900 block of North Richardson Avenue) is a convenient place to leave your car to explore the northern area of Downtown Main Street on foot. Parking lots at Pioneer Plaza (entrances from West 4th or 5th Streets) or behind the Courthouse (entrance from the 200 block of East 5th Street) are good places to park to explore the middle area. The UFO Museum (114 North Main Street) or Petroleum Building parking lots (across Richardson Avenue from the Petroleum Building) are convenient for the southern area. Parking places are usually available along the street as well. There are no parking meters, but police sometimes enforce the two-hour parking limits that have been in place since 1920, two years before Roswell's main streets were paved.

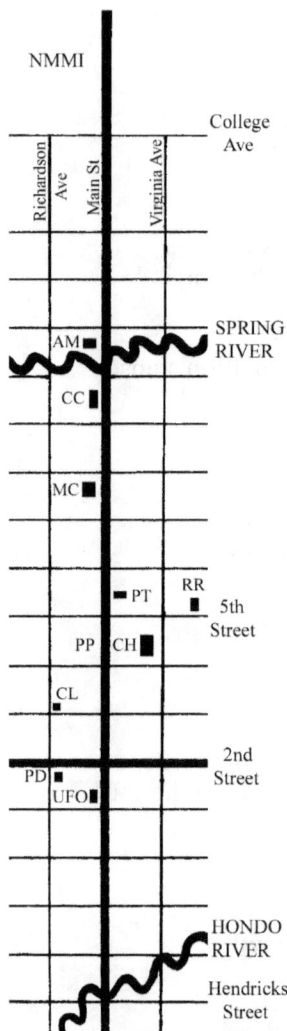

KEY

AM	Art Museum
CC	Civic Center
CH	Courthouse
CL	Carnegie Library
MC	McDonald's
PD	Police Department
PP	Pioneer Plaza
PT	Pecos Trails Bus Station
RR	Old RR Depot
UFO	UFO Museum

North of the Courthouse

1300 Block, North Main Street
East Side

1315 **Farley's Food, Fun, and Pub**. This restaurant and bar with pool tables, specializing in juicy burgers and other informal food, becomes a lively spot in the evening, especially with occasional live music on the patio when it's warm. 627-1100. Open for lunch and dinner every day, holidays variable.

West Side

1300 **Los Amigos**. Delicious steak tacos, chunky chicken enchiladas, and crispy sopaipillas draw folks to this newly opened Mexican restaurant. If you're puzzled by the scene painted near the door, it used to be a restaurant called A Taste of Europe. 623-8352. Open Sun and M for breakfast and lunch; Tu-Sat for breakfast, lunch, and dinner; holidays variable.

1200 Block, North Main Street
West Side

1208 **Pasta Café**. Roswell's "Italian bistro" has a pleasant atmosphere, good Italian food, occasional live dinner music, and a yummy Roswell version of tiramisu. Try not to fill up on the flavorful bread. Reservations are a good idea on weekends. 624-1111. Open for lunch and dinner every day, closed Christmas.

1100 Block, North Main Street
East Side

1113 **Cattle Baron Steak and Seafood Restaurant**. Delicious steaks and prime rib, a huge soup and salad bar, a hearty array of free goodies during happy hour in the bar, and interesting "cattleman" décor that gives tourists a glimpse of the Old West make this one of the few restaurants where reservations are suggested on weekends. 622-2465. Open for lunch and dinner every day, closed Christmas.

East on 11th Street
Bus Station (1100 North Virginia Avenue). Roswell's small intercity and interstate bus station is behind Wendy's on Main Street. 623-0947. Open M-F 7-5, SS and holidays 8-3.

1000 Block, North Main Street
West Side

1000 **Roswell Museum and Art Center.** Roswell's wonderful and free art museum includes important Southwestern art, an extensive collection of Western artifacts, exhibits on space and the work of rocket pioneer Dr. Robert Goddard, and a planetarium.

In 1937 WPA workers constructed the original adobe building, with its entrance on 11th Street at the back of the current structure, in Pueblo Revival style including a flat roof and large visible ceiling beams called vigas. The original ten massive vigas with carved corbels underneath the ends, along with tin chandeliers, wooden furniture, and other decorations created by traditional New Mexico artisans commissioned by the WPA, remain in the Founders' Gallery, the original portion of the Museum that today contains the paintings of Peter Hurd (1904-1984) and Henriette Wyeth (1907-1997).

Roswell native Peter Hurd studied with famous illustrator N.C. Wyeth, served as a combat artist in World War II, and returned to New Mexico to paint landscapes and portraits in the Hondo Valley west of Roswell where he lived with his wife Henriette Wyeth, N.C. Wyeth's eldest daughter and an internationally known artist who specialized in painting portraits and flowers. Hurd is best known for painting President Lyndon Johnson's Official Portrait because LBJ rejected the work saying it was "the ugliest thing I've ever seen."

Since 1937 the museum and its holdings have grown steadily. Highlights of its extensive collection of Southwestern art include those Hurd and Wyeth paintings (in one favorite Hurd painting, *The Oasis*, with Capitan Mountain in the background, two boys enjoy a dip in the only pool available to ranch youngsters) and works of early artists from Santa Fe and Taos such as the most valuable painting in the museum, *Ram Skull with Brown Leaves*, by Georgia O'Keefe (1887-1986). Other galleries display changing exhibits from the permanent collection or touring art shows. The colorful fiberglass western sculptures of Luis Jimenez (1940-2006) are always popular.

Two other exhibits in the museum appeal to different interests. Robert Goddard (1882-1945)—"The Father of Modern Rocketry"—perfected multistage liquid-propelled rockets during his experiments in Roswell from 1930 to 1942. The Robert Goddard Space Collection contains some of his early rockets and a recreation of Dr. Goddard's Roswell workshop, using all his original equipment from the 1930s. Esther Goddard attended dedication ceremonies for this wing in 1959 when German rocket scientist Wernher von Braun gave the dedication speech. She returned in 1964, accompanied by America's first astronaut, Alan Shepard, and Gemini and Apollo astronaut Eugene Cernan, for First Day of Issue ceremonies in the museum for a commemorative air mail stamp honoring her late husband. Former New Mexico Senator and astronaut Harrison Schmitt, the last person to walk on the moon, later donated the spacesuit from his 1972 Apollo 17 flight to the space exhibit that also contains a real moon rock. One of Dr. Goddard's rocket launch towers stands outside at the northeast corner of the museum with a replica rocket in place.

In another area of the museum, the Rogers and Mary Ellen Aston Collection of the American West presents magnificent Spanish, Native American, and Wild West artifacts arranged by themes. A true enthusiast could spend hours here studying the hundreds of items. Small bronze sculptures of western subjects by Roswell oilman Rogers Aston (1918-1999) are on display here as well.

The Museum Store sells a large selection of Southwestern books and non-tacky souvenirs, including Roswell's official city pin featuring a UFO of course. 624-6744. www.roswellmuseum.org. Free admission. Open M-Sat 9-5 (Store: 10-5), Sun and holidays 1-5, closed Thanksgiving, Dec 24 and 25, and Jan 1.

Goddard Planetarium (Richardson Avenue and 11th Street), built adjacent to the Museum in 1967, presents programs through the schools, and occasionally offers public shows, especially during the UFO Festival, for a small admission fee.

Summer art students painted the mural *Puedo ver el futuro—I can see the future* on the east wall of the **Art Annex** (used for art classes) across 11th Street from the Museum. Are those space ships in the middle window?

900 Block, North Main Street

Here the **North Spring River**—usually just called the Spring River—flows (?) between the Roswell Museum and Art Center and the Civic Center, looking rather like a moat. The "drawbridge" over the moat leads to the Museum entrance. Completed in the 1990s, the bridge's cost of $16,000 was much more than that of the original Museum. Nearby a metal dragonfly overlooks the river and a very odd nest clings to the museum wall.

Today the Spring River is a mere trickle but in 1885, when Roswell consisted of nine buildings, the Spring River here was "forty feet (12 m) wide and two feet (0.5 m) deep, crystal clear and rapid flowing." All the water for early Roswell came from this river. This location was the only fordable spot near town and wading was the only way to cross until January 1892 when the Town awarded a $550 contract to build the first bridge. Irrigation wells dried up the springs that once fed the Spring River so that now it only really flows after a heavy rain.

West Side

William F. Brainerd Plaza, named in honor of a former longtime Roswell mayor, stretches from the Spring River to the Civic Center.

Tiles inset in artist Susan Wink's 1997 curved benches and planters entitled *Oasis* on the north side of the plaza represent different aspects of life in Roswell. Can you find a spur, rattlesnake, rocket, Courthouse dome, cow head, baseball, barbed wire, centipede, derrick, paint brush, tractor, dragonfly, wagon wheel, UFO, Conquistador helmet, pencil, trophy, car, deer-track, horseshoe?

The **Chaves County Fallen Heroes Memorial** near the center of Brainerd Plaza honors fifteen law enforcement, fire, and medical personnel who have "fallen in the line of duty." This includes Barney Leonard who not only organized the world's first—and only—Armed Motorcycle Cavalry (p 85) but also served as Roswell's first motorcycle police officer in spite of having lost a hand during the Philippine Insurrection. He died in a shootout with an escaped convict in southeast Roswell in 1934.

912 **Roswell Civic and Convention Center**. Built in 1996 to host trade shows, conferences, concerts, and ceremonies, this building also houses the Roswell **Visitor's Center** that opened here in 2007 after operating in the old Conoco Service Station on Pioneer Plaza for several years. Maps, brochures, and information about area attractions are available, as are ten free Internet minutes.

The boxy portion of the Civic Center closest to Main Street incorporates the original two-story brick structure of the Pecos Valley Coca Cola Bottling Company that operated here from 1937—when this portion of the building was constructed—to 1993.

Children under the direction of former Artist-in-Residence Martie Zelt created the 10' by 32' (3 m by 10 m) mosaic, *Roswell: strata/city/skies*, in the lobby, depicting features of the Roswell area. I Spy—a heart, a fish, Texas, a lion, a fault, a silver dome, a green dome, a fractured Zia sun sign . . . What can You Spy?

Vendors display their wares inside and outside the Civic Center during the UFO Festival, the Chile-Cheese Festival, and other celebrations. When President George W. Bush gave a speech here in 2004, even he got into the spirit of the UFO Capital, remarking, "I understand you had reports this morning of an unfamiliar aircraft. No worries, it was just me." Civic Center, 624-7686. Visitor's Center, 624-7704. Open M-F 8:30-5:30, SS 10-3, closed Thanksgiving, Christmas, New Year's Day.

700 Block, North Main Street
East Side
723 **(Holsum Bakery site, future site of the UFO Museum).** Lester Reischman (1892-1977) came to Roswell in 1940 and bought the Bowman Baking Company. With his son Gene, Reischman who also had interests in oil companies and banking, operated the renamed Holsum Baking Company on this site for many years, supplying products throughout eastern and southern New Mexico and west Texas. Reischman Park in the 300 block of North Main Street is named in his honor.

The UFO Museum has broken ground on this site for its new home—the baking company closed and its building was demolished in 2003—but completion plans are currently indefinite.

East on 7th Street
Fat's Burritos. (704 North Virginia Avenue). A popular burrito stop. 623-8979. Open M-F for breakfast and lunch, closed SS and holidays.

West Side
700 **McDonald's Restaurant (NMMI site).** The only UFO themed restaurant in the chain carries out this theme inside and out. The space mural facing the south parking lot is also fun. NMMI operated in buildings—long gone—on this site in 1894 and 1895, before moving to its current location. 622-2322. Open for breakfast, lunch, and dinner every day; closed Christmas.

600 Block, North Main Street
East Side
601 **(Former Zia Sports Building).** This unusually shaped building began life in the 1920s as a rooming house, but many businesses have occupied it since. The Parquay Grocery Store located here from 1941 to 1943 had grocery shelves around the inside walls and an Art Deco soda fountain in the center. Advertising signs formed the top portion of the roof and rotated in a circle. Photos from the early 1940s showing the building with a radio antenna on top make it look like Roswell's first spaceship. Recently it has become an Alien Haunted House with a small admission fee during the UFO Festival.

The Courthouse Area and Pioneer Plaza

500 Block, North Main Street
East Side

515 **Pecos Trails Bus Station**. This building with Art Deco touches including curved ("streamlined") walls containing glass brick sections, currently serves as headquarters for Roswell's Pecos Trails Transit city bus system but was Roswell's intercity and interstate bus station from 1948 until the 1990s. A large neon Zia sun sign flickers on the ceiling of the lobby that also holds public restrooms and a water fountain. 624-6766. Offices open M-F 8-12, 1-5, closed SS and city holidays. Buses run M-F 6-10, Sat 7-10, Sun 10:30-6:30, holidays variable, no buses on Christmas.

505 **What's Cooking**. A number of different restaurants—and a few other businesses—have operated here over the years. This current take-out restaurant features homemade soups, salads, sandwiches, and pies. 623-3445. Open M-F 10:30-4:30, closed SS and holidays.

East on 5th Street

107 **The Gallery**. The Roswell Fine Arts League sponsors this cooperative gallery featuring different local member artists each month. 625-5263. Free admission. Open M-Sat 10:30-4:30, closed Sun and holidays.

123 **First National Bank in Roswell (Gilder Hotel site)**. Completed in 1908 (and demolished in 1966), the elegant Gilder Hotel with 25 rooms boasted Ionic columns supporting its fourth-floor balcony. Roswell citizens hosted a banquet here in February 1916 honoring General John J. "Black Jack" Pershing after he inspected Roswell's National Guard force and the NMMI Corps of Cadets, just a few months before he led the Punitive Expedition into Mexico chasing Pancho Villa, then led U.S. forces into World War I. The after-dinner speaker delighted the banquet goers—but embarrassed the guest of honor—with tales of General Pershing's escapades as a young soldier at Ft. Stanton.

In 1928 Guy Nickson, former manager of the Gilkeson Hotel on 3rd Street, purchased the hotel and renamed it the Nickson Hotel. It was here that Charles and Anne Morrow Lindbergh spent the night of September 15, 1934 on their visit to Dr. Robert Goddard. The visit quickly became "a field day" for the town, as hundreds gathered to see the famous couple—much to Lucky Lindy's amazement and annoyance.

201 **(Roswell Hotel site).** Today a parking lot, this was once the location of the grand, three-story Roswell Hotel, the closest hotel to the Santa Fe Railroad Depot. Demolished in 1972, the hotel was built in the 1890s of precast concrete blocks made in Roswell and finished to look like stone.

Wide porches originally surrounded the two lower floors. Its lathe-turned porch spindles and hipped roof with dormer windows gave it an elegant Queen Anne style. Each of its twenty-three rooms was equipped with an ornate iron bedstead, a chest of drawers with a mirror, a cane-backed rocking chair, and a washstand with a bowl and pitcher. The second floor even had a bathroom. Its lobby, with three fabric-covered couches and a pot-bellied stove, soon became a gathering place for socializing and gossip. It was here in the dining room that served meals family style that the men of National Guard Battery A ate during their training prior to heading for the Mexican border to protect against Pancho Villa in 1916, and again prior to shipping out to France during World War I.

209 (Former Santa Fe Railroad Depot). J.J. Hagerman's Pecos Valley Railroad Company constructed a two-story frame building to serve as the passenger and freight depot on this site when the tracks arrived in Roswell in 1894.

Fire destroyed the original depot in 1904. Makeshift arrangements (three railroad cars parked on a siding—one for a passenger waiting room, one for offices, and one for a freight warehouse) served in its place until a red brick, hipped roof Santa Fe Railroad Depot was completed on this spot later that year by the company that had taken over the financially strapped Pecos Valley Railroad in 1901.

It was here at the new depot that famous orator and three-time Democratic presidential candidate William Jennings Bryan disembarked in 1909, fresh from the Artesia Alfalfa Festival 40 miles (65 km) to the south, to present a series of lectures sponsored by the Chautauqua Society. As this was a major event for a small town in the middle of nowhere, the city fathers had arranged an elaborate welcoming ceremony including celebratory speeches and patriotic music from the town band. The train arrived ahead of schedule however, and Bryan had already left for his lodgings at the Gilkeson Hotel before the greeters arrived.

Remodeling in the 1940s turned the hipped roof of that 1904 station into a flat-roofed, stuccoed building. Now only the deserted freight portion of the depot stands along the railroad tracks on the north side of 5th Street, still sporting the Roswell sign. The long-empty passenger section burned in 2001. Brick paving still in place suggests that it must have been a lovely spot at one time, however.

Atchison, Topeka and Santa Fe Railroad. Roswell owes its railroad to the innovative and financially disastrous visions of industrial tycoon James John Hagerman (1838-1909) who hoped to turn the Pecos Valley into an agricultural paradise.

Hagerman made his fortune mining iron and producing steel in Michigan, then mining silver and building railroads in Colorado. When Carlsbad promoter Charles Eddy interested him in the agricultural potential of the Pecos Valley, Hagerman committed that fortune and his energies to a grand scheme for irrigating Southeastern New Mexico.

Of course an agricultural paradise needs a railroad to transport its bountiful produce to national markets. In 1890 Hagerman organized the Pecos Valley Railroad and started constructing a line north from Pecos, Texas, a stop on the Texas and Pacific Railway, which was a fairly unimportant line between El Paso and San Antonio. The "Pea Vine," as his railroad was affectionately, or derisively, called—people said it "began nowhere and ended nowhere"—reached Carlsbad in 1891 and Roswell in 1894. By then Hagerman's irrigation scheme was in disarray and the nationwide financial crisis of 1893 had deflated his profits from other ventures. In spite of impending bankruptcy, he managed to arrange financing to complete his railroad on to

Amarillo in 1899, and Roswell had its connection to major transcontinental rail traffic.

Trains don't stop in Roswell anymore, although several freights a day pass slowly through town, blowing their lonesome whistles and blocking traffic.

West Side

500 Bank of America (Opera House site, Lea house site). Security National Bank, later taken over by Bank of America, built this second tallest skyscraper in Roswell in 1963.

Captain Joseph Lea had previously built an adobe house with a pitched shingle roof on this corner in the early 1880s, although he never actually lived in it. William Cosgrove, an early Roswell Postmaster, lived here with his wife for a short time and in early 1884 he moved the Post Office to this house where he also sold clothes and shoes briefly. Captain Lea's sister Ella and her second husband Milo Pierce then lived here from 1884 to 1889. At times Captain Lea stayed with them after the death of his wife Sallie in 1884.

Frank Lesnet, who ran Roswell's Federal Land Office—and disappeared mysteriously in 1893 along with $10,000 in Land Office funds—and his family lived here in early 1891. Then when Goss Military Institute opened in September 1891 Colonel Goss took over the house. He lived here and also used it as a reception area and infirmary for the school.

Most of the early adobe buildings in Roswell, including this one, were later replaced by other structures. From 1902 to 1904 the Roswell Opera House stood on this site. This two-story frame building had a stage 45' (14 m) wide and a seating capacity of 800. Roswell's attempt to import culture, or at least vaudeville shows, was never financially successful however, although several local organizations did use the auditorium for theatrical productions and other gatherings. The Opera House mysteriously burned in April 1904 and was never rebuilt.

500 Pepper's Grill and Bar. Located in the Bank of America building, this popular Mexican and American grill with fun chile murals in the dining areas features Margarita specials, Monday night football in the bar, and live music on the patio some summer evenings—in addition to good queso, flavorful enchiladas and tacos, huge rotisserie chicken salads, and chocolate-mint hard candies at the cash register, where t-shirts with the chile pepper logo may be purchased. Reservations wouldn't hurt on weekends but there is always room for more on the patio. 623-1700. Open M-Sat for lunch and dinner, closed Sun except open for Mother's Day and Easter, holidays variable.

West on 5th Street

108 (National Guard Armory site; Lea cow corral, bunkhouse, and peach orchard site). When Captain Lea owned this entire block in the 1870s he built a large adobe corral to confine his milk cows in this currently open area. At times as many as twenty cows supplied milk and butter for his boarding house. He also planted a peach orchard and built a bunkhouse for his ranch hands between the corral and what would later become 5th Street.

In 1904 forty men meeting at the old Courthouse across Main Street from here organized Battery A of the New Mexico National Guard First Field Artillery Unit. Many of these men had been part of the group of twenty-four from Chaves County who served as Rough Riders under Teddy Roosevelt in 1898.

On this site in 1909 the State constructed Roswell's first National Guard Armory designed by the Rapp brothers in the same Military Gothic style they proposed for NMMI. The National Guard and many other community groups used the Armory much like a Civic Center until fire destroyed it in 1963. The Guard also used open land west of today's Enchanted Lands Park for artillery practice in the early Twentieth Century and later used land along the Spring River just east of Main Street—and the building at 1101 North Virginia Avenue that is today's Community Little Theater—for meetings and training as well.

In 1961 the National Guard built a new Armory at 4203 West 2nd Street, used today by the State Police as headquarters for the Roswell area. Finally, in 1988 they constructed their current Armory at the RIAC (p 111).

400 Block, North Main Street
East Side
401 Chaves County Courthouse (Lea horse corral site, old Courthouse site). In the 1870s Captain Lea built a large horse corral with adobe walls five feet (1.5 m) high here across Main Street from his home. When the Territorial Legislature split Chaves County off from Lincoln County in 1889, Captain Lea donated this full city block for the Courthouse.

The Legislature named Chaves County in honor of Jose Francisco Chaves (1833-1904), the son and grandson of governors of Nuevo Mexico, who reached the rank of Lieutenant Colonel in the Union Army fighting first Confederates, then Navajos. Chaves later became a rancher, a lawyer, and New Mexico's Territorial Delegate to the United States Congress from 1865 to 1871. He remained a powerful leader in the New Mexico Republican Party until an unknown assassin shot him in 1904. A bronze bust of Francisco Chaves by sculptor Robert Summers, who also sculpted the large statue of John Chisum across the street in Pioneer Plaza, stands in the Rotunda of the new portion of today's Courthouse.

The first Chaves County Courthouse (a photo of it hangs in the Roswell Public Library lobby) was completed on this site in 1890. Although it stood three stories high with a four-story tower, it quickly became too small for the growing county government.

In 1911 Chaves County officials hired the Rapp brothers, architects from Trinidad, Colorado, who had recently completed the National Guard Armory and the master plan for the buildings and campus of NMMI, to design a new Courthouse. Both the Rapp brothers and County officials went "all out" on this new Courthouse, designed in the then-popular Beaux Arts Classical style. The County spent the outrageous amount of $164,000 on its construction completed in 1912, the year New Mexico became the 47th state. Builders drove over one thousand $10-apiece pine pilings down to solid-rock strata for the foundation. They constructed the walls of bricks fired locally, possibly at

Thomas Howard's brickyard at 7th Street and Virginia Avenue, but imported tile for the intricately patterned floors. The builders included all sorts of shields, medallions, garlands, and other folderols around both rectangular and arched windows, and with green terra-cotta tiles created the only domed courthouse in New Mexico. They even decorated the ribs between the tiled areas of the dome with garlands—check it out with your binoculars. Amazingly, the Rapp brothers' original design was even more ornate!

Inside the Courthouse, black-and-white tiled floors in a Greek key design, marble stairs, white columns, decorative moldings, brass chandeliers, and an impressive dome set with a stained-glass skylight continued the Beaux Arts motif. Even the circuit-breaker boxes were trimmed with classical designs.

Word is, the people of Chaves County spared no expense on their Courthouse because statehood was fast approaching and they knew the Federal Government would take over all county financial obligations as soon as New Mexico became a state. Therefore, their fancy new Courthouse would cost the people of Chaves County nothing!

Builders also constructed a separate—but much less ornate—jail behind the Courthouse. In the 1930s they added a jail annex that connected the jail to the Courthouse and also contained the Sheriff's Office. It was here that Mack Brazel came to report finding strange debris in July 1947. A few months later, future Grand Ole Opry and Country Music Hall of Fame star Lefty Frizzell wrote his first two hits, "I Love You a Thousand Ways" and "If You've Got the Money, Honey, I've Got the Time," while serving his time in this lockup.

A separate Juvenile Detention Center was added on the southeast corner of the Courthouse in 1974, on the spot where the only legal execution in Chaves County had taken place. In 1896 Eugenio Aragon and Antonio Gonzales were convicted of killing another local resident, Charlie Van Sickle, during a robbery. They were sentenced to hang. Aragon committed suicide in the Chaves County Jail, but Sheriff Haynes executed Gonzales on September 24, 1896. Prior to the hanging, Sheriff Haynes constructed a high fence around the gallows to shield the public from this spectacle, although some claimed he built the fence so he could charge admission. Today, the Juvenile Detention Center remains, but the Chaves County Jail and Annex at the rear of the Courthouse were demolished after a new Chaves County Detention Center (at East Brasher Road and South Atkinson Avenue) was completed in 1996.

The west half of the Courthouse, facing Main Street, is the same one completed in 1912. The east half of the current Courthouse was added in matching style in 2004. This enlarged building holds a total of nine courtrooms for District and Magistrate Courts, as well as various county offices—and some of the nicest public restrooms in Roswell. The District Attorney's Office occupies the basement, where some have claimed to hear the ghostly laughter of children playing. The Jean Willis Museum, dedicated to the recently retired Court Administrator in appreciation of her sixty years of service (1946-2006) seems never to be open, but so far has few exhibits inside.

Although the Courthouse has been the scene of many interesting events, the visit of soon-to-be-indicted Vice President Spiro Agnew probably drew the largest crowd. On an October afternoon in 1972, with the Courthouse's dominating central entrance as a backdrop, Vice-President Agnew campaigned to send Pete Dominici to his first term in the Senate, and touted the virtues of President Richard Nixon to a cheering crowd of 8,500 supporters standing "rib-to-rib" on the lawn. Agnew made no mention of those "nattering nabobs of negativity" attacking his boss. Instead, discussion focused on the citizens of Roswell and Chaves County who "have just stood out in Republicanism and Republican activity"— and still do today.

This same impressive entrance with its broad marble steps topped by massive Ionic columns is just decorative these days. The only public entrance to the Courthouse is around on Virginia Avenue, but the strict dress code will keep most tourists out—no shorts, no sweats, no tank tops, no flip-flops, no cell phones, in addition to no weapons. 622-2212. Open M-F 8-12, 1-5, closed SS and holidays.

Courthouse Lawn. On the northwest corner of the lawn, the anti-aircraft gun used by the New Mexico National Guard during World War II is dedicated to members of New Mexico's 200th Coast Artillery who fought the first battle of that war on December 8, 1941 and were liberated from death camps on August 15, 1945. This New Mexico National Guard unit, including men from Roswell, had been mobilized to the Philippines in 1940. After the Japanese overran General Douglas McArthur's position, more than half of the 1,800 New Mexicans among his troops died as POWs, many during the infamous Bataan Death March. Their sacrifice is commemorated by an eternal flame in front of the Bataan Building in Santa Fe, and in many other ways throughout New Mexico, as well as in the highly acclaimed book *Beyond Courage* by Roswell author Dorothy Cave.

Near the anti-aircraft gun are granite markers dedicated to the "Men and women of Chaves County" who fought in the Persian Gulf War, and to veterans of all wars who "Made the supreme sacrifice." The Ten Commandments marker has stood unchallenged since the Fraternal Order of Elks donated it to Roswell in 1973. The flagpole in the center of the lawn is dedicated to "Those who answered our country's call," while the anchor on the southwest corner of the lawn honors "The men and women of New Mexico who serve in the Navy."

The Courthouse lawn is the site of occasional festivals, prayer rallies, and protest gatherings. A Farmer's Market operates on Saturday mornings mid-July through September. Piñatafest booths set up here in September. Huge cottonwood and elm trees between the walkways are the last of a grove of 10 different species planted in 1922 to create an "urban forest." The largest American sycamore in New Mexico stands among them in front of the south wing of the Courthouse.

East on 4th Street
124 **KOBR-TV Building**. Enjoy beachcombing? The limestone façade of this building contains interesting marine fossils that remind us that the Pecos Valley was once a shallow inland seabed. Can you find small clams, larger ribbed cockleshells, and cross sections of tiny spiral gastropods?

KOBR-TV started life in 1947 (an important year for Roswell) as Radio

Station KSWS, just in time to play a part in the Roswell UFO Crash story (pp 28, 64). In 1953 the company initiated Southeastern New Mexico's first television station, KSWS-TV, which became today's Channel 8.

212 **Roswell Wool**. Although early Hispanic farmers in the Roswell area raised a few sheep for their own use and Captain Lea later owned a number of the animals, large-scale sheep ranching didn't begin here until 1878 when Judge Edmund Stone and his sons "grazed" a herd of 1,500 sheep down from Colorado—evidently there is no such thing as a "sheep drive"—to his ranch on the Berrendo River, four miles northeast of Roswell in the area of today's Country Club. The trip took three months. Although relations with cattlemen were never close, ranchers like John Chisum seem to have tolerated sheep on the fringes of their range. Gradually sheep ranching outpaced cattle ranching in the Pecos Valley as sheep are able to graze on poorer land than cattle.

Early ranchers raised sheep primarily for their wool, which they took to the closest market: the railroad town of Las Vegas, New Mexico, 200 miles (322 km) to the north. The road to Las Vegas was mainly two wagon wheel ruts, sometimes a foot deep, with the only fuel for cooking or campfires along most of the desolate route being dried cow chips. The Jaffa-Prager Mercantile Company on Main Street accepted consignments of wool and freighted it to Las Vegas in huge mule-powered wagon trains—the returning wagons bringing merchandise for their store—but independent sheep ranchers often banded together to form their own smaller oxen-powered wagon trains for the long trip.

After the railroad reached Carlsbad in 1891, much of the wool was freighted there, only an 80-mile (130 km) trip. Roswell first became the gathering point for wool from miles around when the railroad reached here in 1894. Wagon trains loaded with wool, each wagon pulled by ten or twelve burros, arrived regularly from outlying towns such as Lovington 100 miles to the east—a three and one-half day trip. When the railroad through Roswell reached Amarillo in 1899, sheep ranching expanded even more as ranchers were able to sell their sheep to feedlots in Kansas, in addition to just selling their wool.

Roswell has remained the center of the wool trade in Southeastern New Mexico with various Roswell companies buying and selling wool over the years. By 1900 John Rhea's Roswell Trading Company and Harold Hurd's Roswell Wool and Hide Company were each carrying on one-quarter of a million dollars of business a year. Roswell Wool, today the largest wool warehouse in the United States, has operated under various names at this location since 1965. Wool buyers from all over the world attend sales of wool and mohair from New Mexico and out of state growers here in January, February, April, May, October, and December. 622-4460.

West Side
426 **Old Conoco Service Station**. Constructed in the 1920s, this is one of the few stations left in New Mexico built in the Tudor Cottage style that became Conoco's trademark during that era. It was renovated in 1997 and housed the Roswell Visitor's Center for several years. Controversy abounds as

to its future now that the Visitor's Center has moved to the Civic Center.

400-424 Pioneer Plaza (Smith house, gambling hall, and store site; Lea boarding house and store site; Goss Military Institute site; Pioneer Block site). This block has been the heart of Anglo Roswell since its founding shortly after the Civil War. An early settler built the first structure in downtown Roswell as a trading post and makeshift hotel for drovers on the Goodnight-Loving Trail in the late 1860s. Only a few Hispanic farmers and shepherds and occasional nomadic bands of Comanches and Mescalero Apaches lived in this area at the time. The 15' by 15' (4 m x 4 m) adobe building stood on the spot in the center of the block along today's Main Street where gray paving tiles outline a brown square containing the red Zia sun sign.

Van Smith

Thirty-two-year-old C. Van Smith (1837-1914), a professional gambler from "back east," bought this land and the adobe building on it in 1869. He immediately added three rooms and a sleeping loft to the hotel—and some say, brothel—where he also dealt poker, faro, and three card monte. He then constructed a larger adobe building a little to the south (today, the cement area with park benches on the northwest corner of 4th and Main Streets) for a store and laid out two parallel half-mile (0.8 km) tracks for horseracing angling to the southwest. His gambling operation also included pits for cockfighting (legal in New Mexico until 2007), dog fighting, and badger baiting. Smith named this lively and popular rest stop on the Goodnight-Loving Trail "Roswell" in honor of his father, Roswell Smith, and established the first Post Office in the area inside his store in 1873.

John Chisum

Van Smith never got a statue to honor him, but fellow Roswell pioneer John Chisum (1824-1884) did. The center of Pioneer Plaza holds that larger-than-life bronze sculpture of Chisum, himself a larger-than-life character in Roswell's early history—loved by many, hated by some, and played by John Wayne in the 1970 movie *Chisum*. He built the first cattle empire in Southeastern New Mexico, opening this area to settlement and growth in the 1860s and 1870s. Texas sculptor Robert Summers portrayed Chisum herding his lead steer "Old Ruidoso" who sports Chisum's famous "Jinglebob" earmarks—created by slitting the animal's ears their entire length so that the lower portions dangle in an unmistakable mark of ownership.

Born in Tennessee, John Chisum began cattle ranching in Texas as a young man and supplied beef to the Confederacy during the Civil War. After the war he drove cattle into New Mexico looking for new markets. Shortly before Van Smith was setting up shop to entertain cowboys in Roswell, Chisum began following the Pecos River northward to Fort Sumner and the Hondo River westward from Roswell to Fort Stanton to sell beef to the Army for its men and their Navajo and Apache captives.

Chisum claimed vast stretches of grazing land in Southeastern New Mexico, mostly by his mere presence rather than any legal formalities. By 1875, when the 51-year-old cattleman established his headquarters at South Spring River Ranch four miles southeast of "downtown" Roswell, he was known as the "Cattle King of the Pecos." His ranch, often called the "Jinglebob Ranch" because of the earmark he used to identify his cattle, became a popular social center for this part of the Territory (p 130).

Captain Joseph Lea

In 1877, two years after John Chisum located at South Spring River Ranch, 36-year-old Tennessee native and former Confederate Army Colonel Joseph Lea (1841-1904)—"The Father of Roswell"—moved his wife and young son into the four-room adobe house in the middle of this block formerly owned by Van Smith (who had moved on to greener gambling pastures) and began putting together his own cattle and mercantile empire: the Lea Cattle Company. Captain Lea soon owned all of what would become downtown Roswell—his claims were backed by the proper paperwork—and then began extending his holdings to the north and northwest of town. He turned his home into a boarding house, as pictured in an old photo hanging in the lobby of the Roswell Public Library, and opened a grocery and dry goods store in Van Smith's old store. Captain Lea, as he was usually known because he spent most of his time in the Confederate Army at this rank, rapidly became a powerful figure in Southeastern New Mexico. Lea's home came to rival that of John Chisum as a center of social activities in early Roswell.

Enter Billy the Kid

One of John Chisum's hands on his South Spring River Ranch was teen-aged Billy the Kid (1859-1881) who was born in New York City but grew up in Silver City, New Mexico. Controversy surrounds almost all aspects of Billy's life and death. Some viewed him as a cold-blooded killer, but many New Mexicans, especially Hispanics and women, thought him a charming, fun-loving young man—and a good dancer. (The townspeople of Santa Fe even serenaded the 21-year-old during his brief stay in jail there in 1880.)

In 1878 John Chisum joined with John Henry Tunstall and Alexander McSween in trying to break (or take over) the monopoly that Lawrence Murphy and J.J. Dolan held on mercantile goods in Lincoln and on government contracts to supply beef to nearby Fort Stanton and the Mescalero Indian Reservation. Over the course of several years, the Lincoln County War—as this struggle was called—led to the deaths of at least 19 people who were killed by ranch hands and gunslingers working for each faction while terrorizing Anglo and Hispanic settlers throughout Lincoln County, which at that time included all of Southeastern New Mexico. Billy's strong sympathies lay with the Tunstall-McSween-Chisum faction. In April 1878 after Billy and a group of Regulators (as those working for that faction were called) ambushed and killed Sheriff Brady, who supported the opposing faction, Governor Lew Wallace placed a $500 reward on Billy's head.

Enter Sheriff Pat Garrett

Violence continued back and forth for several years. Finally, former buffalo hunter Pat Garrett (1850-1908) became Sheriff in 1880 and began trying to track Billy down. He succeeded in December of that same year. Billy was captured after a shootout, tried and convicted of murder, then sentenced to hang, but in April 1881 he escaped from the Courthouse in Lincoln—killing two deputies in the process—before Sheriff Garrett could carry out the execution.

Exit Billy the Kid

It took Pat Garrett three months to find Billy again. Acting on a tip, Sheriff Garrett and Deputy John Poe headed for Fort Sumner, stopping to buy ammunition at Captain Joseph Lea's store here on the corner of today's Pioneer Plaza. This time, on July 14, 1881, Sheriff Garrett shot and killed Billy, then buried him next to his two pals (if that's the story you want to believe).

Both Pat Garrett and Billy the Kid remain controversial figures in Southeastern New Mexico. Even today they stir up as many arguments and strong feelings as some controversy about a crashed space ship. The extent of Chisum's role in the Lincoln County War is also debated but there is no denying that he encouraged Billy the Kid to protect Jinglebob interests. By the time the violence got out of hand here in Lincoln County, he did support Sheriff Garrett's efforts to bring Billy to justice however.

Captain Lea Again

Throughout the Lincoln County War Captain Joseph Lea remained a strong, steady influence that kept Roswell "neutral" while conflict and lawlessness reigned throughout the rest of the county. Once the Lincoln County War ended, Captain Lea encouraged others to come to Roswell, donating land to many new settlers and businesses. His wealth and political strength continued to grow, and after the death of John Chisum in 1884 he became the most powerful man in Southeastern New Mexico, using his influence to help carve Chaves County out of Lincoln County in 1889 with Roswell as its county seat.

Captain Lea convinced Robert Goss to open a military school in Roswell in 1891 (p 80). He donated five acres (2 ha) and several buildings in this 400 block of North Main Street for the campus, including a 14' by 25' (4 m by 8 m) shed over a portion of the acequia that brought water from the Spring River to the property, thus allowing the Goss Military Institute to describe itself as one of only two schools in the country with a Natatorium. The campus remained here until 1894 when it moved three blocks north; in 1898 it moved to its current location on North Hill.

When Roswell incorporated as a City in 1903, the people elected Captain Lea as its first mayor but he died shortly thereafter at the age of 62. Three successive structures at NMMI, Lea Avenue in Roswell's Historic District, and later, Lea County on the State's eastern border were all named in Captain Lea's honor.

Pioneer Block

In 1900 John Poe, Pat Garrett's deputy who had later served as Lincoln County Sheriff, bought the land along this part of Main Street, including Van Smith's (and later Captain Lea's) original adobe store on the corner of 4th and Main Streets. He built more stores north from 4th Street naming the group of buildings "Pioneer Block." The original Van Smith hotel, later Captain Lea's home and boarding house, was demolished in 1913 to construct additional buildings in the block. A variety of businesses operated here over the next ninety years.

One such business, the *Roswell Daily Record,* was located at 424 North Main Street in the northernmost building next to the Conoco Service Station from 1925 to 1971, when it moved to its current location at 2301 North Main

Street. It was here that the RAAF Information Officer Lt. Walter Haut delivered his press release on July 8, 1947 announcing the "capture" of a flying saucer, and here where that evening's edition carrying the famous headline "RAAF Captures Flying Saucer on Ranch in Roswell Region" was printed.

In 1992 the UFO Museum, mainly a collection of newspaper clippings at the time, opened its doors in the southernmost section of the Pioneer Block, on the corner of 4th Street, where Van Smith's original store had stood. Although John Poe had demolished part of that original building in 1900, the adobe north wall of Smith's original store was still in use.

Pioneer Plaza

In 1997 and 1998 the City of Roswell demolished all the old buildings in the Pioneer Block to construct Pioneer Plaza and the current parking lot for City Hall. No one thought to save any of the rubble until it was too late. If interesting artifacts were found they disappeared into private collections. Today, Roswell uses Pioneer Plaza as a gathering place for festivals and celebrations. Gray paving tiles around the red Zia sun sign set in a brown background at the front of Pioneer Plaza mark the former location of Van Smith and Captain Lea's house, the first building in Anglo Roswell. The current cement square with park benches on the corner of 4th and Main Streets marks the location of Van Smith's—and later Captain Lea's—store where Sheriff Pat Garrett bought that ammunition he used to shoot Billy the Kid (if he did shoot Billy the Kid).

West on 4th Street

110 **Martin's ("mar-TEENS") Capitol Café**. One of Roswell's most popular restaurants, Martin's, or The Capitol (it's called both) serves great green chicken enchiladas with blue corn tortillas (a Northern New Mexico specialty) and the biggest sopaipillas in town. 624-2111. Open M-Sat for breakfast, lunch, and dinner; closed Sun; holidays variable.

South of the Courthouse

300 Block, North Main Street
East Side

327 **Hispano Chamber of Commerce (former Citizen's National Bank)**. Built in 1900, this structure originally housed Citizen's Bank, organized by John Poe, Pat Garrett's deputy and later sheriff of Lincoln County, along with businessmen Nathan Jaffa and John Rhea, and other investors. The front of the building was constructed of hard brick imported from Texas, while the sides and back were built with softer local brick, although all areas visible from the street have since been covered with stucco. The old side walls and bricked-up arched windows are visible from the alley between Main Street and Virginia Avenue. There's a nicely framed view of the Courthouse from the alley too—except for the power lines.

Citizen's Bank served Roswell, especially local ranchers, for many years. It merged with the former Roswell National Bank (organized in 1903, changing its name to American National Bank with H.P. Saunders as President in

1906) in 1920 and became Citizen's National Bank. Unfortunately, the collapse of the livestock industry in the early 1920s led to its failure in 1923 and prompted the suicide of one major stockholder, John Rhea. John Poe died about the same time with his death also rumored a suicide, but this was never confirmed.

Roswell insurance agent and musician Bobby Villegas founded the Hispano Chamber of Commerce in 1987 to promote small businesses and those owned by women, Hispanics, and other minorities in Roswell. In addition to business activities, the Hispano Chamber sponsors community activities such as Piñatafest, celebrating the September 16th beginning of the successful struggle of Mexico—which included all of New Mexico at the time—to gain independence from Spain in 1821. Along with other organizations and the City, the Chamber also sponsors S.O.Y. ("Save Our Youth") Mariachi, a musical and educational youth organization, also founded by Villegas, whose members learn local and regional mariachi music and perform frequently at events around town. 624-0889. Open M-F variable hours, closed SS and holidays. www.roswellhispanochamberofcommerce.com.

Between the two side entrances of this building along 4th Street, a patch of fine-pebble sidewalk paving is one of the few remaining reminders of someone's bright idea back in the 1980s to pave downtown Roswell sidewalks with this "poolside" material. It didn't last. A later attempt at downtown beautification produced our current brick crosswalks and sidewalk inserts, which are actually attractive and seem to be holding up well. The jury is still out on these newly landscaped (?) medians on North and South Main and West 2nd Streets covered with river rocks and blue glass pellets. In spite of being impossible to cross without breaking an ankle, the medians are supposed to help "Keep Roswell Beautiful." It will take a few years to know whether their fate is more like that of the brick inserts or the pool pavement.

313-315 (**Former J. C. Penney's Building**.) This is one of the few downtown buildings retaining some of its original design, remnants of once-interesting architectural detail that are best viewed from across the street. The round areas high on the facade were once windows with the panes divided into pie-shaped sections.

J.C. Penney's was the first national department store chain to move into Roswell—the beginning, so long ago, of the end for many local merchants. The empty storefronts along Main Street today testify as to how many businesses Downtown Roswell has lost to the Mall at the north end of town—where you can now find J.C. Penney's.

305 **Pecos Flavors Winery**. Here is a comfortable, welcoming spot for tasting and purchasing New Mexico spirits including the Pecos Flavors Winery Galactic Series (Cabernet Sauvignon, White Zinfandel, Muscat); Pecos Applause (a sweet white) and Pecos Pleasure (a red table wine); Billy's Blush from Tularosa Vineyards for more "local color"; and Alien Amber Ale from Sierra Blanca Brewery. Gourmet snacks, Alien Jerky in several flavors, and Alien Dust (dip mixes) also tempt. Fancy New Mexico souvenirs and a delightful little children's book (ages 4-8) *T is for Tortilla* by Jody Alpers, one of the owners, are also for sale. The location hosts occasional local musical talent. 627-6265. Open M-Th 10-7, F and Sat 10-8, closed Sun and Christmas.

East on 3rd Street

118 **Billy Ray's Restaurant and Lounge**. Karaoke nights, occasional comedy nights, and Friday night live bands entertain patrons here. 627-0997. Open M-Sat for lunch (mainly sandwiches) and Tu-Sat for dinner (steaks and Mexican food), closed Sun, holidays variable.

West Side

312 **New Mexico Energy Library**. An interesting but unlabeled model of an oil-drilling rig is on display in one front window, while a rock and mineral collection occupies the other.

308 **L. J. Reischman Memorial Park.** When the building occupying this space burned in 1977, the owner donated the land to the City for a park in honor of his father, Lester Reischman (1892-1977), who moved to Roswell in 1940 and operated Holsum Bakery for over sixty years at 723 North Main Street, the future site of the UFO Museum. This park is a pleasant place to sit and try to figure out the mural—a vision of Roswell, of sorts—if it isn't too hot.

300 **J. P. White Building (former Allison Building, second Masonic Lodge site)**. Masons used the upper floor of the two-story red-brick building constructed on this site in 1893 as their Lodge, after the first one at 208-210 North Main Street burned in the Great Fire of 1893. They rented out the lower floor to businesses and the Post Office. The original building was demolished in 1909 with the two-story Allison Building replacing it in 1910. In 1928 Roswell cattleman and entrepreneur J.P. White purchased the structure, changed its name, and added two additional stories. In 1930 he added another story over half of the building, and completed that floor in 1947, resulting in today's five-story office building. The metal sheath added in 1963 covers all the windows and architectural features, but does give the building something of an other-worldly look that fits in with Roswell's UFO theme.

West on 3rd Street

111-119 **Kraft and Hunter Building**. The Hobson-Lowe Meat and Storage Company was the first to occupy this building in 1904 and also manufactured ice on the premises. Over the years it has held a restaurant and creamery; businesses selling appliances, furniture, typewriters, cigars, stationery, racquets, real estate, insurance, and clothing; professionals including attorneys, insurance agents, and abstractors; and several billiard halls. It even contained the U.S. Post Office from 1909 to 1913.

In early Roswell, hotels commonly operated on the second floor of buildings that housed other commercial businesses downstairs. The Plaza Inn occupied the second floor of this building from 1918 to 1966. The Roswell Building and Loan Association, founded in 1901 (and now Pioneer Bank at 306 North Pennsylvania Avenue), occupied part of the building from 1926 until 1970. Its vault is still in place and used as a storage area for legal documents.

Some of the more ornate architectural details have been lost over the years but second floor iron window railings and detailed moldings near the roofline are still interesting. Old photos of the building are on display in the entryway to the Kraft and Hunter Law Offices, along with several old plats of the area showing businesses formerly occupying each structure. The "Buggy Repository" sounds intriguing.

121-123 **Brewer Building**. This building retains even more of its architectural detail near the roofline than the Kraft and Hunter Building next door. Completed in 1908, it housed undertaking businesses for many years, including the original Ballard Funeral Home. In 1944 it became the Community Service Center for personnel from the Roswell Army Air Field. Dances took place on the second floor with its lovely hardwood floors. Since Walker Air Force Base closed in 1967, the Artist-in-Residence Program, attorneys, and currently an oil company have found office space here.

From the alley between Main Street and Richardson Avenue the building's interesting rear doorway and arched windows are visible, as are similar bricked-up structures in the Kraft and Hunter Building next door.

127 (**Former Carnegie Library**). Nineteenth-century industrialist Andrew Carnegie became a philanthropist in later life, using his vast fortune to build 2,800 public libraries throughout the country, including this one opened in 1906. The Roswell Woman's Club, that had begun the project in 1897, raised money to buy the land and purchase the books, while Carnegie provided $10,000 to construct the building. It sits empty now and is available for purchase; its role as a library ended in 1978.

200 Block, North Main Street

Do you feel an eerie presence the closer you get to the UFO Museum? Like alien eyes are watching you? Check out the street lamps from here to 1st Street—and a few other places along Main Street.

East Side

211 **Bullock Park**. Tiny Bullock Park is dedicated to J. Dixon Bullock, who operated the jewelry store next door founded by his father Oscar and currently owned by his son Don.

209 **Not of This World**. Tourists find this espresso bar and Internet café with its comfy couches, space-themed murals, and fifteen minutes of free Internet a restful stop for drinks, sandwiches and snacks. Board games, magazines, and occasional live local music make it a popular evening hangout for teens, especially on Friday nights when it becomes a "Christian dance club." 627-0077. Open 6:30 a.m.-11 p.m. every day, holidays variable.

205 **Roswell Landing**. This souvenir shop has the usual UFO merchandise, but the t-shirt slogans seem more clever and the books more "far out." Its fascinating miniature scenes of daily alien life are, unfortunately, not for sale, but information about a proposed resort, Earth Station Roswell, is available to prospective investors. Open M-Sat 9-7, closed Sun, holidays variable.

201 **Ginsberg Music Company (*Pecos Valley Register* site)**. James A. Erwin opened the first newspaper in Roswell in an adobe building on this site in 1888 with his 17-year-old brother-in-law, future attorney Louis O. Fullen, working as his "printer's devil." After several moves, mergers, and name changes, this original *Pecos Valley Register*, published weekly on Saturdays, was absorbed by the *Roswell Daily Record* in 1925.

Benjamin Ginsberg (1897-1981) was born in Iowa and moved to Albuquerque with his family in 1912 where he went to work for the Baldwin Piano Company. In 1917 he and his wife moved to Roswell and he opened his own Baldwin Piano dealership (and confectionary—seems like an odd combination) in what later became the J.P. White Building. After several changes of location, he established Ginsberg Music Company here where it has remained ever since. A successful businessman, Ginsberg helped organize Security National Bank (later bought by Bank of America) and financed the expansion of the Petroleum Building in 1954. He was also active in several service clubs, served as state president of the Elks Club, and became an early member of Congregation B'nai Israel.

Today Ginsberg Music Company is owned by Ben's son Bernard and his wife Hannah and operated by their son Pruitt Ginsberg. 622-5630. Open M-F 9:30-5:30, Sat 9:30-5, closed Sun and holidays.

East on 2nd Street

109 (Former Soo Lee Hand Laundry). Settlers of Chinese origin were rare in early Roswell but around the turn of the Twentieth Century Soo Lee (often written Sue Lee) opened a fine hand laundry in this building, later incorporated into the Ginsburg Music Company (the building, not the laundry). He and his family lived in a back room.

A Roswell old-timer, Ted Hunt—who grew up in Roswell, graduated from NMMI in 1918, became its band director, and wrote its current fight song—remembered that children entertained themselves in early Roswell by going to watch Mr. Lee iron clothes. They were fascinated seeing him take a mouthful of water and deftly spray it on a shirt wherever it was needed as he ran his heavy flatiron over the front, back, and sleeves.

Soo Lee delivered freshly laundered linens and clothing by horse and buggy, and presented his customers with bars of fine hand-made soap at Christmas time. The citizens of Roswell and the surrounding area liked and respected Lee and valued his careful attention to their laundry needs—all except for Count Mancini-Martini, Modern Languages instructor at NMMI, who disliked all Roswell laundries so much for some unknown reason that he sent his dirty clothes out of town by train to be washed elsewhere.

In 1916 competition from the more modern Beaty's Steam Laundry across the street and Roswell Steam Laundry at 515 North Virginia Avenue—that opened in 1899 and remains in business today at the same location as Ameripride Linen and Apparel Services—forced Soo Lee to move down the street to a new building at 119 East 2nd Street and transform into the Soo Lee Steam Laundry. This was evidently a good decision as his continuing entrepreneurial success allowed him to retire to California in 1923.

116 Roswell Space Center (former Beaty's Steam Laundry). Beaty's Steam Laundry, occupying this building from shortly after 1900 until 1924 when it closed, gave the Soo Lee Hand Laundry across the street strong competition. In later years the building held a plumbing and heating company and a paint and glass contractor.

Today the "Off-World Trade Goods" at Roswell Space Center consist of attractive t-shirts designed by the owner-artist, alien salsa and other good stuff, alien marshmallow guns, and numerous other trinkets popular with all types of visitors—you may notice little green footprints on the sidewalk leading here from Main Street. Inside, their Roswell Spacewalk (small admission fee) contains space scenes illuminated by black light "that rival the ice moons of Jupiter." Outside, their Space Mural (a work in progress) and their garbage cans are otherworldly. 627-6868. Open 8-6 every day, holidays variable, closed Christmas.

West Side

226 **Bank of the Southwest (former First National Bank of Roswell)**. Roswell citizens who used banks in 1890 did their banking in Albuquerque, Santa Fe, or Las Vegas, New Mexico, all 200 miles away, as these were the closest towns with such financial institutions.

On July 19, 1890 Edward A. Cahoon and a buddy left Albuquerque driving a buckboard loaded with $50,000 in bundles of bills and sacks of nickels, dimes, and quarters, heading south to open the Bank of Roswell. Two armed cowboys on horseback accompanied them. In the buckboard they also carried a small safe and a contraption never before seen in Roswell: a bicycle.

Cahoon and his buddy made the rounds of Albuquerque saloons the night before they left, telling everyone how they planned to come the usual way down to Roswell. Instead, they came "the back way," following the Rio Grande south through Isleta to Socorro, then across the mountains to Carrizozo, Lincoln, and on into Roswell. Their plan worked. They arrived safely in Roswell with their $50,000—and their safe and bicycle—on July 23. After that hot, dusty trip the first thing the four men did once they had secured their cargo was take a refreshing dip in the Spring River. The Bank of Roswell opened for business three days later, July 26, in the lobby of the Pauly Hotel—on the site of the current UFO Museum.

John Poe, one of the bank investors, constructed a building on this site and the bank moved into it in 1899. It received its Federal charter that same year and became the First National Bank of Roswell—the only bank in Roswell to survive the 1929 bank panic. In 1912, today's current larger building, constructed of white glazed brick and called "The White Sentinel of Main Street," replaced Poe's earlier building. Historic photos of both buildings hang in the Wells Fargo Bank lobby. The building was remodeled in 1951 and again in 1974, then the bank moved to its new location at 400 North Pennsylvania Avenue in the mid-1980s and eventually became Wells Fargo Bank.

Today, Bank of the Southwest occupies the extensively remodeled 1912 building. The white brick has disappeared under tan stucco and the white columns that once flanked its doorways now front the house at 712 North Lea Avenue. When Bank of the Southwest expanded south, it left the architectural detail of the two buildings next to it intact, including the fancy iron columns flush with the façade from Roken Iron Works in St. Louis. Decorative moldings along the top under the tan paint are best viewed from across the street.

216 **Alien Zone**. This large souvenir shop has an extensive collection of t-shirts and other alien merchandise, as well as cold drinks and snacks. For a fee, tourists can photograph themselves among a variety of life-sized aliens in "Area 51" to show friends at home what they really discovered in Roswell.

627-6982. Open 9:30-5 every day, closed Christmas and New Year's Day.

204 **Planet Roswell.** The t-shirts, postcards, books, and giant UFO flying discs in this small souvenir shop are worth a stop. A favorite t-shirt slogan: "What happens in Roswell—didn't happen." 627-3300. Open M-Sat 9-7, closed Sun, holidays variable.

200 **Cover-Up Café (Joyce-Pruitt Company Grocery Store site, Montgomery Ward site).** This UFO-themed café in the center of the alien action has recently closed. Are you in the market for a business?

The Joyce-Pruitt Company bought out the successful Jaffa-Prager Mercantile Company in 1896 and moved to this location where it sold groceries and dry goods for several decades. Montgomery Ward Department Store operated here from 1933 to 1966. Denny's Restaurant constructed the current building and served meals here from the 1970s through 2002.

West on 2nd Street

128 **Roswell Police Department: L. O. "Tommy" Thompson and L. M. Hall Law Enforcement Center (former Roswell Automobile Company, former Roswell State Bank).** Former cowboy, buffalo hunter, and gambler James W. Stockard (1859-1924) moved to Roswell in 1894, acquired hotel, saloon, gambling, and livery stable businesses, and bought Pat Garrett's ranch on the Hondo River east of town where he raised racehorses and wolfhounds. At the turn of the century, a trip from Roswell to Santa Fe on the newly completed railroad took three days over a circuitous 500 mile (800 km) route through Amarillo, Texas and Trinidad, Colorado. When the New Mexico Central Railroad connected Torrance, a town 111 miles (177 km) northwest of Roswell, with Santa Fe directly in 1903, Stockard and various backers formed the Roswell Automobile Company to transport passengers on a daily automobile stage line to the train depot in Torrance—only a nine-hour drive over primitive roads that Stockard had scraped across the prairie.

Stockard built a two-story cement brick "complete automobile garage" on this site in 1904 to service his stage line equipment. The second story contained offices and a large apartment for him and his wife. (From 1906 to 1908 when Stockard served as Mayor of Roswell, those second floor offices became City Hall.) Although Stockard began selling Thomas and Kissel Kar automobiles downstairs in 1905—thus establishing the first automobile dealership in Roswell two years after the first automobile, a 1902 Oldsmobile owned by an early doctor, made its appearance in town—he soon switched to more popular Buicks. In that same year Stockard negotiated a contract to carry the U.S. Mail on his stage line that was now operating three brand new two-cylinder, 27-horsepower Buicks (one of which is pictured crossing Macho Draw in an historic photo in the Roswell Public Library lobby). On January 10, 1906 he initiated the world's first Automobile Mail Route, cutting two days off the time needed for mail delivery in and out of Roswell.

J.W. Stockard sold his interest in the Roswell Automobile Company in 1910 but it continued to operate here for many years. Roswell State Bank opened in one room of the building in 1946, and then expanded to take over the whole building, until they razed it in 1958 to replace it with this current structure. When First Interstate Bank took over Roswell State Bank it enlarged the building. Then in the mid 1990s the bank moved to its current location (400 North Pennsylvania Avenue, where it was taken over by Wells Fargo Bank) and the Roswell Police Department took over this current building.

In Roswell's early years the Lincoln County Sheriff, headquartered in Lincoln 50 miles (81 km) to the west, provided law enforcement in Roswell, such as it was. Buffalo Soldiers from Fort Stanton made Roswell's first arrest in 1878 while maintaining peace during the Lincoln County War. After Chaves County split off from Lincoln County in 1889, C.C. Fountain won the first election for Chaves County Sheriff—defeating former Lincoln County Sheriff Pat Garrett—and opened the first Sheriff's Office in the new county seat at Roswell. When Roswell incorporated as a town in 1891 it hired Henry Wright as the first Town Marshall to enforce town ordinances—the beginning of the local Roswell Police Department.

Several colorful characters have held the post of Town Marshal—later called Chief of Police—over the years: dime-novel styled Charlie Perry from 1893 until 1894 when he became Sheriff—from which position he later absconded with tax monies; one-armed reformed outlaw J.J. Roscoe who made the rounds from 1904 to 1906 on his "very fine sorrel horse" with a cartridge belt wrapped around his waist, a double-action Colt .45 on his left hip, a sawed-off 12-gauge shotgun in a scabbard strapped to one side of his saddle, and a Winchester .30-30 repeating rifle in the scabbard on the other side; and Barney Leonard, really only a Deputy, who began patrolling the streets single handedly (literally) on his Harley-Davidson motorcycle in 1912.

The Roswell Police Department acquired its first automobile in 1930, the same year it and the Fire Department moved into a building at 108 West 1st Street (now a parking lot), and its first radio dispatch system in 1940, just a year after it moved into the newly completed City Hall at 415 North Richardson Avenue. By 1948 when longtime Police Chief "Tommy" Thompson took over the department it included 10 officers and had begun dealing with felonies as well as enforcing city codes. By the time his successor, L.M. Hall, completed his tenure in 1978 the force had grown to more than 30 officers operating in three divisions: patrol, traffic, and detective units.

Police Headquarters moved into a building at 519 East 2nd Street (now also a parking lot) in 1962. In 1973 it moved from those quarters to the former Terminal at the old Municipal Airport in northwest Roswell. Then in 1993 it moved here, from where 98 officers protect Roswell citizens today.

When the City took over this building and remodeled it for the Roswell Police Department, it named the structure the "James W. Stockard Building" in recognition of Stockard's early "accomplishments and pioneering spirit" at this location. After the Police Department moved in they followed police tradition and, with the Stockard family's gracious support, renamed the Building the "L.O. 'Tommy' Thompson and L.M. Hall Law Enforcement Center" in honor of two of their own who were admired for their outstanding contributions to the Police Department and the community.

The plaque naming the building for Stockard remains in the entrance-way, which is on the south side. A small museum off the lobby contains interesting historic Police Department photos, uniforms, and awards, as well as a plaque dedicated to Roy Woofter, the only Roswell Police Officer ever killed in the line of duty—in 1911.

131 **Roswell Chamber of Commerce**. Designed to promote area businesses, this organization also provides tourist information in the building lobby. 623-5695. www.roswellnm.org. Open M-F 8-5, closed SS and holidays.

100 Block, North Main Street
East Side

127 **She's So Unique (former *Pecos Valley Register*)**. The Pecos Valley's first newspaper, the *Pecos Valley Register,* which started publishing in 1888 across 2nd Street from here, moved into this building in 1899. After various configurations it finally merged with the *Roswell Daily Record* in 1925. The building was later occupied by Hall-Poorbaugh Press, Malone Motor Company, Yucca Drug and Photo Shop, Marcus Shoes, and just previously to the current boutique, by Shepler's Saddle Shop and Western Wear that sported a life-sized horse statue on the roof. No one seems to know what happened to the horse when Shepler's closed—another Roswell mystery.

115-117 **Roswell Home Furnishings (Jaffa-Prager Mercantile Company site, former Mabie-Lowrey Hardware Company, former Wilmot Hardware Company)**. This location was originally the site of the largest mercantile business in early Roswell—the Jaffa-Prager Mercantile Company, Roswell's first department store. Like many German Jews in the Nineteenth Century, four Jaffa brothers emigrated from Prussia to Trinidad, Colorado, by way of Pennsylvania, in the 1870s where they established a grocery business. Three brothers of the next generation, Nathan, Harry, and Joseph Jaffa, came to Roswell. Nathan established a mercantile business in 1886, first on a small scale at John Chisum's South Spring River Ranch, then on this site near "downtown" Roswell. Sidney and William Prager joined him and his brothers a year later to organize the Jaffa-Prager Mercantile Company, selling groceries and dry goods and dealing in wool and hides. All members of the firm were civic minded and supported the growth of Roswell. Their business thrived over the next ten years. In fact, when early settlers got around to naming streets, they decided that this important store marked the beginning of town, so they called its location the corner of 1st and Main Streets. In 1896 the Jaffa-Prager Mercantile Company sold their successful business to the Joyce-Pruitt Company but Nathan Jaffa and William Prager continued to play important entrepreneurial roles in the growth of Roswell well into the Twentieth Century.

Jay Mabie, father-in-law of famous western music performer of the 1920s, '30s, and '40s, Louise Massey Mabie, founded the Mabie-Lowrey Hardware Company in this current building in 1912. Its intricate architectural details remain hidden underneath the current metal and stucco façade.

During the 1920s before radio came to Roswell, the Mabie-Lowrey Hardware Company set up a large baseball diamond sign on their porch roof.

Crowds gathered along the street to hear them broadcast each World Series game over a loud speaker, based on information from the wire at the *Roswell Daily Record* office, with announcers reporting the play-by-play action and providing "color" while they moved markers around the bases on the sign.

A young man named Dan Wilmot became an officer of the Mabie-Lowrey Hardware Company in 1922, following such Roswell notables as William Prager, Nathan Jaffa, and Sheriff John Poe. Wilmot helped run the business until 1942 when he took it over, changing its name to the Wilmot Hardware Company which remained in operation until the 1970s. It was Dan Wilmot and his wife Grace who reported seeing a flying saucer zoom over their house shortly before the 1947 UFO Crash (pp 26, 73).

101 (**Former Green Lantern Bar**). This building served as a billiard hall for much of its nearly 100 years of existence, although in the 1920s a proprietor named Hing Lee sold Chinese merchandise here. By 1941 it had become a bar—first the Dinty Moore, then the Green Lantern owned at one time by Bob Crosby, "The King of the Cowboys." Although now just a dilapidated building with an unlit green lantern neon sign out front, it served a lively clientele well into the 1980s. Soft Roswell-made brick used in its construction is visible in the exposed north wall.

West Side

126 **Roswell Alien Corner**. Once called the Apache Gallery—there's still a painting of Geronimo on the wall around back—this business found that UFO merchandise sells better. It still carries some souvenir Native American pottery, Mexican imports, rocks and minerals, dolls, and other interesting items in addition to alien souvenirs. Need a cow skull? Or an alien skull? This is the place.

One of the first permanent structures in Roswell, this two-story local-made-brick building was constructed as the El Capitan Building in 1894 and housed the Roswell Drug Store for many years. The upstairs contained rooms for rent, which reportedly are still intact (but closed off and creepy). The current metal façade covers the usual fancy architectural details of that era but the original structure can be glimpsed by peeking up under the façade outside the front door. Bricked-up windows and the old tin roof on the building next door are visible from the alley. 627-7489. Open M-Sat 9-4:30 in winter, 9-8 in summer, Sun 12:30-4, holidays variable, closed Christmas.

114 **International UFO Museum and Research Center (former Plains Theater, Pauly Hotel site)**. As Roswell's primary tourist destination, the UFO Museum welcomes thousands of visitors from around the world each year, ranging from serious researchers to curious fun seekers to confirmed skeptics. In addition to exhibits about the Roswell UFO crash, the Museum presents information on other UFO sightings, crop circles, ancient astronauts, alien abductions, Area 51, government cover-ups and conspiracies, and just about every other UFO- or alien-related topic. You can even have your photo taken here by a professional photographer with a UFO backdrop, for a fee.The Museum's goal is not necessarily to provide answers, but to stimulate questions. It also contains the world's most complete UFO research library with books, pamphlets, magazine articles, original documents,

and memorabilia related to UFOs, as well as Internet access for the benefit of researchers and a marvelous mural painted by Roswell High School art students. Various controversies have arisen within the Museum itself over the years, but it remains a dynamic institution.

Many of the UFO Museum exhibits consist of newspaper clippings and other documents, with some three-dimensional displays, art, and a wall of fun UFO cartoons—were you expecting real aliens? Overall, the museum appeals more to adults than children, as many of the exhibits require detailed reading, but a real devotee could spend hours and hours here. The autopsy scene props from the 1994 Showtime movie *Roswell* is the kids' favorite, except for the Gift Shop, of course. The building is cleverly arranged to exit visitors through this Gift Shop, which has more alien and UFO merchandise than you could ever imagine—t-shirts, including official UFO Festival shirts, mugs, posters, door mats, shot glasses, Christmas ornaments, baseball caps, stickers, refrigerator magnets, key chains, action figures, DVDs, and lots of books, just to name a few.

The large 1997 mural on the Museum's south wall facing the parking lot, *Be in(g) Touch*, recalls a similar scene from the Sistine Chapel and has stirred up some controversy of its own.

This location on Main Street has catered to visitors and residents alike since Roswell's early years. An adobe cantina—one of many "thirst emporiums" in early Roswell—hosted fun-seeking pioneers on this spot in 1885.

In early 1890 Allene O'Neal, a former actress who claimed to have been on stage at Ford's Theater when President Lincoln was assassinated, opened Roswell's first real hotel in a new adobe building erected here. She named the hotel after her "benefactor," P.F. Pauly, builder of the first Chaves County Courthouse, who financed the project. The Pauly Hotel was "The Only First-Class Hotel in the City" as its old ad read, and in July 1890 E.A. Cahoon opened Roswell's first bank, eventually called the First National Bank of Roswell, in the hotel lobby.

When James Stockard, an early Roswell "wheeler-dealer," took over in 1898 he changed its name to the Grand Central Hotel, adding a gambling operation and the fancy saloon pictured in an 1897 photo in the Wells Fargo Bank lobby. Later owners operated it as the Bankhead Hotel after World War I, until fire in the spring of 1937 completely destroyed the building. The location served as a used car lot before the Plains Theater was constructed on the site in 1947. This movie theater remained in business until 1978, then the building stood more or less vacant until the UFO Museum moved here in 1997.

The *Roswell Morning Dispatch*, a now-defunct newspaper that started as the *Southwestern Dispatch* in 1925 and was absorbed by the *Roswell Daily Record* in 1950, operated in the building to the south of the hotel from 1931 to 1949 (it survived the fire). The UFO Museum has taken over this space for its Gift Shop but hints of the building's once elaborate façade are still visible outside above the windows. It was here that Lt. Walter Haut delivered one of his press releases about the Flying Saucer Crash in 1947. The Museum charges an admission fee. www.roswellufomuseum.com. 625-9495. Open 9-5 every day except Thanksgiving, Christmas, and New Year's Day.

West on 1st Street

102 **El Toro Bravo Bakery**. A colorful variety of Mexican pastries is available here along with tamales by the dozen. Use the tongs to place your selections on a tray and take them to the cashier. 627-5701. Open M-Sat 8 a.m.-9 p.m., Sun 7 a.m.-9 p.m., holidays variable.

108 **Starchild**. This shop sells simple UFO crash scenes created with "genuine Roswell rocks" and cans of Alien Pate and Alien Sausages, in addition to the usual alien ID cards, t-shirts, aprons, etc., etc. 627-6990. Open 8:45-5:30 every day, later in summer, holidays variable.

100 Block, South Main Street
East Side

115 **Roswell Seed**. John Gill (1848-1923) was born in Tennessee but at the age of 46 brought his family to Roswell in 1894 to open a furniture store and undertaking business—two businesses that often went together in that era because the furniture maker also built caskets. When Gill got so fat that he was turned down for insurance, he decided he needed more exercise so he sold his store to a Mr. Dilley and bought a small ranch outside of town. After several slimming years on the ranch he opened Roswell Produce and Seed Company in the 100 block of North Main Street about 1898 and hired Mr. Dilley to build seed bins and counters for the new store.

Gill began publishing his Seed Catalogue in 1903, sharing his advice about what to plant and when to plant it in the Pecos Valley, in addition to listing seed for sale. By 1909 John Gill's son Walter had become a partner. They changed the company name to Roswell Seed and moved the store two blocks south to where it remains in business today, still using the seed bins and counters Mr. Dilley built over 100 years ago.

Walter Gill later revised the Seed Catalogue, as did John Gill's grandson Verdi Gill. This old-fashioned, family-run business continues to publish the Seed Catalogue every year, and Jim Gill, John Gill's great-grandson, continues to dispense advice to local gardeners and serious farmers alike. 622-7701. Open M-Sat 8-5, closed Sun, holidays variable.

West Side

102 **El Toro Bravo Restaurant.** The small Mexican buffet here is both flavorful and moderately priced, as are items from the menu. Occasionally live music entertains during the evening on weekends. 622-9280. Open for lunch and dinner every day, holidays variable.

106 **Alien Zone II**. This souvenir shop is similar to the same owner's Alien Zone at 216 North Main Street with clever alien t-shirts and trinkets. The spooky (PG rated) alien exhibits in the dark "Hangar 84" area are great fun, and free!—definitely worth a visit. Open 9:30-5 every day. Closed November-March.

400 Block, South Main Street

Hondo River Bridge. In the 1800s herds of pronghorn grazed in the fields south of here, coming to the river to drink. One of the few places early settlers found bushes and trees, the riverbanks also supported thick growths of grapes that pioneers made into delicious jams, jellies, and occasional batches of wine.

Thickets here also provided good hiding places, as Roswell's fearless and second-most-famous sheriff, Charlie Perry, discovered one afternoon in September 1890. When two rowdy Griffin brothers began causing a disturbance in town, Charlie Perry, at that time a Deputy U.S. Marshal, was called in to deal with the problem. The Griffin brothers immediately took off south out of town. Perry recruited two able-bodied men to assist him and headed out after the two ruffians, but he and his small posse got only as far as this spot where the Griffins were waiting in ambush, hidden among the trees and bushes along the Hondo River. Perry killed both Griffins in the following shootout while neither he nor his two men were injured. This and several similar incidents set Perry on his way to becoming a Wild West sensation "back east" as a dime-novel-style hero rivaling his mentor, Sheriff Pat Garrett—that is until the day in June 1896 when he absconded with $7,639.02 in Chaves County tax funds.

Chapter IV. Downtown Historic District

Original houses in the Roswell area were made of adobe or even sod. Log cabins were rare as the closest trees grew in the mountains 75 miles to the west—until settlers began planting them around their new homes. The arrival of the railroad in 1894 allowed "exotic" building materials like brick, glass, and lumber to be brought in more easily, and newly arriving Roswell residents then began to build with these new materials in the familiar styles of their hometowns farther east: Georgian, Queen Anne, Colonial Revival, California Mission, Hipped Box, Mediterranean, Prairie, and Greek Revival among others.

As Roswell grew during the late 1800s and early 1900s, patterns of settlement emerged. Hispanics generally lived south of the Hondo River on the east side of town. The small number of African-Americans tended to cluster along the Hondo River east of Main Street, but some lived interspersed in mainly Hispanic or Anglo areas. Working-class Anglos lived close to the business district, while wealthy Anglo merchants, bankers, and cattlemen built their larger, more expensive homes along wide avenues farther west. As the business district expanded in the second half of the Twentieth Century, homes in some of these residential areas, such as the 300 and 400 blocks of North Pennsylvania and North Kentucky Avenues, were replaced by businesses, but most of the area remains residential: today's Downtown Historic District.

A detailed walking or driving map of the Downtown Historic District is available free at the Visitor's Center at or the Historical Center.

Broad lawns and stately cottonwood, elm, poplar, mulberry, and pecan trees give the Downtown Historic District a Midwest feel and create a friendly habitat for birds and the squirrels whose ancestors early Pecos Valley developer J.J. Hagerman reportedly imported from "back east." White-winged, Mourning, and Inca Doves are common here. In March and October Turkey Vultures gather for migrations in large numbers, often roosting in trees in the Downtown Historic District or riding thermals over the pecan orchards, creating a sometimes eerie atmosphere.

Sidewalks in the Downtown Historic District stamped with dates like 1909, 1910, and 1914 are in pretty fair condition for something that has been walked on for almost 100 years. The older ones have a brownish cast. Is it from age, or just different materials? A walk along the alleys as well as the sidewalks gives a different perspective on some of the houses and uncovers a few hidden gems.

This guide to the Downtown Historic District—covering a little more than the actual Historic District—starts on Richardson Avenue, the first street west of Main Street, and works its way west. The description of each street begins on the north and proceeds southward, also covering sites between each street and the next street to the west.

Richardson Avenue and One Block to the West

Richardson Avenue, 600 Block North
West Side
West on 6th Street
215 **Rhea house.** John W. Rhea ("RAY"), Roswell banker, President of the Roswell Trading Company, and partner in the Rhea-White Ranching Company in the Sacramento Mountains 100 miles (161 km) to the west, built this

Hipped Box style house in 1905. The wide, wrap-around porch was a pleasant place to sit and catch a breeze on a hot summer evening. In recent years this house has been converted to office space used by attorneys and medical professionals.

Around 1912 noted African-American cowboy Addison Jones and his wife Rosa Haskins Jones lived in the small house on the back of the lot—now 605 South Pennsylvania Avenue—while Mrs. Jones worked as a domestic in the Rhea household. "Old Add" was famous as an expert bronco buster and a "walking encyclopedia" of cattle brands.

Downtown Historic District

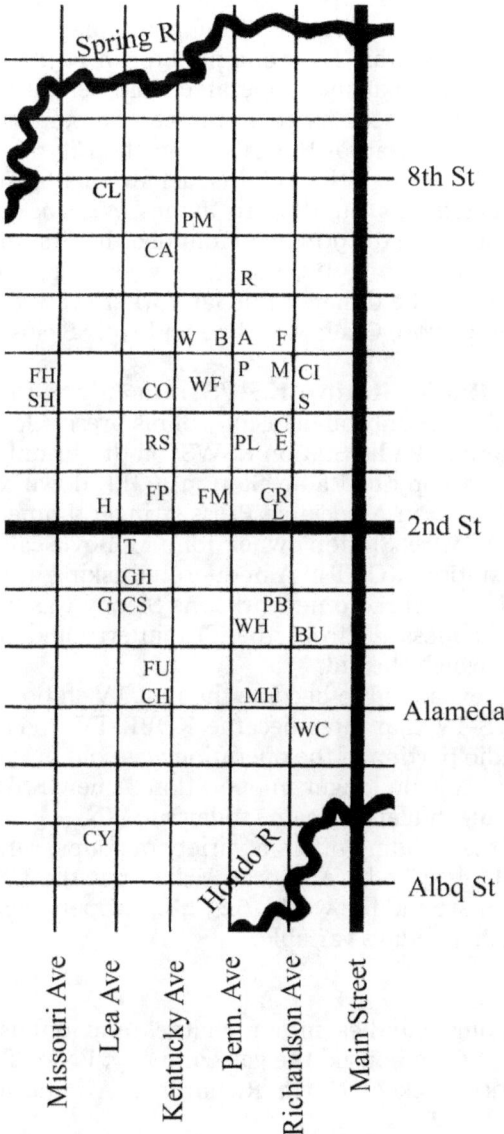

KEY

A	St. Andrews Episcopal Church
B	1st Baptist Church
BU	Burritos and More
C	Cobean Stationery Co.
CA	Cahoon house
CH	Church house
CI	City Hall
CL	Former 1st Nat. Bank columns
CO	Corn house
CR	Copy Rite Building
CS	Christian Science Church
CY	Crosby house
E	Elegante Hair Salon
F	Federal Building
FH	1st Hinkle house
FM	1st United Methodist Church
FP	1st Presbyterian Church
FU	Fullen house
G	Garrett house
GH	Gill house
H	Historical Center
L	La Posta Restaurant
M	Municipal Court
MH	Massey house
P	Post Office
PB	Petroleum Building
PL	Public Library
PM	Poe-Mossman house
R	Rhea house
RS	School Adm. and Educ. Center
S	Schlotsky's Deli
SH	2nd Hinkle house
T	Tinnie Merc. Store and Deli
W	Former Woman's Club
WC	Wilson-Cobb Library
WF	Wells Fargo Bank
WH	Wilmot house

Richardson Avenue, 500 Block North
West Side

500 **Federal Building.** This 1967 building was designed to suggest Native American motifs—seemingly more Central American than North American. It houses the Federal Bankruptcy Court and offices for Social Security, Medicare, the IRS, and the 10th District Circuit Court of Appeals where Federal judges occasionally hear cases. Like all Federal buildings, security here has tightened since September 11, 2001.

Richardson Avenue, 400 Block North
East Side

415 **City Hall**. WPA workers constructed this solid, no-nonsense building with Art Deco cement panels on the façade. As one of the many plaques inside the structure emphatically states, it was "Built and paid for in 1938-39." From 1939 to 1962 the Roswell Police Department operated from here, along with other City officials. Today it only houses City government offices, including that of the Mayor—the ceremonial head of the City—and the City Manager who actually runs things. "In recognition of his achievements and pioneering spirit" the City dedicated this building to James W. Stockard (1859-1924), mayor of Roswell from 1906 to 1908, who founded the first motorized mail delivery route in the world in 1905, the same year he opened Roswell's first auto dealership. In 1915 he donated this land where City Hall was eventually built to the City. 624-6700. Open M-F 8-12 and 1-5, SS closed, holidays variable.

401 **Schlotsky's Deli (former Radio Station KSWS).** On July 8, 1947, RAAF Information Officer Lt. Walter Haut brought a copy of his press release about the crashed flying saucer here to Radio Station KSWS, on the air only a few months, after first delivering a copy to Radio Station KGFL down the street. Station manager George Walsh, an Associated Press stringer, immediately sent the information to the AP wire. Station owner John McBoyle called Lydia Sleppy at their sister radio station, KOAT in Albuquerque, asking her to put the story out to the ABC and Mutual radio networks. As Sleppy was typing the story onto the teletype a message from the FBI interrupted her transmission telling her to cease—which she did.

In 1953 Radio Station KSWS expanded to become the first TV station in Southeastern New Mexico, KSWS-TV that later became KOBR-TV, today's Channel 8 in Roswell. The AM radio portion of the operation was sold in 1965 and eventually became KRSY, which is no longer in operation. A new KSWS radio station went on the air in 1965 and later became today's KCKN.

The restaurant currently in the building offers a variety of soups, sandwiches, and pizza. Munch a "Schlotsky" where George Walsh put the UFO Crash story on the AP wire to flash around the world. 623-4840. Open M-Sat for lunch and dinner, Sun for lunch, holidays variable.

West Side

403 **Municipal Court**. This Court handles minor charges and offenses against City laws in a building that once housed the gas company, PNM. The flowerbeds that brighten the 400 block of North Richardson Avenue are

courtesy of former Municipal Court Judge Hector Pineda who frequently sentenced offenders to gardening as community service. 624-6725.

400 (**First Christian Church site**). The Disciples of Christ organized their first Christian Church in Roswell in 1892, as the town's third church. The congregation constructed their first building here in 1895, replaced it with a more modern building in 1918, and in 1957 moved to their current location at 1500 South Main Street. The 1918 building was then demolished, and the site remains a parking lot.

Richardson Avenue, 300 Block North
East Side

315 (**U.S. Post Office and Federal Building site**). A photo of the solid two-story Post Office and Federal Building that once stood in this parking lot hangs in the Roswell Public Library lobby. The Post Office opened that new building here in 1913 and left for its current location at 415 North Pennsylvania Avenue in 1961. Newly established Roswell Community College took over the structure from 1963 to 1967, then it was demolished in 1971.

West Side

320 **Cobean Stationery Company**. The Cobean family founded this store in 1916 at 208 North Main Street. Today, third-generation family members operate this office supply business with a small but worthwhile bookstore—the oldest continuously operating bookstore in New Mexico—in the back. They stock many local authors and a good selection of books about New Mexico, including such gems as *UFOs and the Murder of Marilyn Monroe*. You won't find that one on Amazon! 622-1541. Open M-F 8-5, closed SS, holidays variable.

310 **Elegante Hair Salon (former Radio Station KGFL)**. Walt Whitmore, Sr. established Roswell's first radio station, KGFL—which he said stood for "Keep Good Folks Listening"—in a building no longer standing at 507 North Main Street in 1931. The radio station moved to 502 West 2nd Street in 1937, then moved to this location in 1943. KGFL remained the only station in town until KSWS went on the air in 1947. Over the years at least three interesting events have been connected with Radio Station KGFL and its influential owner who died in 1951.

In 1933 Walt Whitmore paid to put up a singing group from California called the O-Bar-O Cowboys at Greenhaven Tourist Court, site of today's Poe Corn Park, in exchange for them performing daily on KGFL radio. The group became quite popular locally—their first success on an otherwise disastrous Southwestern tour. As this was the depths of the Depression the musicians still had trouble finding enough money to eat, so Leonard Slye, the group's leader, asked listeners to bring them food. He especially challenged ladies to bring lemon pie, saying no one could make lemon pie as good as his mother's. Local woman Arline Wilkins took up the challenge. She brought two lemon pies to the station, at that time located on Main Street, and struck up a friendship with Slye, discovering that her family farm was just down the street from the tourist court where he was staying. The two stayed in contact even after the group moved on—eventually to Hollywood—and in 1936 Miss

Wilkins and Mr. Slye, who had changed his name to Roy Rogers, were married here in Roswell in her family home at 701 East 2nd Street (which was later moved to 920 E. 2nd Street and is now the office of Michelet Homestead Realty). Their happy marriage lasted ten years until Arline died of an embolism in 1946. Roy Rogers later married Dale Evans and together they starred in a series of popular western movies and TV shows, but he always described Roswell as "where I got my start" on his Happy Trails.

In another interesting connection, KGFL news reporter Frank Joyce was the first to interview Mack Brazel about the UFO debris he found on the Foster Ranch north of Roswell in July 1947. Station owner Whitmore found the story so intriguing that he drove to the Foster Ranch, picked up Brazel, and brought him back to Roswell to record an interview—confiscated by the military before he could broadcast it. Then when RAAF Information Officer Lt. Walter Haut brought his press release about the crashed saucer to the station here in this building, Joyce, a United Press stringer, put it on the UP wire where it made worldwide headlines. In a later interview here, Brazel changed his story after spending several days in military custody, saying the debris came from a weather balloon, but when the subject of "little green men" came up Brazel angrily muttered, "They weren't green!"

Finally, during that same summer of 1947, it was here at KGFL that future Grand Ole Opry and Country Music Hall of Fame Star Lefty Frizzell first went on the air, broadcasting his daily half-hour musical radio show from this studio—until a jail sentence interrupted his career.

In 1974, after 43 years of broadcasting, Radio Station KGFL finally went off the air.

Would you like to get your hair done where Mack Brazel muttered "They weren't green!" and Lefty Frizzell began his on-air musical career? The current building tenant, Elegante Hair Salon, welcomes walk-in clients if space is available. 624-0505. Open M-Sat 10-7, closed Sun, holidays variable.

West on 3rd Street

200 **(Gilkeson Hotel site)**. In 1906 Roswell's largest and most magnificent hotel opened on this site, expanding to include most of the block along 3rd Street two years later. A photograph in the Roswell Public Library lobby of famous Chautauqua lecturer and three-time Democratic presidential candidate William Jennings Bryan speaking to a crowd from the hotel's large second-floor balcony in 1909 shows its two-story Ionic brick columns and gives an idea of its elegance.

In 1943 Roy Norton purchased the establishment and renamed it the Norton Hotel, but in 1966, with the days of the downtown hotel long past, it was demolished and the site became today's parking lot.

Richardson Avenue, 200 Block North
West Side

210 **Copy Rite Building**. Hall-Poorbaugh Press opened its doors at 127 North Main Street in 1914, moved its printing operation to this location in 1924, and finally went out of business here 76 years later in 2001. Today a more "up to date" printing company occupies the building. Former Artist-In-

Residence Matt Berinholtz and Roswell High School art teacher Robin Einhorn organized artists from the Unity Center Teen Program to paint the *Printing Aliens* mural outside on the building's north wall in 1997. 623-4196.

West on 2nd Street
201 **La Posta Restaurant (former Elks Lodge)**. David Tomlinson, the same contractor that built the J.P. White house, now the Historical Center, completed the two-story portion of this building in 1908. He was Mrs. White's father. Originally surrounded by lovely gardens until the one-story addition replaced the landscaped grounds, this building served as the Elks Lodge—organized in Roswell in 1906—until 2002 when the Elks moved to 1720 North Montana Avenue. The restaurant currently occupying the building serves a large and diverse Mexican buffet—something for everyone. 622-1147. Open M-Sat for breakfast, lunch and dinner; Sun for breakfast and lunch; holidays variable.

Richardson Avenue, 100 Block North
West Side
West on 1st Street
200 **Roswell Petroleum Building (Prager house site)**. Beginning in the late 1920s small wildcat oil companies drilled everywhere in Southeastern New Mexico. Some drilling produced gushers and instant millionaires; some produced dry holes and failed businesses. At first, drilling was random and wells were shallow—only a few thousand feet deep at most. As the science developed throughout the 1930s, '40s, and '50s, site selection came to depend on sophisticated technology. Wells went down as much as 20,000' (6000 m) and geologists, engineers, and bankers replaced seat-of-the-pants wildcatters.

The first four floors of the Petroleum Building, Roswell's first skyscraper, were completed in 1952 to provide much needed office space for Southeastern New Mexico's growing oil and gas industry. Four more floors were added two years later and the eight-story tan brick Petroleum Building is currently the third tallest in town. Although larger oil companies have moved their offices out of Roswell, many geologists, land men, and other smaller oil-related companies continue to operate here.

The house of Roswell pioneers William and Anna Sidney Prager that originally stood on this site was moved to 1706 West Juniper Street in 1952 to make room for the new building. Will Prager was a successful Roswell merchant: a partner in the Jaffa-Prager Mercantile Company at 114 North Main Street and later owner of Price and Company, a general merchandise business that operated successfully at 306 North Main Street for over fifty years. Anna Prager was always prominent in Roswell women's civic activities and the Pragers hosted frequent social gatherings. The oldest active Jewish congregation in New Mexico, B'nai Israel—currently meeting at 712 North Washington Avenue—which was organized by Prager's partner, Nathan Jaffa, began meeting here in the Prager home in 1903.

The Petroleum Building's eighth floor balcony provides a wonderful overview of Roswell's downtown area with NMMI in the distance—the best view in town unless you have your own hot air balloon or UFO.

Munchies Pizza and Subs, the current café on the first floor, serves a good, really cheap pepperoni pizza special. 627-0776. Open M-Sat for lunch and dinner, closed Sun, holidays variable.

Richardson Avenue, 100 Block South
East Side

119 **(Jaffa house site)**. Roswell merchant and banker Nathan Jaffa (1863-1945), his wife, and their three children lived where the parking lot across Richardson Avenue from the Petroleum Building is located today. Jaffa, who with William Pager and their brothers, owned the Jaffa-Prager Mercantile Company at 114 North Main Street, had health problems and believed the high mineral content in the water from his shallow well aggravated his difficulties. In 1890 he had a deeper well drilled on his back lot in the hope of finding purer water. At 250 feet (75 m) he struck Roswell's first gusher: artesian water. Initially the well only attracted mild curiosity, but gradually the implications of this new water source dawned on Roswell residents. Others drilled artesian wells in the area, and soon the abundant water supply led to an agricultural boom.

In 1889 Nathan Jaffa had become Chief of Roswell's first Volunteer Fire Department, which unfortunately was unable to quell the Great Fire of 1893 when much of the business section burned. In spite of this, Jaffa was elected Roswell's first mayor—then called Chairman of the Board of Town Trustees—in 1891 when Roswell incorporated as a town. He served another term as mayor from April to December 1903—long before New York City elected Abe Beam as its first Jewish mayor in 1974. In that same year, 1903, although there were only thirty-six Jews in Roswell, Jaffa organized a Jewish synagogue and a Sabbath school, Congregation B'nai Israel, and served as its first leader. Jaffa Street in southern Roswell is named in his honor.

127 **Burritos and More**. Tasty burritos, eat-in or "to go." 622-4447. Open M-Sat for breakfast and lunch, closed Sun, holidays variable.

Richardson Avenue, 200 Block South
West Side
West on Alameda Street

209 **Louise Massey house**. As a teenager in 1917, life-long musician and performer Louise Massey (1902-1983) married Roswell native Milt Mabie (1900-1973) who worked at his father's Mabie-Lowrey Hardware Store on Main Street. Together they organized a family band, Louise Massey and the Westerners, that was "discovered" in 1928 when they auditioned for a Chautauqua agent who was in Roswell. The band toured the U.S. and Canada, sang on NBC Radio, and performed in the Tex Ritter movie, *Where the Buffalo Roam*. Their song "White Azaleas" sold three million copies and "My Adobe Hacienda," that Massey wrote about her home in the Hondo Valley, became a worldwide hit upon its release in 1947.

Milt and Louise Massey Mabie moved into this 1925 Gable with Box style house when they retired to Roswell in 1973 and lived here most of the rest of their lives.

Richardson Avenue, 300 Block South
East Side

301 **Wilson-Cobb History and Genealogy Research Library**. Although it is open only limited hours, this library's collection of materials about families from all areas of the country, but especially the East and South, free computer access to Ancestry.com, and occasional genealogical "mini-seminars" make it an important resource for those interested in genealogy and family history. 622-3322. Open MWF 1-4, closed holidays.

Pennsylvania Avenue and One Block to the West

Pennsylvania Avenue, 700 Block North
West Side

West on 7th Street

311 **Poe-Mossman house**. John Poe (1850-1923), described as a tall and quiet but forceful man, was one of the deputies present when Pat Garrett shot and killed Billy the Kid. Later when he succeeded Garrett as Sheriff of Lincoln County, he and his bride Sophie lived upstairs in the Lincoln County Courthouse, using the room where Billy the Kid had been imprisoned as their bedroom. Sophie Poe's only complaint: she hated walking up and down the stairs every day that were still stained with the blood of Deputy J.W. Bell whom Billy had shot and killed during his escape.

Sophie Alberding Poe (1862-1954) had met John Poe in Roswell in 1882 while she was working in Captain Joseph Lea's boarding house on Main Street. Her older brother, who worked as a ranch hand for Captain Lea, got Sophie the job after their parents died while she was still a teenager.

In later years John and Sophie Poe moved from Lincoln to Roswell where Poe became a successful merchant, then President of the First National Bank that he helped E.A. Cahoon found (p 54). Later still, he constructed the Pioneer Block on Main Street (p 48) and he and businessman John Rhea founded Citizen's National Bank (p 49). Poe Street in southern Roswell is named in his honor.

When John Poe built this Queen Anne style house in 1895 it was called "the most beautiful home in Roswell" because of its gracious shade trees, vine-covered walls, and carefully tended rose gardens. (Surely the original roof did not have the current striking shingle pattern, or did it?) Some claim that it was the first house in Roswell to have indoor plumbing, although the same claim has been made for the Rhea house on 6th Street and for the house at 604 North Pennsylvania Avenue.

Two of the original outbuildings remain in the back yard. The two-story hipped roof barn, built at the same time as the house of locally-made brick (visible in a hole in the east wall), provided ample space—and a good view through all the little windows—for the family horses. The northeast corner also held a workshop and tack room. A stairway gave access to the second floor hayloft on the inside while the large hinged second floor doorway on the alley permitted easy loading of hay and feed into the loft. The small frame laundry house between the main house and the barn was probably a later addition.

John and Sophie Poe soon became the best-traveled residents of Roswell, spending the whole year of 1913 on a leisurely tour around the world. They filled their home with art collected during these extensive travels. Mrs. Poe always wore the latest, most expensive, fashions and enjoyed playing the aristocrat—a far cry from the teenaged orphan working in the Lea family boarding house.

Unfortunately, when John Poe died at the age of 73 he left his 61-year-old widow with few financial resources. Having to sell her treasured home and look for ways to support herself, she turned to writing about their past adventures, publishing several volumes about their travels as well as her most successful book, *Buckboard Days*, a 1936 account of her husband's career in the Wild West.

Burton "Cap" Mossman (1867-1956), bought this house from Sophie Poe in 1923. A wild, reckless, and quick-tempered Western lawman, former Rough Rider, and the first Captain of the Arizona Rangers, Mossman had retired from the Rangers in 1902 to get into the cattle and sheep business in New Mexico. He eventually came to own the Diamond A and Circle Diamond ranches west of Roswell, after a number of additional "Wild West" adventures. A 56-year-old reclusive widower by 1923, Mossman and his two young children lived here by themselves until he married his secretary, Ruth Shrader, in 1925. She later made the first donation to the Roswell Museum and Art Center's permanent collection, a watercolor by Santa Fe artist Olive Rush entitled *Weird Land*. After her husband's death in 1956, Mrs. Mossman continued to live here with her stepdaughter until her own death in 1969.

Pennsylvania Avenue, 500 Block North
East Side

505 **St. Andrews Episcopal Church**. Although Roswell women organized an Episcopal Guild in 1889, St. Andrews Episcopal Church was not formally organized until 1891. The second church in town, it met originally in the Courthouse. The Parish Hall (just east of the steeple) that the congregation built in 1899 in Gothic Revival style with pointed-arch windows is now the oldest church building still standing in Roswell. John Gaw Meem, a Santa Fe architect famous for his efforts to preserve "Santa Fe Style," designed the 1950 sanctuary and steeple additions with Romanesque rounded-arch windows. St. Andrew's Episcopal School, at one time including pre-school and kindergarten through 6th grade, operated here from 1957 to 2008.

West Side

500 **First Baptist Church**. The first Baptist Church in Roswell, organized in 1894 as the fourth church in town, erected its first building in 1895 on the southeast corner of Fourth Street and Pennsylvania Avenue next to the (no longer existent) first Methodist Church where the Roswell Public Library now stands. Rock for that building came from the quarry on Six Mile Hill west of Roswell. In 1907 the congregation moved to a new red brick building on this current site and Roswell artist Florence Morris remodeled the old rock building, a picture of which hangs in the Roswell Public Library lobby, into her

home and studio. It was demolished in 1962. The current tan brick building on this site was completed beside the red brick church in 1962, and the older building was demolished in 1985. First Baptist Church's Living Christmas Tree service is a staple of the Roswell Christmas Season.

Pennsylvania Avenue, 400 Block North
East Side

415 **U.S. Post Office**. Roswell's central Post Office was constructed in 1961. A branch Post Office is located at 5904 South Main Street near the entrance to the RIAC. 623-9868. Open M-F 7:30-5:30, Sat 8-12, closed Sun and federal holidays. The lobby with stamp machines is always open.

Van Smith opened the first area Post Office in his store on today's Pioneer Plaza in 1873, naming the new station "Roswell" after his father, Roswell Smith. The Post Office has moved around over the years: 400 North Main Street, 500 North Main Street, 300 North Main Street, 111 West 3rd Street, 315 North Richardson Avenue, and even for a short time at Postmaster Ash Upson's homestead one and one-half miles (2.4 km) east of town during the Lincoln County War when he tried to settle down rival factions by threatening to do away with a Post Office in Roswell entirely. It worked—briefly.

West Side

400 **Wells Fargo Bank (third Masonic Temple site)**. This tallest skyscraper in Roswell, eleven stories and a penthouse, was built in 1984 and is even identifiable on the Roswell skyline from a hill on US 285 20 miles (32 km) north of town. Unfortunately, there is no public access to the beautiful view from the upper floors.

The banking establishment that eventually became Wells Fargo Bank started out as the Roswell Bank in the lobby of the Pauly Hotel at 114 North Main Street in 1890. It moved to 226 North Main Street in 1899 where it remained until its move to the current location. The original safe E.A. Cahoon brought by wagon to Roswell in 1890 for the Roswell Bank is supposedly still somewhere inside. Several interesting photos of early Roswell hang in the bank lobby.

In 1909 Roswell's more than 350 Masons—a substantial increase over the eight who founded the Lodge in 1888—built their third Masonic Temple on this site, replacing the one demolished at 300 North Main Street to build the Allison (later J.P. White) Building. A picture of this three-story red brick Greek Revival building, fronted by four white columns, each three and one-half feet in diameter and twenty feet high, hangs in the Roswell Public Library lobby. Builders incorporated those four columns into the grand foyer of the fourth Masonic Temple at 2903 West 4th Street when they demolished the building in 1964. 622-3441. Open M-Th 9-5, F 9-6, Sat 9-1, closed Sun and federal holidays.

Pennsylvania Avenue, 300 Block North
East Side

301 **Roswell Public Library**. This attractive 1975 building, remodeled in 2002, with authors' names in metal lettering around the roofline, has a comfortable reading lounge with magazines and newspapers, free Internet access, a fun children's area with papier-mâché sculptures, and a Southwest Section containing interesting books about Roswell. It also maintains materials devoted to local genealogy and family history. The pendulum clock on the wall across from the circulation desk came from the original Carnegie Library at 127 West 3rd Street. Interesting historic photos of Roswell hang in the lobby, which also contains restrooms and water fountains.

Ceramic tiles for Susan Wink's *Tree of Knowledge* on the southwest lawn were made by the Roswell community. The 2008 sculpture celebrating the library's 2006 Centennial represents its deep roots in Roswell and its significant contribution to growth and knowledge in the community.

The plaza surrounding the north entrance is named in honor of Frances Bear Kyte and her mother Grace Thorpe Bear, widow of H. M. F. Bear who bought the *Roswell Record* in 1902 and changed it from a weekly to a daily paper and its leanings from Republican to Democrat. After he died in 1905 Mrs. Bear and his former partner, Charles Mason, continued to publish the paper until 1945. Mrs. Bear helped establish Girl Scouting in New Mexico in 1922 as President of the Roswell Woman's Club. The charming sculpture in Bear Plaza is L. Deane Trueblood's *Reading Bench*.

The white marble pedestal, topped with remains of a sundial marking "the bright hours only," on the northeast edge of the plaza was originally erected by the Woman's Club in 1909 at the Carnegie Library. Puzzle: Can you figure out why this sundial would not tell accurate time, even if its shadow-casting gnomon were still present? Hint: hold a pencil or stick in place and read the time. 622-7101. www.roswellpubliclibrary.org. Open M-T 9-9, W-Sat 9-6, Sun 2-6, closed holidays.

Pennsylvania Avenue, 200 Block North
West Side

200 **First United Methodist Church**. The first Methodist Episcopal Church, South congregation in Roswell was established in 1887 as the town's first organized religious group. In 1888 they constructed the first church in the Pecos Valley, an adobe building at 311 North Pennsylvania Avenue where the Roswell Public Library now stands. A photo of it is on view in the Library lobby. In May 1897 the congregation moved to a new rock church with stained-glass windows on this current location. The original adobe building on Pennsylvania Avenue was remodeled and used as a home until it was demolished in 1962. A red brick building replaced the rock church on this site in 1921, using some of the stained-glass windows salvaged from the rock church. In 1982 the current stone building was completed alongside of the red brick building, which was then demolished. Stained-glass windows from both the stone and red brick churches illuminate the current sanctuary. A lovely carillon plays each day over the lunch hour.

The Cowboy Bell—the first bell in the first church in Southeastern New

Mexico—currently mounted inconspicuously in a wall niche inside the secluded courtyard on the east side of the church, was a gift from cowboys profoundly moved by a Sunday revival meeting in Roswell in 1894 held by famous Texas evangelist Abe Mulkey. Some say the cowboys' generosity was meant to assuage guilty consciences after a Saturday night in Roswell's bars, dance halls, and other establishments of entertainment. The bell called parishioners to services for 88 years until the current sanctuary was completed in 1982.

Pennsylvania Avenue, 100 Block South
East Side

105 **Wilmot house**. As recounted in that famous July 8, 1947 front-page story in the *Roswell Daily Record*, Roswell hardware store owner Dan Wilmot and his wife Grace saw a large, glowing, flying saucer pass overhead while they were sitting on their front porch here on the evening of July 3, 1947 (p 26). Today the house's owner operates a grooming service for toy dogs.

Kentucky Avenue and One Block to the West

Kentucky Avenue, 600 Block North
West Side

612 **Cahoon house**. As President of the First National Bank (p 54), Edward A. Cahoon (1862-1934) completed this impressive Tudor style half-timbered stucco and brick house with a steeply pitched roof for his family in 1929. Cahoon was ambidextrous and enjoyed producing two different "authentic" signatures, always signing personal papers with his right hand and business papers with his left. Cahoon Park, Cahoon Armory at NMMI, and Cahoon Avenue in the southeastern part of town were all named in his honor.

Oilman, rancher, environmentalist, and philanthropist Robert O. Anderson (1917-2007), former President of Atlantic Richfield Oil Company who presided over the discovery of the Prudhoe Bay Oilfield and the construction of the Trans-Alaska Pipeline, lived here in the 1950s and '60s with his wife and six children. In an attempt to keep the house cool during Roswell's sweltering pre-air-conditioned summers, Anderson would open all twenty windows each night to let in cool air. Then the millionaire oilman would rouse himself at 4:30 each morning to close all twenty windows trapping the cool air inside.

Kentucky Avenue, 500 Block North
East Side

501 (**Former Woman's Club building**). Roswell women organized the Woman's Book Club in 1895 to bring civilization to Roswell by obtaining "the best current literature" to stay informed on "literary and social issues" at a time when Sheriff Perry still patrolled our dirt streets with his six-guns. Two years later the renamed Roswell Woman's Club began its drive to establish a public library, and finally succeeded in 1906 with the help of Andrew Carnegie (p 52). All early civic-minded "society ladies" in Roswell participated ac-

tively in the Woman's Club, although husbands initially opposed such a dangerous organization.

Woman's Club President Grace Thorpe Bear, Publisher and Society Editor of the *Roswell Daily Record*, organized the club's effort to construct a building of its own in 1930. Once completed, this building became a center of social activities and a meeting place for other civic organizations. During World War II the USO held dances here. In 1976 the Woman's Club sold this California Mission Revival style building to the First Baptist Church and moved into a building at 2801 West 4th Street that they sold in 2000. Once again operating without a clubhouse, the Woman's Club remains an active civic and social organization today, supporting the Historical Society and providing scholarships to ENMU-R students.

Kentucky Avenue, 400 Block North
West Side

412 **Corn house**. Built prior to 1904 and purchased by pioneer farmer Martin Corn's son Wade in 1917, this Southwestern Vernacular style house with stucco walls, a flat roof, decorative arches, and decorative red roof tiles is currently owned by a great-granddaughter of Martin Corn. The carved tree trunk out front represents a recent art form to appear in Roswell—another can be seen at 100 North Washington Avenue, and a huge one stands in front of the Adult Center at 807 North Missouri Avenue. This carved tree trunk depicts bears at a honey tree.

Kentucky Avenue, 300 Block North
West Side

300 **Roswell Independent School District Administrative and Educational Services Center**. Built as Roswell Junior High School in 1929, this building's sturdy red brick construction, numerous tall windows, and Art Deco touches would identify it as a school in any neighborhood in America. Inside, hardwood floors, high ceilings, and transomed doors raise images of no-nonsense education. Today this older building and the 2000 addition on the northwest corner—where the only public entrance is located—house the administrative offices of the Roswell Independent School District (three high schools, four middle schools, twelve elementary schools, and several special programs).

Roswell schools got their start in 1880 when families built the first one-room adobe school three miles east of "downtown" Roswell. They constructed "The Farms" school at that same location when the first building collapsed in 1886. Meanwhile, families in town had built a "Village School" at East Tilden Street and South Sherman Avenue in 1885 that also served as a community center.

Roswell's first public school, the Third Street School (three rooms, made of local brick, seventy-eight students, two teachers, cost of $5,000) was built on this site in 1890. Kentucky Avenue was "out in the country" at that time and the feeling was that walking to this distant location would provide good exercise for the students.

Central School (three stories, made of "imported" Texas brick, twenty rooms counting "water closets," 645 students including the first high-school graduating class of three, 11 teachers, cost of $25,000) replaced the Third Street School on this site in 1901. It was demolished in 1928 to construct this current building, but its photo hangs in the Roswell Public Library lobby.

Inside the current building, Pueblo Auditorium with Classic Revival bas-relief columns, grape leaf light fixtures, and—for some reason—decorative medallions featuring the Scottish rampant lion flanking the stage, was completed in time for 1929 high school graduation ceremonies. As the largest auditorium in town it hosted plays, concerts, and public meetings—and still does.

Some consider the most important event ever scheduled in Pueblo Auditorium to have taken place on Valentine's Day, February 14, 1955, when a yet-unknown Elvis Presley performed onstage as a part of the Hank Snow tour. Exactly how Elvis fits in with UFOs isn't clear, but evidently the photographer who took the first publicity photos of Elvis also filmed the 1947 alien autopsy—at least that's what the Internet says.

The ghost of a little boy supposedly haunts the balcony. He is sometimes visible from below but disappears when any living person enters the balcony. (This is a pretty tame ghost story, but we'll take what we can get. Ghosts seem to be few and far between in most of Roswell—unlike some other parts of the state.)

Photos of Roswell schools through the years are displayed in the auditorium lobby, an exhibit of student artwork decorates the halls, and a 1917 map of Chaves County Schools and School Districts—including Eden Valley, Macho Draw, Eight Mile Draw, and Blackdom—hangs downstairs in the new addition's hallway.

Tucked away in a small courtyard behind the northwest entrance stand tile-covered bancos—New Mexican for "solid benches"—a creation of artist Susan Wink who also created the bancos for Brainerd Plaza. Friends and family made the colorful individual tiles that form this 2004 *Community Quilt* mosaic in remembrance of educator and much loved Director of Special Education, Sandy Pickens (1944-2000).

Basketball made its debut in Roswell on this spot in 1902 when a group of energetic young ladies attending Central School ordered a rulebook for the sport that had been invented only eleven years earlier. After giving a tea to raise money to purchase a ball, they enlisted the boys to build backboards and a local blacksmith to forge hoops. Never having seen an actual game, they nevertheless organized themselves into several intramural teams, laid out a basketball court behind the school, and began playing in the afternoons. 627-2500. Open M-F 8-5, closed SS and school holidays (but open during the summer).

Kentucky Avenue, 200 Block North
West Side

200 **First Presbyterian Church**. The first Presbyterian Church in Roswell was organized in 1899 as the town's fifth church. The congregation met in the Baptist rock church on the corner of 4th Street and Pennsylvania Avenue until they constructed their own building in 1901 at 3rd Street and Pennsylvania

Avenue, where the Bank of Commerce now stands. It burned in 1932. They built this current Gothic Revival structure with a steeply pitched slate roof—looking somewhat like fish scales—in 1937.

West on 2nd Street
412 **Tinnie Mercantile Store and Deli**. The deli portion of this business serves interesting and delicious sandwiches and salads along with gourmet snacks and desserts. Travelocity has identified Tinnie's as a "hidden gem." In the 1980s Walter Haut, the RAAF Information Officer who wrote the press release about the 1947 UFO Crash, was operating an art gallery and framing shop in this building when publication of the first book about the Crash, called *The Roswell Incident*, made him a sudden, and initially a somewhat reluctant and embarrassed, celebrity. 622-2031. Open Tu-Sat 10-5, closed Sun and M, holidays variable.

Kentucky Avenue, 200 Block South
West Side
200 **Fullen house**. Long-time Roswell attorney Louis O. Fullen constructed this Mediterranean style house with its striking tile roof prior to 1912. Although he later served as District Attorney, at age 17 Fullen became the "printer's devil" and only employee of Roswell's first newspaper when his brother-in-law, J.A. Erwin founded the *Pecos Valley Register*.

210 **Church house**. Joshua P. Church (1862-1917), early Roswell entrepreneur and "character," built this Queen Anne style house with all its roof variations and dormer windows—and a foundation that has recently been rebuilt with an added basement—for his wife Amelia in 1895. He also built a greenhouse for her behind their house, a location used continuously by florists ever since, including by today's House of Flowers at 405 West Alameda Street.

Church's wife, Amelia Bolton (1862-1957), was born in Ireland but grew up in Lincoln, New Mexico. After various adventures and two brief marriages—she outlived both husbands, the second a prominent Lincoln citizen whose actions triggered the Lincoln County War—Amelia Bolton Forest Fritz at age 29 married 29-year-old Joshua P. Church in 1891 and moved with him to Roswell. Church had already been a gold prospector, a Lincoln County Deputy Sheriff, and a South American business promoter when he bought an interest in Roswell's Pauly Hotel and became its manager shortly before his marriage. The newlyweds lived in the hotel for several years, then moved to this house and sold the hotel. At various times Church also owned the Oriental Saloon at 106 North Main Street, the Oriental Drug Company and Billiards Hall at 213 North Main Street, and (briefly) an automobile dealership in El Paso. He was a partner in the first (1894, unsuccessful) and the second (1899, successful) telephone company in Roswell. Although he was a devoted husband, he often ran into problems with alcohol that affected his health, and he died of tuberculosis in 1917.

Amelia Church remained a widow for 40 years this time. A leader in church circles and civic clubs for over sixty years, she was instrumental in founding the Roswell Museum and Art Center in 1937. Mrs. Church loved horticulture and became an authority on Pecos Valley flowers and plants. Her untiring efforts led to plantings of flowers and trees throughout Roswell, including a lovely rose garden that once surrounded the Art Museum, before building expansion covered the area. She organized garden clubs and was active in the Roswell Woman's Club and the Historical Society, as well as being an early member of St. Andrews Episcopal Church. A bronze-colored bust of her appears in the Historical Center as one of the four most important early citizens who contributed to Roswell's civic improvement and development.

Lea Avenue and One Block to the West

Lea Avenue, 700 Block North
West Side
712 **(Former First National Bank columns)**. The white columns on this Greek Revival style house built in 1910 once flanked the entrances to the First National Bank of Roswell at 226 North Main Street.

Lea Avenue 200 Block North
West Side
200 **Historical Center for Southeast New Mexico (former White house)**. Inspired by Frank Lloyd Wright's Prairie Style that emphasizes broad horizontal lines reflective of wide-open spaces, Roswell building contractor David Tomlinson constructed this fourteen-room "mansion" for his son-in-law J.P. White in 1910. White had commissioned the house for his bride who was Tomlinson's daughter.

James Phelps White (1856-1934) was born in Texas, the nephew of Major George Littlefield who was a hugely wealthy Texas cattleman. Twenty-five-year-old White came to New Mexico in 1881 to manage some of his uncle's ranching operations, the LTF, that covered a good part of the state. J.P. White soon began acquiring his own land and cattle herds and quickly became the largest rancher in eastern New Mexico and western Texas. He was the first in this area to dig water wells out on the range and put up windmills to pump water to the surface for his cattle. By 1920, 64-year-old White was the wealthiest man in the Pecos Valley. When cattle drives proceeded down 2nd Street toward the railroad stockyards, J.P. White would stand in his second-floor window and count his "money" as it thundered by.

White and his family lived and breathed cattle. When he and his brother Tom traveled "back east" to do some sightseeing, they agreed that Niagara Falls "would make a mighty fine place to water a herd."

Today White's former home houses the Historical Society for Southeast New Mexico. A tour of the house showcases White family antiques in the parlor and dining room and a well-stocked vintage kitchen including an icebox and range. Bronze-colored busts of the four people who "contributed most to the development and civic improvement of Roswell," created for the Roswell Museum and Art Center in 1937 by WPA artist J.R. Terken, decorate the staircases: John Chisum and Joseph Lea stand near the top of the main stairway while Amelia Church and J.J. Hagerman guard the top of the back stairway. Exhibits featuring "King of the Cowboys" Bob Crosby, Roswell Army Air Field, the Bataan Death March, the history and culture of Mariachi music, Roswell's 1956 Little League World Championship Team, and many other topics of local history fill the upstairs bedrooms.

Lou Tomlinson White was quite a socialite when she could get to "society." The green brocade dress she wore to Governor Hinkle's 1923 Inaugural Ball in Santa Fe is on display downstairs. She lived in this house until her death in 1972 at the age of 92, and some say she still does. When displays appear mysteriously rearranged, workers just assume that they didn't please finicky Mrs. White's sense of style.

The two-story carriage house northwest of the main building originally contained an upstairs hayloft and an apartment for servants. Downstairs, three stalls accommodated horses and a milk cow while an enclosed area held the buggy, then later the family automobile. Later still, the family built a garage just for autos south of the carriage house. The large round cistern on the northeast corner of the carriage house collected rainwater from its roof. Soft rainwater was a welcome change from highly mineralized ground water for both drinking and washing.

The recently opened Museum Archive Center next door contains thousands of documents and photographs pertaining to the history of Roswell and the Pecos Valley. The sweet bronze statue of the *Little Gardener* by Gary Price in front of the Archive Building honors Dora Lewis McKnight (1904-1997), founder of the Roswell Morning Garden Club. Books about Roswell and New Mexico history and small, inexpensive "Pecos Valley Diamonds" are available in the Museum Gift Shop. 622-8333. Office open M-F 10-4; Museum open 1-4 every day, holidays variable; Archives open MWF 1-4.

Lea Avenue, 100 Block North
East Side
101 **Gill house**. When John Gill (1848-1923) opened Roswell Seed, currently at 115 South Main Street, and moved his family into town from his small ranch in 1898, he built this Queen Anne style house with a wrap-around porch, perfect for sitting outside on a hot summer evening to visit with neighbors. Although the house is no longer owned by the Gill family, Roswell Seed still is (p 60).

Lea Avenue, 100 Block South
East Side
101 **First Church of Christ, Scientist.** The congregation constructed this church in 1922 in the highly formal Georgian style unusual for Roswell. Previously members had met at the home of Mrs. F.M. Eaton at 111 South Kentucky Avenue since the church's founding in 1908.

West Side
102 **Elizabeth Garrett house.** Ask any New Mexican—native or otherwise—to sing the New Mexico State Song, and you are likely to get some hemming and hawing and maybe some desultory humming. Some will actually know that it is called "O, Fair New Mexico," and those who do can usually tell you that it was written by "Pat Garrett's blind daughter."

Elizabeth Garrett, the composer of this pleasant but forgettable song, was born in 1885 near Ruidoso, one of seven children of Apolinaria Gutierrez Garrett and Sheriff Pat Garrett, the man who shot Billy the Kid. Accidentally blinded as a very young child, Elizabeth grew up on the Garrett ranch just east of Roswell with no intention of living a handicapped life. She attended school in Austin, Texas, and then studied music in Chicago and New York.

Elizabeth Garrett toured the country, giving concerts in which she sang and accompanied herself on the piano. Traveling with a seeing-eye dog—quite a novelty at that time—she visited Helen Keller who dedicated one of her books to this serene but determined young lady. Garrett then returned to Roswell to teach piano and voice, and to defend the reputation of her often-maligned father. She lived here in "La Casita," her five-room adobe Pueblo Revival style house which she called her "dream home," with its flat roof, vigas, and roof drain spouts called "*canales*." In later years she subsisted on a small pension resulting from her State Song, and died in 1947 after an injury sustained in a fall.

Lea Avenue, 500 Block South
West Side

500 **Crosby house.** This Queen Anne style house with an ornate gable and eaves was home in the 1920s and '30s to rancher and rodeo performer Bob Crosby (1897-1947). Roswell's "King of the Cowboys" won the World Champion Cowboy title in 1925, '27, and '28, and appeared in the 1937 Tex Ritter movie *Trouble in Texas* as a rodeo contestant. His trophies are on display in the Cowboy Hall of Fame in Oklahoma City but the Historical Center here in Roswell maintains an exhibit of his memorabilia. Bob Crosby Arena at Eastern New Mexico State Fairgrounds is named in his honor. Crosby later moved to a house at 7 Riverside Drive and at one time owned the Green Lantern Bar at 101 North Main Street. One evening in 1947 while driving home to his ranch near Kenna he died when he crashed his Jeep into a draw—that has since been named for him—just east of the Pecos River on U.S. 70.

Missouri Avenue and One Block to the West

Missouri Avenue, 400 Block North
West Side

406 **First Hinkle house**. James F. "Jim" Hinkle (1862-1951) came to New Mexico as a 24-year-old cowboy in 1886. He later became active in ranching, banking, and politics, serving in the Territorial Legislature and as Mayor of Roswell, then as Governor of New Mexico in 1923 and '24—the first governor from the southeastern part of the state. Hinkle and his family lived in this Southwestern Vernacular style house with its flat roof, stuccoed walls, and a porch with an arched entry and tiled roof while their new house next door was being built.

400 **Second Hinkle house**. Jim Hinkle built this Queen Anne style house with an irregular roof, wrap-around porch, and covered breezeway leading to the carriage house in 1904.

Chapter V. New Mexico Military Institute (NMMI)

Founded in 1891 as Goss Military Institute, this is the only state-supported, co-educational, college-preparatory high school and junior college in the United States. Its eight hundred male and female cadets come from all over the United States and many foreign countries. Junior college graduates have the opportunity to receive a commission in the United States Army.

Isaac and William Rapp, brothers and architects from Trinidad, Colorado, designed a master plan for the NMMI campus and its buildings in 1908 in an architectural style that is a variation of Gothic Revival called Modified Gothic, Military Gothic, or Scottish Castle. Crenulated rooflines recall medieval castles manned by archers who hid behind the higher areas while shooting at attackers through the lower notches. All buildings are constructed of Kansas buff brick that became available—and eventually put local brick kilns out of business—when Roswell's railroad finally connected with the transcontinental railway system in 1899. Many of the buildings sport the Rapp brothers' trademark octagonal turrets. Even the modern Toles Learning Center has stylized ones. (Trivia Question: Exactly how many octagonal turrets are there on campus?)

Locals call the school NMMI ("NEH-me"), "The Institute," or even the "Toot Farm." The uniformed cadets strung out along Main Street headed to the Mall on Saturday afternoons are the "Toots," of course. The junior college athletic teams are the Broncos, while the high school teams are the Colts.

NMMI often brags about its famous alumni such as Conrad Hilton, founder of the Hilton Hotel chain; Sam Donaldson, ABC newsman; Samuel Marmaduke, founder of Hastings; Peter Hurd, American artist; Tony Lama, Jr., founder of Tony Lama Boots; Roger Staubach, former Dallas Cowboys quarterback; Owen Wilson, popular young actor; and Paul Horgan, two-time Pulitzer Prize-winning author. It denies rumors that Jessica Jaymes, *Hustler* magazine's 2004 "Honey of the Year," is an alumna.

History

In 1890 Captain Joseph Lea—"The Father of Roswell"—enrolled his son Wildy ("WILL-dee") in Fort Worth University, a premier military school of the day. Captain Lea was so impressed with his son's education there that he convinced the superintendent, Robert S. Goss, to come to Roswell and start a military school here.

Goss Military Institute opened in September 1891 with thirty-eight students and six instructors on land provided by Captain Lea in the 400 block of North Main Street, today part of Pioneer Plaza. The school provided the only high school education in Southeastern New Mexico, focusing on military training as well as academic subjects.

Mabel Day Lea, Captain Lea's third wife, insisted that the school be open to girls as well as boys, as she herself had a school-aged daughter from her previous marriage. Of the first thirty-eight cadets, twenty were female students who were not subject to the same military discipline as the boys but did drill daily with wands instead of rifles.

Financial difficulties soon led the citizens of Roswell to seek support for the school from the Territorial government, which finally agreed to take over the military school. In 1894 the newly renamed New Mexico Military Institute moved a few blocks north to the corner of Main and 7th Streets, near the present-day McDonald's.

In September 1898, after some additional serious financial difficulties that required closing the school for several years, NMMI again relocated, this time to its present-day site at the top of North Hill on forty acres donated by Pecos Valley developer J.J. Hagerman. The school reopened with eighty-two students in a three-story red brick building housing classrooms, dormitories, and even a basement swimming pool: the first Lea Hall. To the disgust of everyone connected with the school except Mrs. Lea, much of the student body remained female until 1899 when most were excluded. Legal considerations opened enrollment to females again in 1977. Hispanics have long attended NMMI. The first African-American cadet was admitted in 1966 with so little controversy that the cadet, Edward Colbert, Jr., remarked, "I never even knew it wasn't integrated until I read it in the paper."

Since its early years NMMI has survived expansions, crises, and changes of emphasis, and today remains committed to providing a high quality education. NMMI graduates have gone on to serve in all areas of business, industry, education, and the professions, as well as in the military, where graduates have distinguished themselves as leaders in all conflicts, many giving their lives for their country.

NMMI Organizational Structure

The Superintendent of NMMI, serving as the President and CEO, is responsible to the Board of Regents—the supervisory board appointed by the Governor of New Mexico—for all aspects of the school's operation. All faculty are supervised by the Academic Deans who report to the Superintendent, as does the Commandant who is responsible for disciplinary issues as well as for overseeing health and safety, cadet housing, and military training.

Four Squadrons of three Troops each, plus a Headquarters Troop (the band), with commissioned and non-commissioned cadet officers leading each Troop, make up the Regiment of the Corps of Cadets, based on the historical composition of a Cavalry Regiment. The highest-ranking cadet from the rising Junior College sophomore class, based on academics, physical fitness, and military leadership ability, becomes the Regimental Commander of the Corps of Cadets. He or she is in charge of all aspects of the Corps of Cadets and reports to the Commandant. The first female Regimental Commander led the Corps of Cadets in 1998, the first African-American in 2003, and the first Hispanic in 2004.

Touring the Campus

NMMI encourages visitors to walk around its lovely campus. While enjoying the shade trees lining each plaza they often have difficulty imagining that the current campus started life as a flat stretch of treeless prairie, but old photos—such as the one of Lea Hall in the Roswell Public Library lobby—confirm this. Prospective students can obtain information from the Admissions Office in the Enrollment and Development Center near Saunders Plaza. To reach visitor parking turn onto Colt Avenue from College Avenue or onto Duty Avenue from Kentucky Avenue. 622-6250, www.nmmi.edu

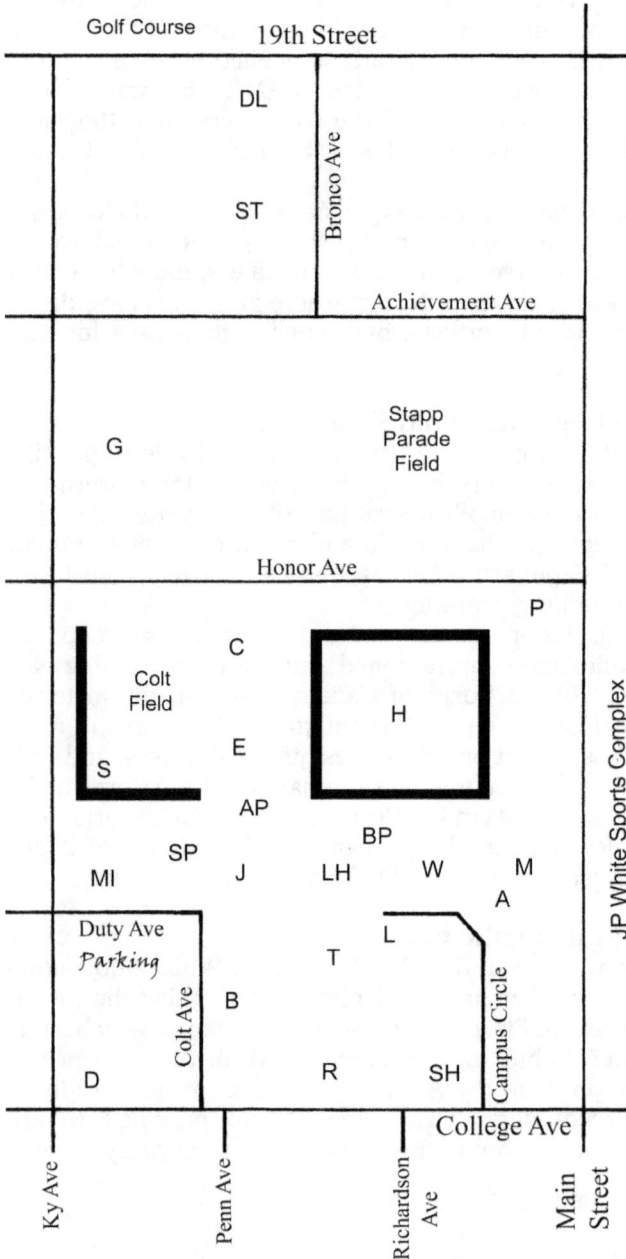

NMMI Campus

Golf Course   19th Street

DL

Bronco Ave

ST

Achievement Ave

Stapp
Parade
Field

G

Honor Ave

P

C

Colt
Field

H

S

E

JP White Sports Complex

AP

BP

SP   J   LH   W   M

MI

A

Duty Ave
Parking

L

T

Colt Ave

B

Campus Circle

D

R   SH

College Ave

Ky Ave

Penn Ave

Richardson
Ave

Main
Street

KEY

A Alumni Chapel
AP Alumni Plaza
B Bates Hall
BP Bronco Plaza
C Cahoon Armory
D Dow Hall
DL Daniels Leadership
      Center
E Enrollment and
      Development Center
G Godfrey Athletic
      Center
H Hagerman Barracks
J JRT-VMV-Hinkle Hall
L Lusk Hall
LH Lea Hall
M McClure Hall
MI Marshall Infirmary
P Pearson Auditorium
R Rock Garden
S Saunders Barracks
SH Superintendent's
      House
SP Saunders Plaza
ST Stables
T Toles Learning Center
W Willson hall

Around Saunders Plaza

Like all campus plazas and pedestrian walkways, construction of Saunders Plaza began in 1983. A large statue of long-time Commandant H.P. Saunders, Jr. sculpted by Roswell oilman and artist Rogers Aston in 1974 dominates this plaza, as Saunders long dominated cadet life. A 1912 NMMI graduate, Saunders became Commandant in 1916, and held the position for the next thirty-one years. He was described as small boned but heavily muscled and athletic, a man of great moral strength and high standards, fair in his discipline of cadets, but quite strict. When highly perturbed, Saunders would let loose with his strongest expletive: "Fiddle-sticks!"

Thompson Memorial Plaza. This small plaza just northwest of Saunders Plaza remembers R. Dan Thompson, Class of 1940, "a soldier, polo player, coach, and friend" and is dedicated to NMMI's two National Intercollegiate Championship polo teams. Although staff and students had played polo almost from the beginning of the school it only became a major sport at NMMI in 1924. On a visit to his cadet son (Will Rogers, Jr., later a well known actor) in 1937, humorist Will Rogers, himself quite a horseman, even played a chukka of polo here—actually, he played on the polo field that once existed across Main Street between today's baseball field and the Wool Bowl. NMMI won their two national championships by beating Princeton in 1952 and Yale in 1954. However, just one month after winning their second championship, NMMI dropped polo as a sport—because of its expense—in spite of strong objections from students, staff, and alumni.

The solid bronze **Chukka Bell** hanging in the small tower on Thompson Memorial Plaza started life on an Illinois Central Railroad locomotive in 1854 and over the years served to signal dinnertime on a southern farm and quitting time at a Mississippi lumber mill. A parent donated the bell to NMMI in 1940 to signal time at polo matches on the field across Main Street. In 1962 the bell was moved to the front of Luna Natatorium—now the Enrollment and Development Center—then here to Thompson Memorial Plaza in 1984.

The Chukka Bell commemorates two young men who "played great polo" and died in accidents on the NMMI polo field: Cadet Owen Speer and former cadet Hal T. Niemann who was playing for the University of Oklahoma. Superstition has it that if the bell rings nowadays, a cadet will die—although this has never happened.

Saunders Barracks. Also named for H.P. Saunders, Jr. and called "The Slab," Saunders Barracks was first constructed as a cadet dormitory in 1964. The original building was torn down in 1994 and the current "Slab" was completed in two phases, one in 1994 and one in 1998.

Marshall Infirmary. This hospital opened in 1918, just in time for the deadly worldwide flu epidemic. Two-thirds of cadets were affected by the illness, but only three died. Red Cross nurses and local doctors helped, but fellow cadets cared for each other. Classes were dismissed for six weeks of quarantine, with nightly movies—silent, of course—relieving boredom. In 1965 the hospital was dedicated to Dr. I.J. Marshall, a long-time NMMI physician. Campus police offices are also located here.

Around Alumni Plaza

Alumni Memorial Plaza, whose outline is in the shape of the New Mexico flag's Zia sun sign, is dedicated to William D. DeSanders, a B-17 pilot and member of the class of 1940. His larger-than-life statue sculpted by Roswell oilman and artist Rogers Aston stands in the middle of the plaza. Bronze statues also sculpted by Aston of soldiers from the First and Second World Wars, Korean War, and Vietnam War at each of the four corners of the plaza commemorate the alumni who served in those conflicts. Aston's close attention to detail reflects careful research. For example, his World War I doughboy accurately carries a P-17 rifle rather than the Springfield .03 that many assume they used.

JRT-VMV-Hinkle Hall. This complex of three interconnected buildings was completed over a span of 55 years.

The J. Ross Thomas Memorial Building (facing east) was constructed first, opening as the new PX in 1933. Today it contains the Post Office, barbershop, and a game room. Thomas, a VMI graduate and "lunger," joined the faculty in 1909, teaching mathematics for over twenty years before finally dying of tuberculosis in 1930. The cadets, who both feared and idolized him, dedicated the 1932 Bronco yearbook to the memory of this instructor described as having "a broad smile and even broader ears."

In 1955 the second portion of the building (facing north) was completed and dedicated to three students who had drowned during the 1954 Final Ball: Donald Vertrees, Wood Moore, and Perry Vlahopoulas. Called VMV Hall from the first initial of each of their last names, today this building contains a ballroom used for small banquets and a bowling alley on the floor below. Two large photos of NMMI in past days hang in the entranceway.

The final portion of the complex, Hinkle Hall (facing south and sometimes irreverently called "Tinkle Hall") was completed in 1988. A stained-glass window over the entrance highlights NMMI's dedication to "Duty, Honor, Achievement." Major Wayne A. Whiting's huge painting of El Capitan dominates the entryway, where smaller portraits of James Hinkle and his two NMMI alumni sons, Rolla and Clarence, also hang. The upper lobby contains photos and brief histories of campus buildings, while the lower floor houses a game room. Visiting dignitaries, including John Farrer, Conductor of the Roswell Symphony Orchestra, stay in comfortable suites on the top floor. The building is dedicated to the family of James Hinkle, former Roswell Mayor, New Mexico Governor, long-time NMMI supporter, and member of the Board of Regents. In addition to his two sons, eight of his grandsons and at least nine of his great-grand children have attended NMMI.

Enrollment and Development Center (former Luna Natatorium, former McBride Military Museum). From its earliest days in 1891 NMMI has always had a swimming pool. Luna Natatorium, with its impressively detailed Military Gothic features, was built over an outdoor pool on this site in 1918 and named in honor of former cadet Antonio Luna who died at Fort Bliss in 1916. During the 1930s, bathing suits were not allowed in Luna Natatorium because they were considered unhygienic. Female employees entered the area at their own risk—of embarrassment. Until 1985 when the pool was filled in, some claimed to hear the Splashing Ghosts of three cadets who drowned here under unusual circumstances in 1954.

In 1985 NMMI converted this building to office and exhibit space, renaming it the McBride Military Museum in honor of former cadet and New Mexico National Guard Lt. General Douglas L. "Ladd" McBride, who contributed financially to the project.

In 2006 NMMI again renovated the building and renamed it the Enrollment and Development Center. It now houses the offices of Admissions, Financial Aid, the NMMI Foundation, and the Alumni Association. At present the museum exhibits related to NMMI and U.S. military history are in temporary storage, but will eventually be displayed on the second floor, and will hopefully include one of Sergeant Barney Leonard's Harley-Davidson motorcycles with a machine gun mounted on the sidecar. ("Sarge," a weapons instructor at NMMI, put together an eight-cadet, four-vehicle Armed Motorcycle Cavalry squad in 1915, but was unsuccessful in convincing General Pershing to take the unit on his pursuit of Pancho Villa into Mexico the next year.) Currently, football memorabilia from Roger Staubach, an autographed picture of actor Owen Wilson, and a photo of a polo player by famous New Mexican photographer Laura Gilpin are among the items displayed.

Around Bronco Plaza

Joullian Centennial Bronco Plaza centers around a large bronze statue of a bronco, the school mascot. Shaded benches memorializing alumni, family, and friends surround the statue. This plaza was dedicated in 1991, the Centennial of the school's founding, and named for alumnus Edward C. Joullian, III, Oklahoma City oilman, former President of the Boy Scouts of America, and Chairman of the Centennial Committee—who also donated one million dollars to the Centennial Celebration Fund. Cadets and staff buried a time capsule under the pavement on the northern side of the plaza to be opened at the Bicentennial, September 3, 2091. The Centennial Flame north of the time capsule burns on special occasions. Another plaque inscribed with the words of the NMMI Alma Mater, "Old Post," is set in the south side pavement of Bronco Plaza.

Lusk Hall. Completed in 1938 as the Headquarters Building and Library—explaining the inscriptions of "Headquarters" on the east wing and "Library" on the west wing—today Lusk Hall with its four-faced clock tower houses administrative offices. In 1965 the building was dedicated to the memory of Ewing Lusk who came to NMMI in 1911 to teach mathematics and surveying. As a young man his work as a surveyor for a railroad in Oklahoma and an irrigation company along the Texas coast convinced him that he liked hot weather better than cold, and Roswell was the ideal spot. After a brief stint as Principal of Roswell High School, he served as Principal of the NMMI High School Division for twenty-nine years and as Superintendent in 1951 and 1952. Students dedicated the 1922 and 1944 Bronco yearbooks to him.

In 1961 Ruby Saunders Crosby, wife of a prominent Roswell businessman, donated a carillon for the Lusk Hall tower in memory of her brother H.P. Saunders, Jr., long-time NMMI Commandant.

Lea Hall. Today's Lea Hall, built in 1937 on the site of the old Headquarters Building, houses academic classrooms and offices for the humanities. Designed to mirror Willson Hall across Bronco Plaza, it honors Captain Joseph Lea, "The Father of Roswell," who is also "The Father of NMMI," as he was responsible for its founding in 1891, donated the land for its first campus, and provided much support over its early years.

This is the third building on the NMMI campus given Lea's name. The first Lea Hall, a three-story red brick building, stood just northeast of where the Commandant's House (2 Campus Circle) stands today. A photo of this building hangs in the Roswell Public Library lobby. This first structure erected on the current campus contained classrooms, dormitories, a laundry, a kitchen, a dining room, and even a basement swimming pool. The first Lea Hall survived a twenty-four-inch hole blasted through one wall when a Cadet Taliaferro set off a cannon late one night, but it did not survive a fire in 1909.

The second Lea Hall, also three stories high but built of the standard Kansas buff brick adopted by that time, was completed in 1910 in what is now the northeast section of Hagerman Barracks. It contained classrooms, science labs, the library, and a small collection of military memorabilia, including the key to the blockhouse on San Juan Hill, donated by "Captain Jack" Fletcher, long-time NMMI Band Director. He had led the band that played patriotic music when U.S. troops raised the Stars and Stripes over the Governor's Palace in Havana at the conclusion of the Spanish-American War.

Willson Hall. Willson Hall's elaborate architecture made it the most impressive building on campus at its completion in 1927. Constructed on the old parade ground site where Cadet Conrad Hilton once marched disciplinary tours for writing "vulgar and obscene" comments on another cadet's paper, it currently houses natural sciences, math, social sciences, and business administration classrooms and offices, but originally also contained the library—which seems to have moved around quite a bit over the years.

Mathematics instructor James W. Willson, Superintendent from 1901 until his death in 1922, was one of the most influential early figures in setting NMMI's future course. A proud Virginian and a graduate of the Virginia Military Institute, Willson set out to create the best military school west of the Mississippi. He established the strong military character of NMMI, based on the VMI model, focusing more on military training and discipline than on academics. He placed such emphasis on sports, which he greatly enjoyed, that he once refused to hire a prospective faculty member because the applicant didn't play baseball—until 1910 staff as well as students played on the athletic teams. He did hire several fellow VMI graduates, including "Deke" Pearson, who became a later influential Superintendent, and J. Ross Thomas, the long-time demanding but beloved mathematics instructor.

Hagerman Barracks. The original section of this main cadet barracks makes up the southern half of the west side of today's quadrangle. It was completed in 1908, the first building constructed in the Rapp brothers' Military Gothic style. Its Sally Port—a wide gateway to a fort or castle that permits the passage of a large number of troops at one time—was built in 1925 and quickly became the symbol of NMMI. Other sections were added over the years until the quadrangle stood complete in 1952. In addition to dormitories, "The Box," as it is called, also contains the Commandant's office.

J.J. Hagerman, industrialist and railroad tycoon, was an early promoter of development in the Pecos Valley. He donated land for the current NMMI campus.

Toles Learning Center. The J. Penrod Toles Learning Resource Center, completed in 1985, contains the Paul Horgan Library, as well as an auditorium, a TV production studio, a computer center, and counselor offices. Several artworks by alumnus Peter Hurd and other artists decorate its walls. Stretching along the balcony, *The Encounter*, by local artist John Meigs (1916-2003), a protégé of Peter Hurd, portrays a street scene in early Roswell.

Businessman and lawyer J. Penrod Toles graduated from NMMI in 1948 and married a daughter of H.P. Saunders, Jr., longtime NMMI Commandant. He joined the Board of Regents in 1971, and became president of the Board in 1974, an office he held until he resigned in 1982.

Paul Horgan (1903-1995), a 1923 NMMI graduate, served as librarian from 1926 to 1944. He won two Pulitzer Prices: one for *Great River: The Rio Grande in North American History* (1954) and one for *Lamy of Santa Fe* (1975), a biography of the pioneer archbishop, whom Willa Cather fictionalized in *Death Comes for the Archbishop*.

When Horgan first became librarian here he reorganized the library using the Dewey Decimal System. The previous part-time librarian, Bandmaster "Captain Jack" Fletcher, had also instituted a new organizational scheme when he took over the library in 1909 from Modern Languages Instructor Count Mancini-Martini. The Count had organized books by size—tall books on one shelf, short books on another. "Captain Jack" reorganized the books by color—red, green, blue . . .

McClure Hall. An academic building containing science and math classrooms, McClure Hall was completed in 1962. John McClure, a much admired instructor, taught chemistry at NMMI from 1905 to 1948, with an early two-year absence to complete graduate work at the University of Chicago. This building, along with Dow Hall, was disappointing to some because it lacked many of the castle-like features of the earlier buildings.

Along Honor Avenue

Godfrey Athletic Center. Gyms, four racquetball courts, a fitness center, and a swimming pool—with tennis courts out back—make up NMMI's current athletic center. Completed in 1980 and dedicated in the middle of a snowstorm Homecoming Weekend that fall, the facility was named in honor of L.T. "Babe" Godfrey, NMMI Class of 1924, an outstanding athlete, teacher, and coach at NMMI for forty years. A bust of Godfrey created by Roswell sculptor Rogers Aston welcomes athletes to the Center. The public may use its facilities for a small fee ($3.00 a day). 624-8286. Open days and evenings during the summer, evenings and weekends during most of the school year—call for exact days and hours.

Colt Field. NMMI's original Polo Field covered this area as well as the land where Godfrey Athletic Center now stands. A small section, about where Honor Avenue runs today, also served as the football field, although baseball, played on the eastern half of today's Stapp Parade Field, was a much more popular sport. Perhaps this was because NMMI's early Twentieth Century baseball teams won frequent championships and beat every school and town team within 400 miles, while the football team lost its first intercollegiate game in 1907 to the "Farmers" of the Agricultural College in Las Cruces by a score of 28 to 0.

Ewing Lusk's surveying class, with the help of two mules, laid out and graded an oval cinder track around the football field in 1918 and the polo field moved across Main Street.

In the 1920s and '30s NMMI played its football games at (no longer existent) Thorne Park on East 2nd Street. Beginning in 1935 they played in de Bremond Stadium near today's Civic Center. When the Wool Bowl on Grand Avenue east of the campus was completed in 1963, NMMI football games moved there.

Today NMMI football teams play most of their games here at Colt Field but occasionally still use the Wool Bowl for special events.

Cahoon Armory. This building houses the athletic department offices and contains a gym used for basketball games, and in the past for dances. Built in 1927, it was dedicated in 1929 to Roswell businessman and banker E.A. Cahoon, who served for thirty-nine years on the Board of Regents. It is called an Armory because at one time the National Guard used it as such. Older cadets try to scare RATS—new cadets—with ghost stories about its Bloody Tower.

Ghost stories do abound on campus. One of the most popular concerns "Missing Troop J"—this one has even made it to the Internet. It seems there is no Troop J in the Corps of Cadets out of respect for members of an early Troop J, all of whom died fighting to protect NMMI and Roswell during the Indian Wars. It is even said that the faces of these young men can sometimes be seen staring out of the clock tower on Lusk Hall. One big problem with this story: the Apache Wars in New Mexico and Arizona ended with the final capture of Geronimo in 1886. It wasn't until five years later that Colonel Goss founded Goss Military Institute—that became NMMI—as a secondary school whose original students were mainly girls but included boys as young as seven. Not until World War I, by which time NMMI had expanded to include a junior college, did volunteers from NMMI fight with the National Guard and U.S. Army. But ghost stories are still fun, and quite a number of them, most equally implausible, make the rounds here late at night.

Stapp Memorial Parade Field. In 1980 NMMI named this new parade field in honor of Thomas B. Stapp, who graduated in 1931 and soon joined the faculty. After cadets dedicated the 1945 Bronco yearbook to him, he served as Commandant from 1946 to 1953.

In December 1997 former President Gerald R. Ford reviewed the Corps of Cadets from the grandstand on Stapp Field, and then became the first recipient of the Will Rogers Award, NMMI's premier honor, named for the American humorist who is an "honorary alumnus." NMMI invites the public to occasional parades on Stapp Field during the school year, but discourages anyone from picking up pecans under its trees that line Main Street.

Along College Avenue and Campus Circle

Alumni Memorial Chapel. Coach "Babe" Godfrey led alumni in raising $600,000 to build this non-denominational chapel as a memorial to cadets who died in service to their country. Completed in 1975, it soon became a popular spot for weddings. Light from inside illuminates its beautiful stained-glass window entitled *The Creation* so that it is visible to passing motorists at night.

Superintendent's House. At 1 Campus Circle, the steep roof and gabled ends of this 1931 building give it a Tudor look, although it remains consistent with the prescribed Rapp brothers' master plan.

Bronco Statue and Fountain. The small white Bronco statue, the NMMI mascot, was placed here between Lusk Hall and the Rock Garden in the early 1920s.

Rock Garden. Superintendent "Deke" Pearson built this lovely rock garden, topped with a huge chunk of petrified wood, during the 1930s. At one time he kept two small alligators in the pool that filled the rocky basin, but had to enclose it with a wire fence after neighbors across College Avenue complained about finding alligators in their shrubbery.

Bates Hall. This dining hall and cadet store was built in 1918 and later named in honor of the Carlsbad hotel operator, R.L. Bates, who became the first Commissary Officer to use the building. Cadets dedicated the 1939 Bronco yearbook to him, so the food must have been good.

Dow Hall. An academic building constructed for military science in 1957, Dow Hall contains a shooting range as well as classrooms. Some complained because this building—along with McClure Hall east of Willson Hall—lacks the towers, turrets, and other castle-like features of the Military Gothic architecture. It does still have parapets and was built of Kansas buff brick, so the Rapp brothers' master plan remains in force. Roswell attorney and former Lieutenant Governor of New Mexico Hiram Dow, a 1905 NMMI graduate, was a long-time member of the Board of Regents.

Along North Main Street
Pearson Auditorium and Brown Music Center. Virginian D.C. "Deke" Pearson, who served as Commandant for four years beginning in 1905 and then became Superintendent in 1926, serving in that position for twenty-one years, built this auditorium that seats over 1,000 people in 1940. Colonel Pearson was the first Superintendent to be seriously interested in academics, as opposed to military discipline and sports.

In 1941 Superintendent Pearson purchased a Wurlitzer organ from the Sunshine Theater in Albuquerque and installed it in the auditorium. The organ was refurbished in 1983 and occasional organ concerts are scheduled today.

Pearson Auditorium hosts five concerts a year of the Roswell Symphony Orchestra (founded in 1959, with all professional musicians since 1970), as well as presentations by various Armed Forces Bands, ballet troupes, opera companies, and other entertainment for cadets and the public. Some say Superintendent Pearson still keeps a watchful eye on the goings on in his auditorium through his haunting, or haunted, portrait in the auditorium lobby. Varying fees are charged for events.

The adjoining W.P. Brown Memorial Music Center, completed in 1983, is used for band practice. Brown, a Phoenix businessman and alumnus, provided the money to renovate the organ in Pearson Auditorium. The Brown Music Center contains an interesting portrait of that wonderful old NMMI character, Bandmaster "Captain Jack" Fletcher who led the NMMI band for forty-one years. "Captain Jack" had been a Bandsman in the British Army for ten years and a Bandmaster in the United States Army during the Spanish-American War prior to coming to NMMI in 1902. Retiring in 1943, he has the longest faculty tenure on record, and he probably also holds the record for most luxuriant moustache.

Pedestrian Overpass. The pedestrian walkway built over Main Street in the 1960s is open again after several years of repair. It seems a tractor-trailer heading south was just a *little* too tall to clear the bridge.

J.P. White Parade Grounds and Sports Complex. In 1929 NMMI bought this area, located across Main Street from the main campus, and named it after Roswell businessman and cattle rancher J.P. White, who served on the Board of Regents from 1907 to 1930. Today it includes a sports complex and the NMMI baseball field. Baseball games are open to the public for a small admission fee.

Along West 19th Street

Stables. WPA workers built NMMI's stables in 1937. Once a state-of-the-art equestrian facility able to accommodate 140 horses, the stables have remained empty since the last horses left NMMI in 1997, a sad time for the school whose recruiting motto was once "Every boy rides."

Daniels Leadership Center. This new facility with its adjacent ropes course provides leadership training programs to cadets and the Roswell community. Philanthropist R.W. "Bill" Daniels, Jr. (1920-2000) graduated from the NMMI high school program in 1939 and the junior college in 1941. A Navy fighter pilot in World War II, he later became "The Father of Cable TV" as a highly successful leader in that field. In addition to funding this center, Daniels established NMMI's television production studio in Toles Learning Center. Varying fees are charged for programs.

Golf Course and Clubhouse. Superintendent Hugh Milton took over at NMMI in 1947. An Army General during World War II, he had previously served as President of New Mexico Agricultural and Mechanical College—today's New Mexico State University—so one of his first projects at NMMI was to irrigate 140 acres on West 19th Street to raise alfalfa for NMMI's horses. He also set up a hog farm on the property, feeding the nearly 100 pigs from dining hall scraps. Needless to say, this was never a popular enterprise, and he was never a popular Superintendent. In 1956 a later Superintendent, Hobart Gay, who had been General

George Patton's Chief of Staff during World War II, turned the hog farm into an eighteen-hole golf course. This was a much more popular use for the land, and General Gay was a much more appreciated Superintendent—although NMMI no longer holds its annual "Gay Day" celebration to honor him. When the golf course was built, special permission was granted to design the clubhouse in a Modified California Mission style, rather than the standard Military Gothic because it was believed that a crenulated clubhouse would look silly. The par 72 golf course and its driving range are open to public use, with a fee of $25.00 for 18 holes, which includes a cart. 622-6033. Open nearly every day 8-5 but closed Thanksgiving and Christmas.

Chapter VI. Along the Spring River Recreation Trail

In 1984 Roswell's Parks and Recreation Director A.B. Gwinn and City Planner Ivan Hall developed a proposal for the beginning of a Bike Trail that would eventually stretch five miles (8 km) through the center of Roswell, from Enchanted Lands Park on the west to the Spring River Park and Zoo on the east. Hall and others eventually put funding together from seventeen different sources, ranging from state grants to jars of coins collected by children, to complete this popular trail for walking, skating, and bike riding.

West of Main Street

Enchanted Lands Park (Along Riverside Drive between Estrellita Drive and Sycamore Avenue). The west end of the Recreation Trail begins here, surrounded by grassy fields, playground equipment, and picnic tables. The National Guard held artillery practice just west of Enchanted Lands Park during the early years of the Twentieth Century, and the Pest House for quarantining victims of contagious diseases like smallpox was once located in the vicinity.

The southern branch of the North Spring River once flowed steadily through this area from its origin in artesian springs just west of Enchanted Lands Park. The northern branch of the same river arose about one-half mile (0.8 km) to the north and flowed through the draw north of 8th Street and west of Sycamore Avenue. From where the two branches joined just east of Sycamore Avenue, the North Spring River flowed about six miles (10 km) to empty into the Hondo River east of Roswell. Native peoples probably visited this river for centuries, as Mogollon pottery shards were common along its banks in Roswell's early years.

More than 10' (3 m) deep and 40' (12 m) wide in places, the river provided good fishing, swimming, and boating until irrigation wells drastically lowered Roswell's water table by the middle of the Twentieth Century. Today, heavy rains can flood the lower areas of Enchanted Lands Park, but the river only appears as a trickle between the sloping stonemasonry walls farther downstream. Water actually flowing in the riverbed excites comment.

Although officially called the "North Spring River" to distinguish it from the "South Spring River"—now also dry—which once flowed into the Pecos River three miles (5 km) south of Roswell and gave John Chisum's South Spring River Ranch its name, most people today just call this the Spring River.

Littell Crossing, where the Recreation Trail crosses Sycamore Avenue, honors Max Littell (1916-2001), a Roswell realtor, outdoor enthusiast, and one of the founders of the UFO Museum. He helped develop the Enchanted Lands Subdivision in this area in the 1960s.

Kenneth Smith Bird and Nature Center (East of Sycamore Avenue). Built primarily by Boy Scouts, this small sanctuary honors a Roswell birder who donated the money to create a quiet refuge here. Smith was a son-in-law of Lester Reischman, oilman and owner of Holsum Bakery, whose own small park is located in the 300 block of North Main Street.

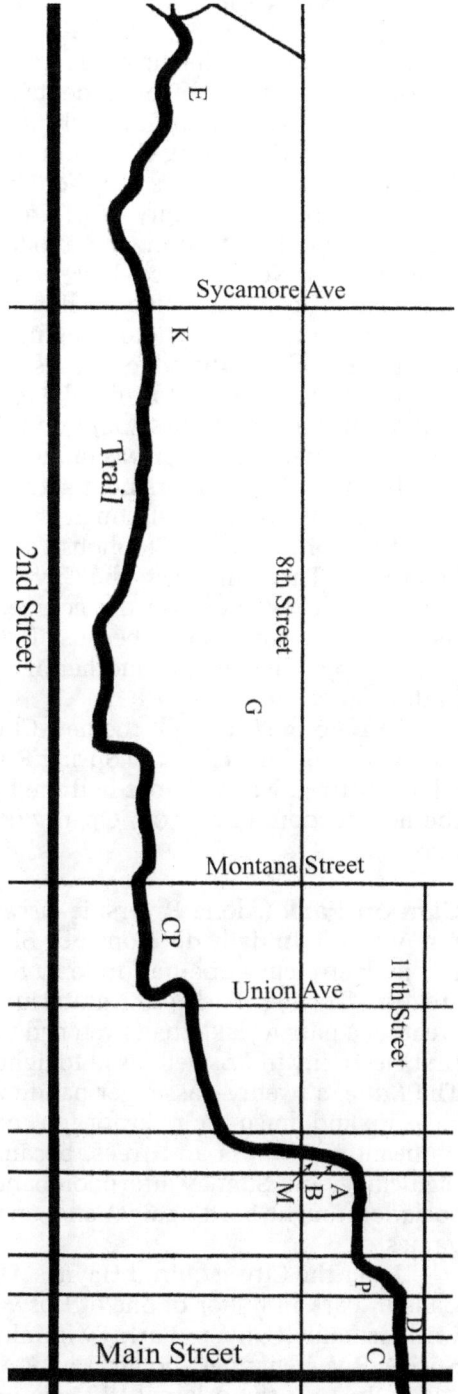

Spring River Recreation Trail (West of Main Street)

KEY

A   Adult Center
B   Boy Scout Hut
C   Civic Center
CP Cahoon Park
D   de Bremond Stadium

E   Enchanted Lands Park
G   Golf Course
K   Kenneth Smith Nature Center
M   Margo Purdy Park
P   POW/MIA Park

2nd Street

Trail

E

K

Sycamore Ave

8th Street

G

Montana Street

CP

Union Ave

11th Street

M   A   B

P

D

C

Main Street

Spring River Golf Course (1612 West 8th Street). The Recreation Trail skirts this par 71 municipal golf course—watch for golf balls! Greens fees are quite reasonable ($11.00 for nine holes, $16.00 for eighteen holes if you walk, $26.00 with a cart) with special rates for students and senior citizens.

In the early years of Roswell's history, visiting families often camped on the north bank of the Spring River in this area, as did the Ninth Cavalry of African-American Buffalo Soldiers sent here in 1879 from Fort Stanton to keep the peace during the Lincoln County War. Later the City established fairgrounds on the eastern end of this section where today residences line Riverside Drive. The first Southeastern New Mexico Fair held here in 1892 included agricultural and homemaking exhibits inside the huge Alfalfa Palace made entirely of hay bales, as pictured in an historic photo hanging in the lobby of the Best Western Sally Port Inn. The fair also featured foot races, baseball games, and horse races.

Hard-packed sand formed the tees and "greens" for the first nine-hole Roswell Municipal Golf Course built on this location in the 1920s. The fairways were mowed prairie. The rough was unmowed prairie.

In 1936 WPA workers built a 37-par, nine-hole course here with actual grass on the greens and tees, although the fairways remained questionable. They also built the stonemasonry Clubhouse southeast of the current tennis courts in Cahoon Park. That same year the City Council recommended against an audacious request to let women use the course. The City Councilors must have changed their minds at some point, because LPGA Champion Nancy Lopez learned to play golf here by following her mother and father around that same nine-hole course in the 1960s.

In 1966 the City built the new Clubhouse at its current location farther west and renamed the facility the Spring River Golf Course. When the "back nine" was added in 1975, Nancy Lopez had the honor of being the first person to tee off on the new section. 622-9506. Open 7:30 a.m. until dark every day except Christmas.

Cahoon Park (Along Riverside Drive between Montana Avenue and Washington Avenue). Initially developed by Sheriff C.W. Haynes in 1892, this 26-acre (10 ha) park stretches one-half mile (0.8 km) along the Spring River. He called his creation "Haynes' Park and Natatorium" and dammed the river at Union Avenue, creating a narrow lake that stretched nearly two miles (3 km) back upstream. The first electricity in Roswell, used to light the park, came from a turbine in the dam. The *Katie,* a twenty-passenger paddlewheel boat with a loud, shrill whistle, gave rides up and down the river for ten cents. Haynes' Dream (as it was called), with its beautiful flowers and trees, became a popular spot for swimming, boating, picnicking, and Sunday afternoon band concerts, but the Roswell Ministerial Association fought hard against allowing alcohol consumption or Sunday baseball games.

Later the City acquired Haynes' Dream and in 1935 renamed this entire area Cahoon Park in honor of one of Roswell's early civic-minded businessmen. WPA workers built Cahoon Park Swimming Pool and its bathhouse and lined the Spring River channel though Cahoon Park with stonemasonry during the late 1930s. In 1974 the original WPA bathhouse was demolished and a new one was constructed, although the original WPA-built diving tower at the northeast corner of the pool remains, used only for storage now. The pool is open to the public for a small fee in the summer.

WPA workers also constructed the lovely Sunken Gardens in Cahoon Park. The City Council named this area "Clyde Fulton Gardens," in honor of the City Manager who designed and supervised construction of the project, because of his "22 years of faithful service" from 1920 to 1941. In 1987 "Roswell Citizens and Jaycees" refurbished these gardens after years of neglect following damage in 1954 floods. This peaceful oasis provides a restful spot for hikers along the Recreation Trail.

In 1946 the Roswell Junior Chamber of Commerce built a Boy's Hut near the swimming pool for Boy Scout and Junior Police Organization meetings. In the 1950s it also housed the area Boy Scout Executive Offices until they moved into their new building on Aspen Avenue. After being used for storage for several years, the building became the Hospitality House serving recreational needs of senior citizens until 1974 when adult activities moved to the Memorial Center on Missouri Avenue. Today the building at 1101 West 4th Street provides offices for the City Parks and Recreation Department (624-6764).

Wide lawns, picnic tables, and playground equipment make Cahoon Park a popular spot for family and group picnics, especially on weekends. Six lighted, well maintained, and free tennis courts are available near the west end of the park. The nearby basketball court began life as the park's only tennis court, built by WPA workers in the 1930s and refurbished for basketball in 1988.

Large, dark Mississippi Kites nest in the trees throughout Cahoon Park during the summer and occasionally dive at park visitors who come too close to their young.

Margo Purdy Park (800 North Missouri Avenue). This small but attractive park was named in honor of a woman long active in the Roswell Parks and Recreation program. Shaded benches and a water fountain offer a pleasant rest stop for hikers and bikers. Equipment for its horseshoe pits and shuffleboard courts is available from the Adult Center across the street.

Boy Scout Hut (808 North Missouri Avenue). WPA workers completed this small, brown, flat-roofed structure in 1937 with building materials donated by local lumberyards and one hundred dollars from the Kiwanis Club. Old light poles from the baseball field at Thorne Park on East 2nd Street became its vigas, which are the exposed roof beams characteristic of this Pueblo Revival style architecture. The Scout Hut has since expanded several times, always with donated materials and labor.

Roswell Boy Scout Troop 2, organized at the First Methodist Church in 1916 just nine years after Lord Baden-Powell founded Boy Scouting in England, still meets here regularly. Troop 2 was the first Boy Scout Troop ever to tour Carlsbad Caverns. In 1922, after descending in a guano bucket—used by the company that mined the rich fertilizer deposits—the boys followed Caverns' discoverer, cowboy Jim White, on a torchlight tour through the giant rooms, then spent the night underground camping among the fantastic formations.

The bend in the Spring River here was a popular spot for full immersion baptisms early in the Twentieth Century. Parishioners lined the sloping banks singing hymns while the principals waded in the deep, clear water where bubbling artesian springs added to the river's flow.

Roswell Adult and Senior Center—A Veterans' Memorial (807 North Missouri Avenue). This building was completed in 1950 as the Chaves County Youth Memorial Center, dedicated to those who served in World War II. In 1974 youth programs moved to the Yucca Recreation Center on Richardson Avenue and adult activities moved here from the Hospitality House in Cahoon Park.

The Adult and Senior Center sponsors activities for those 18 and over but is especially popular with Roswell's retirees. Classes of all sorts proceed year around and the building provides space for card games, pool tournaments, club meetings, dances, woodworking, and other crafts. Varying fees are charged for classes and events.

Two wooden sculptures welcome visitors at the entrance to the Adult Center. On the left is a strange reptile (lizard? dinosaur? Komodo dragon?) that emerged from the woodworking shop. On the right a Sheriff waves from 20' (6 m) atop an amazing composite sculpture of *All Things Under the Sun*. Also called *The Oldest Citizen*, referring to the 180 year-old cottonwood from the riverbank across the street that Rex Branson and his nephew Jeremy Crow carved to create the work, this sculpture has stood here since the artists completed it in May 2004—although some believe they are still adding to it, as new creatures seem to appear with each examination. Can you find four different species of reptiles? Six species of birds? Seven species of hoofed animals? Six different types of tools? Four types of vehicles? Or maybe even more have appeared. 624-6718. Open M-F 8 a.m.-9 p.m., Sat 11:30-9, closed Sun, holidays variable.

The stone arch to the south of the building is all that's left of the 1949 structure erected by the Church of the Nazarene when it moved here from its earlier location on Washington Avenue. The rest of the building was demolished in early 2008 to make room for expansion of the Adult Center. The Church of the Nazarene had previously moved to a new location on Sycamore Avenue and the building had been used by various religious and community groups in recent years.

POW/MIA Park (912 North Pennsylvania Avenue). WPA workers completed stonemasonry walls lining the Spring River banks through Cahoon Park in the late 1930s. German Prisoners of War continued the work in this area and farther downstream during the 1940s.

The United States Army established the Roswell Prisoner of War Internment Camp in the Orchard Park area thirteen miles (21 km) southeast of Roswell in 1942. It held 4,800 prisoners until after the end of World War II in 1945, mostly German troops from General Rommel's North African campaign. The POWs generally believed they were treated well and some even returned with their families after the war to settle in the Roswell area. Prisoners were allowed to earn one dollar a day working on farms and ranches or completing public construction projects. Several guards usually accompanied large groups of prisoners, but individuals or small groups working on farms or ranches were simply dropped off in the morning and picked up again in the afternoon. The camp recorded few escape attempts, not because the prisoners feared the guards, some suggested, but because they were amazed and intimidated to see that every farmer and rancher carried a rifle in his truck.

Here, between Kentucky and Pennsylvania Avenues, the POWs incorporated a German Iron Cross design into the north wall of the riverbank. Angry citizens soon covered it with buckets of cement, but in the 1980s City workers removed the cement and dedicated this small area as POW/MIA Park, to commemorate all Prisoners of War and those Missing in Action.

Members of the German Air Force, the *Luftwaffe*, who used the spacious airport runways at the RIAC to practice take-offs and landings in the 1990s, donated a portion of the Berlin Wall to the park to commemorate today's friendship between our two countries. We know that the portion on display here came from the west side of the wall because only on the west side could people get close enough to cover it with graffiti. The east side of this wall, built to prevent Soviet-bloc citizens from escaping to freedom in the west, was a no-man's land—anyone approaching it was shot.

de Bremond Stadium (1000 North Richardson Avenue). Another WPA project, de Bremond Stadium was constructed of the same rock as the river walls, all of which came from a quarry on Six Mile Hill west of town. Once the stadium was completed, Roswell High School and NMMI played their football games here until the Wool Bowl opened in 1963. A plaque just south of the stadium names seven future NFL players who got their starts in de Bremond Stadium, including Roger Staubach of the Dallas Cowboys. Today, Roswell schools play soccer and middle school football games here.

In 1935 the City named the stadium to honor Colonel Charles de Bremond (1864-1919), born in Switzerland, who arrived in Roswell in 1894 and soon became a successful sheep rancher. He commanded Roswell's National Guard Battery A of the First Field Artillery during World War I, leading the unit, including fourteen NMMI cadets, through the fighting in France. Although twelve soldiers were wounded, all survived to return to Roswell after the Armistice. The names of the five officers and 192 men of Battery A inscribed on a tablet at the southeast corner of the stadium interest those researching family history.

Roswell Museum and Art Center (1000 North Main Street). This free museum offers Southwestern art, Western artifacts, and a space exhibit containing pioneer rockets, a space suit, and a moon rock (p 35).

Roswell Civic and Convention Center, and Brainerd Plaza (912 North Main Street). Many of Roswell's civic celebrations, including a portion of the UFO Festival, take place here (p 37).

East of Main Street

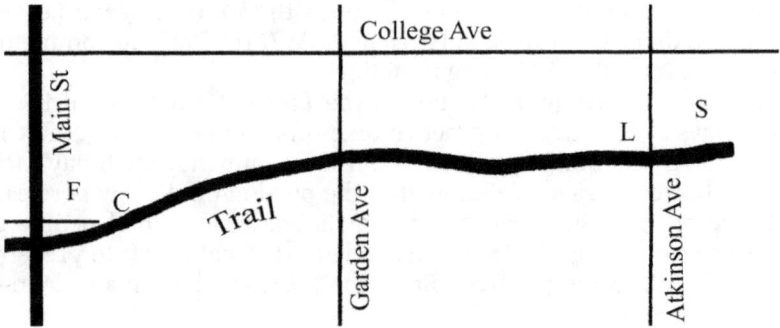

Spring River Recreation Trail
(East of Main Street)

KEY

C Charlie's Park
F Former City Park

L Loveless Park
S Spring River Park and Zoo

(Former City Park) (North of the river between Main Street and the AT & SF Railroad tracks). Early Roswell citizens used the large open area stretching from the river north to 12th Street here as a park where they played baseball and held picnics and square dances. Later it became a fairground for Hay Carnivals and Cotton Festivals. The pink building at 1101 North Virginia Avenue, originally built to hold fair exhibits—old timers claim it was the pig barn—but now home to the Roswell Community Little Theater (five performances a year, including one during the UFO Festival, 622-1982), juts out into the street because Virginia Avenue was only a footpath when the building was first constructed. At one time National Guard troops trained here and used the pink building for meetings. Boys in the Babe Ruth League played baseball in the park here until 1963 but foul balls crossing Main Street created a dangerous situation. In that year the League moved to a ballpark at Stiles Field (Bland Street and Wyoming Avenue) in southwest Roswell.

Today the City Sanitation Department occupies the eastern portion of this former park while several restaurants (Arby's, Wendy's, Cattle Baron), the Roswell Community Little Theater, and the Bus Station occupy the western portion.

During Charlie Ortega's tenure as Sanitation Department Chief he planted trees and tended the small landscaped area along the Recreation Trail where the Sanitation Department headquarters begin. When he retired, the City named the area **Charlie's Park** in his honor.

Charles Loveless Memorial Park (Blashek Mill site) (1200 North Atkinson Avenue). East of Charlie's Park the Bike Trail follows a rather uninteresting stretch of river through an area of businesses and warehouses—although interesting birds and dragonflies do live here—then emerges in Loveless Park. In 1984 the City dedicated this park to the memory of a long-time Roswell citizen whose family donated the land as well as money for the footbridge and picnic shelter. Previously a grist mill stood on this site.

George Blashek arrived in Roswell in 1882 to establish Roswell's first industrial project, a mill to grind flour and cornmeal, on land here given him by Joseph Lea—"The Father of Roswell." Blashek ordered millstones from "back east," had them shipped to the nearest railroad station in Las Vegas, New Mexico, then freighted them by oxcart the 200 miles south to Roswell. The Spring River powered the mill that he and his family operated for the next sixty years. In winter he sawed blocks of ice from the river and stored them, insulated with sawdust, in an adobe shed on the north side of the mill so that ice was usually available until late summer. Unfortunately, no sign of his mill remains today.

Spring River Park and Zoo (1306 East College Avenue). In the 1930s Roswell's zoo began as a small collection of animals in Cahoon Park just west of the swimming pool. In 1966 the zoo—including a bear, a deer, a pronghorn, two ostriches, and a lion whose tail had been bobbed by two drunken airmen—moved to this current location where it had room to expand. The only problem: people living around Cahoon Park missed the early morning roaring of the lion.

The only free zoo in New Mexico, Spring River Park and Zoo boasts a small but interesting collection of native and exotic (although not extra-terrestrial) animals: bears, coyotes, eagles, bison, Sandhill Cranes, foxes, monkeys, deer, mountain lions, and so forth. The native animal exhibits are arranged along "The Capitan Trail" depicting the habitats encountered on a hike from Spring River up to Capitan Peak: river bottoms, prairies, foothills, and mountains.

One of the most popular exhibits in the zoo is the Prairie Dog Town, also inhabited by Burrowing Owls. These prairie dogs, descendants of animals moved from the Wool Bowl area when the stadium was constructed in 1963, often sit on their haunches guarding the entrances to their elaborate system of burrows, communicating with their neighbors through shrill calls. The Burrowing Owls take advantage of the prairie dog burrows for nesting. They come and go as they please, living in the zoo only by choice. One of the few owls active during the day, the small Burrowing Owls often sit near the burrow entrances watching zoo visitors as well.

Another popular area is the Children's Zoo containing child-sized animals such as ponies and goats that appeal to younger visitors. A beautiful antique carousel stands near the Children's Zoo. Choose your steed—or a more exotic mount—and hop aboard before the music starts! A gift to the children of Roswell in 1971 from oil company executive and carousel horse collector Marianne Stevens, this 1927 Spillman carousel made in North Tonawanda, New York, arrived without horses, but Mrs. Stevens also donated the animal figures to fill it. All were carved before 1917 and include a giant chicken, a cow, a deer, and a life-sized St. Bernard, all from France. The rhinoceros is German. The rest are American-carved. The size of the saddles indicates that these figures were designed to hold adults as well as children, as carousels were popular amusements for all ages in the early Twentieth Century.

Marianne Stevens also raised money for the miniature railroad train that takes visitors along the edge of the stocked Fishing Pond (for children under 12 only, no license required) where Canada Geese congregate in winter. It also circles the Longhorn Cattle Pasture with its windmill. Don't forget to scream as you go through the tunnel! The gas-powered locomotive pulling the train is a 1/3-scale replica of the *C.P. Huntington,* the first engine Collis P. Huntington purchased for the Southern Pacific Railroad which he organized in 1871. The half-mile of train track came from an amusement park "back east." City carpenter Ross Delaney built the train station out of timbers from the old Walker Air Force Base stables so the City named it in his honor. Tickets for rides on either the Carousel or the Train (that run daily during the summer and on spring and fall weekends) are only 25 cents.

A footbridge crosses the Spring River just west of the miniature railroad bridge. The two steel "A" frames supporting it were salvaged from the old National Guard Armory (108 West 5th Street) that burned in 1963. They originally supported the roof of that 1909 building (p 42).

Peppermint Playground adjoining the zoo on the east is a popular spot for family picnics with its playground equipment, shade trees, barbeque grills, and picnic tables.

Various activities take place in the zoo throughout the year: an Easter Egg Hunt, Race for the Zoo, Zoo Day Camp, Labor Day Symphony Concert, Boo at the Zoo, etc. Admission to the zoo is free. 624-6760. Open every day 10 a.m. to sunset.

The Recreation Trail ends here at the zoo while the Spring River continues on about one mile (1.5 km) farther east to where it flows into the Hondo River. Plans to extend the Recreation Trail to that location are "in the works."

< Roswell Zoo >

Chapter VII. Along the Hondo River Recreation Trail

The popularity of the Spring River Recreation Trail—and the persistence of City Councilwoman Mary Anaya—led the City to establish this recreational trail in southeastern Roswell beginning in 2003. It follows the Hondo River nearly one and one-half miles (2.5 km) from the Yucca Recreation Center on the west to the 900 block of East 2nd Street on the east, through the heart of the original settlement of Rio Hondo that later became Roswell.

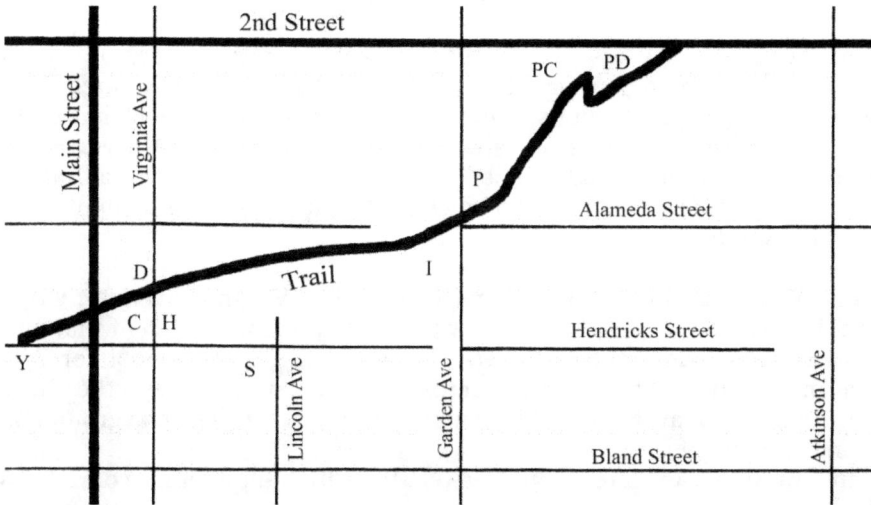

KEY

C	Carver Park	PC	Poe Corn Park
D	Dixon house site	PD	Pan Dulce Bakery
H	Headstart	S	St. John's Catholic Church
I	Iglesia Bautista	Y	Yucca Recreation Center
P	Poe Corn Center		

West of Main Street

Yucca Recreation Center (former Roswell High School) (500 South Richardson Avenue). Completed in 1912 as the original Roswell High School and built in the Rapp brothers' Military Gothic style (as can be seen in photos in the Best Western Sally Port Inn lobby), most of this structure was demolished when the City took over the building to use as a youth recreation center in 1974; Roswell High School had moved to new quarters on West Hobbs Street in 1954. Today only the gymnasiums and a few upstairs rooms remain from the original building; the rest is new construction. The Yucca Center provides a wide variety of year-round sports activities and recreational classes for youth. Varying fees are charged for classes and events. 624-6700.

Main Street

Hondo River Bridge (400 Block South Main Street). Today this bridge is flanked by used-car lots and automotive businesses, but once it was the spot to watch herds of pronghorn as they gathered to drink. It was also the location of the shootout between Deputy U.S. Marshal Charlie Perry and the Griffin brothers (p 61).

East of Main Street

(Dixon house site) (109 East Tilden Street). African-American Joe Dixon worked as a handyman, janitor, and gardener for Amelia Bolton Church (p 76) for many years. Although the house she provided for him at this location no longer stands, it was once a part of an area where several African-American families lived in early Roswell. "Laughin' Joe," as Dixon was called because a brain injury made him susceptible to episodes of uncontrolled laughter, was a popular character in early Roswell.

George Washington Carver Park (400 South Virginia Avenue). Originally named Lovelace Park, because the City purchased it from a man of that name in 1935, this park was located immediately west of Carver School for African-American students that once stood across Virginia Avenue where the Headstart building stands today. School children used the park as their playground, and it took on the name of the school.

In a racially segregated 1939 Roswell, the City built a tennis court—now the basketball court—in this small park at the request of the Roswell Colored Tennis Club and posted a sign "For Colored People Only." In an early stand for civil rights—sort of—Anglo citizens protested that this unfairly discriminated against other races. The sign was changed to read "Colored People Permitted to Use this Court."

Virginia Avenue Bridge over the Hondo River (400 block South Virginia Avenue). Rufus Dunnahoo (1849-1937), who opened Roswell's first blacksmith shop on the southwest corner of 4th and Main Streets, had originally come from Mississippi and settled at Seven Rivers, a few miles north of Carlsbad. He found this notorious rustler hangout too "wild and wooly" for his tastes and in 1881 headed north for Las Vegas, New Mexico, with a wagon caravan. The Hondo River was too high to ford when the caravan reached Roswell but Captain Lea, who had moved to town four years earlier, had several large vigas laid across the river at this spot and covered with smaller saplings so that Dunnahoo and his party could cross. Dunnahoo returned to settle permanently in Roswell a few months later—he liked what he saw on the way through town better than what he found in Las Vegas—and the makeshift bridge here continued to serve travelers for several more years.

Roswell Headstart Center (George Washington Carver School site) (205 East Hendricks Street). The first public "Colored School" in Roswell opened in Smith Chapel on South Michigan Avenue in 1907, then moved across the street to the Colored Masonic Hall where students attended classes for the next 23 years (p 136).

The Roswell School Board let a contact to build a school for African-American students on this site in July 1930. The two-room building was completed shortly after the school year began and the students moved into their new George Washington Carver School for grades 1 through 12. Roswell's African-American students attended school here until the fall of 1952 when the junior and senior high schools were integrated. Elementary students continued to attend Carver School until it closed in 1955.

Today the new building on this site serves as one of Roswell's three Headstart Centers, preparing disadvantaged children for kindergarten.

Chihuahuita

Chihuahuita means "little Chihuahua," and is named after the Mexican state just south of the New Mexico border, as well as its capital city, that was the birthplace of many of its original citizens. The oldest part of Roswell, originally called Rio Hondo, Chihuahuita hugs the south bank of the Hondo River on slightly higher ground than the rest of downtown Roswell, which protected it from the flooding that was once so common. Immigrants from Chihuahua and Hispanics from Northern New Mexico and Texas settled here before Anglo Roswell existed. This was one of the first of several small Hispanic communities of farmers and sheep ranchers that sprang up in eastern New Mexico after it became a part of the United States in 1850 because settlers found empty spaces, plentiful water for farming, and abundant grass for grazing livestock.

Little is known of Chihuahuita's early history. In 1867 it appeared on a U.S. survey as Rio Hondo and contained several adobe buildings, as did the Hispanic settlements of La Plaza de Missouri 15 miles (25 km) to the west and El Berrendo, a few miles to the north.

After the Civil War a wave of Anglo cattlemen, then farmers taking advantage of the Homestead Act and later the discovery of artesian water and the arrival of the railroad, came to dominate the earlier Hispanic inhabitants. Other Hispanic settlements died out, but Chihuahuita persisted.

Two separate societies, one Anglo and one Hispanic, developed in Roswell—and to some extent remain today. Chihuahuita had its own markets, laundries, barber shops, bars and restaurants, curanderas (healers), builders, churches, and schools. In 1902 twenty-four charter members organized La Sociedad Union y Fraternidad Mexicana de Roswell, a mutual aid society for social and financial support in the Hispanic community.

In the early 1900s the Chihuahuita area was platted as the Acequia Subdivision of Roswell and its street names were anglicized. Today Chihuahuita is bounded generally by Atkinson Avenue on the east, Poe Corn Park and 2nd Street on the north, Virginia Avenue on the west, and Bland Street on the south. Many of the oldest houses in this section are made of adobe. Generations have rebuilt, repaired, and added on to the original structures, usually without keeping any records. It is difficult to know just how old some of these houses are, but the oldest are probably at 105, 106, 107, 114, and 115 South Mulberry Avenue (originally called Calle Alamosa); 708, 712, 718, and 901 East Walnut Street; and 715, 717,

719, 721, 725, 729, and 733 East Alameda Street (originally called Calle Camino Real). These houses are all built in the New Mexico Vernacular style: adobe walls but pitched roofs, often covered with tin, rather than the flat-roofed Pueblo Revival style adobe houses usually associated with New Mexico. Houses in Chihuahuita are generally small. Yards are often filled with ornaments and decorations—including a space ship at the corner of Alameda and Elm Streets.

Chihuahuita remains the traditional heart of Hispanic Roswell. Recent interest in renovating and revitalizing this neighborhood is leading to a resurgence of community spirit in the Chihuahuita area, a district that has long been one of the poorer sections of town.

St. John-the-Baptist Catholic Church (506 South Lincoln Avenue). Franciscan priests founded two Catholic churches in Roswell in 1903: St. Peter's for Anglo Catholics and St. John's for Hispanic Catholics. St. John's, built here close to the early Hispanic settlement on the Rio Hondo, was originally named St. John-the-Baptist Mexican Catholic Church. The one hundred thirty families that made up the congregation by 1904 first met in a small building on East Hendricks Street, then moved into this current building in 1916. Brown adobe walls, colorful ceramic tiles, religious statues in niches along its bell towers, and a splashing fountain in a lovely courtyard give this church a Mexican flavor. As a part of its Centennial Celebration in 2003, St. John's parish erected a Memorial Wall inscribed with the names of all deceased church members, along with all the priests who have served the parish over the years. Both of these interest visitors researching family history.

Priests say several masses in Spanish here each week, in addition to those in English. In the days leading up to Christmas the congregation participates in Las Posadas, an Hispanic tradition of traveling from house to house that commemorates Mary and Joseph's search for lodging. The congregation also celebrates the Festival of St. John on June 24 and the Festival of Our Lady of Guadalupe on December 12.

A recently demolished building next door to the church served as a school of eight grades taught by the Order of the Sisters of St. Cisinni from 1922 until the mid-1960s when it closed due to financial and staffing problems. In 2008 the parish broke ground for a new Community Center on this site.

Iglesia Bautista del Calvario (Spanish Calvary Baptist Church) (600 East Tilden Street). Manuel and Francisca Melendez bought the entire north side of the 600 block of East Tilden Street when they moved to Roswell from the Mexican state of Chihuahua in 1912. They gave their son Eduardo this portion when he married fourteen-year-old Urbana Juarez in 1914. The young couple built "La Casa de Adobe" here where they raised their large family—producing three Army Air Corps pilots, a West Point appointee and engineer, a college instructor, an Air Force "Singing Sergeant," a schoolteacher, and a computer programmer—then they donated their land to this church that they helped organize in 1940. Their house no longer stands but the church has become an active community center and is one of the strongest Spanish language Baptist churches in the state. Melendez Park located on the corner of South Garden Avenue and East

McGaffey Street honors Urbana Melendez for her long years of leadership and hard work in the Chihuahuita community.

Poe Corn Center (201 Garden Avenue). The City built Hondo Pool in Hondo Park, just across the Hondo River from the heart of Chihuahuita, in 1955. The bathhouse was also used as a recreation center, but room was limited so the City completed this current pre-fab structure on a concrete slab in 1963 with basketball courts, classrooms, offices, a ceramics room, and a concession area. In 1972 both the Recreation Center and the Park were named for Roswell's Recreation Director from 1958 through 1972, Poe Corn (1909-1972), a son of Roswell pioneer Martin Corn. The Roswell Boy's and Girl's Club currently operates the recreation center, and the pool that is open to the public for a small fee in the summer.

Poe Corn Park (former Hondo Park, Greenhaven Tourist Court site) (606-618 East 2nd Street). Picnic tables, shade trees, and playground equipment make this an inviting rest stop along the Hondo River. The East Side Little League, one of three Little League organizations in Roswell, plays on the baseball fields here.

G. A. Greene opened Greenhaven Tourist Court here along 2nd Street in 1928. Operating until 1971, it also included a Texaco service station, a grocery, and a trailer park at various times. Greenhaven Tourist Court's most famous guest was Roy Rogers, who stayed here with his singing group in 1933 while touring the Southwest (p 65).

The land between Greenhaven Tourist Court and the river was originally called Hondo Park. In 1973, the year after Hondo Park was renamed in honor of Poe Corn, the City acquired the area that had been Greenhaven Tourist Court and added it to Poe Corn Park.

Pan Dulce Bakery (912 East 2nd Street). Flavorful Mexican pastries, burritos, biscochitos (the New Mexico State Cookie), the ever-popular menudo, and much more are available to enjoy here or at a picnic table in adjoining Poe Corn Park. 622-5970. Open T-Sat 5 a.m.-6 p.m., Sun 5 a.m.-2 p.m., closed M, holidays variable.

The Hondo River Recreation Trail currently ends at 2nd Street a little east of Pan Dulce Bakery, but another of Roswell's mysteries appears here. The address of Pan Dulce Bakery is 912 East 2nd Street while the address of the liquor store next door is 620 East 2nd Street. What happened to the 700 and 800 blocks of East 2nd Street? Some suggest alien abduction.

VIII. Roswell International Air Center (RIAC)

In 1940 the United States Army built an airfield and pilot training facility on vacant land just south of Roswell: Roswell Army Air Field where pilots and bombardiers trained throughout World War II. After the war it became home to the nation's only atomic warfare group, with the *Enola Gay*, the airplane that dropped the atomic bomb on Hiroshima, based here.

After the Air Force separated from the Army in 1947 RAAF took the name Walker Air Force Base, in honor of Brigadier General Kenneth Walker of Cerrillos, New Mexico, a Congressional Medal of Honor recipient who died in the Pacific in 1942. It became one of the largest installations operated by the United States Air Force Strategic Air Command.

Walker Air Force Base closed in 1967. The City of Roswell took over the land and facilities and began promoting the Roswell Industrial Air Center to educational and health-care institutions as well as to manufacturing companies, especially those related to aircraft industries. Its 13,000' (4,000 m) runway, along with Roswell's good weather and low volume of air traffic, has made the RIAC a popular location for training airline and military pilots. Private individuals have bought many of the former base quarters as low-cost housing.

Recently the City renamed the facility the Roswell International Air Center. It has also been designated a "Foreign Trade Zone," which brings businesses tax benefits.

Central Area

Entrance. (South end of Main Street). The public entrance and guard box for Walker Air Force Base once stood where Main Street becomes the Esplanade—the landscaped median between the two lanes of Walker Boulevard—just south of the railroad tracks. Today this is the beginning of the RIAC, as the sign indicates.

Just north of the Entrance are three restaurants: **Phillips Kountry Kettle** (American and Cajun), **Anita's** (Mexican), and the very popular **Burrito Express** (burritos, mainly to go).

Burrowing Owls often stand beside ground squirrel holes in open areas east and west of the Esplanade, and the ground squirrels themselves scamper across the lawns during the summer. The railroad tracks, a branch of the main spur from the Atchison, Topeka and Santa Fe line three miles (5 km) to the east, are no longer in regular use. Built in the 1970s to provide rail access to the Bus Plant, these are some of the newest railroad tracks in New Mexico. The government had built the main spur that ends near the Water Tower in 1941 to provide rail access to the RAAF for supplies and heavy equipment.

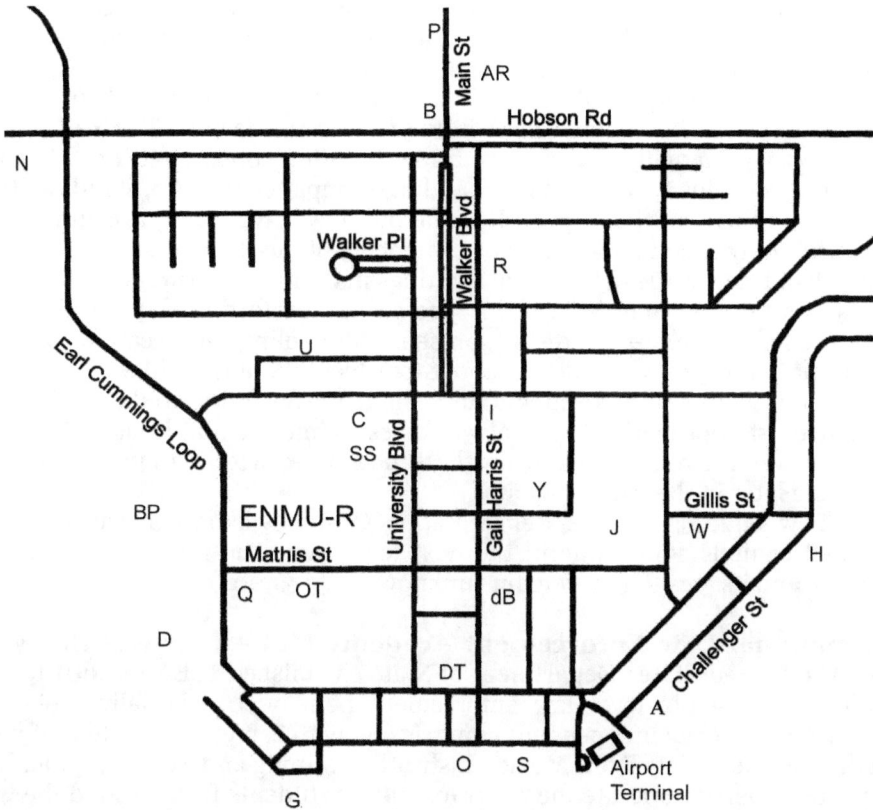

RIAC

KEY

A	AAR Aircraft Services	**N**	National Guard Armory
AR	Anita's Restaurant	**O**	Old Fire Station
B	Burrito Express	**OT**	L.C. Harris OTC
BP	Bus Plant	**P**	Phillip's Kountry Kettle
C	Campus Union	**Q**	Quonset huts
D	Dean Baldwin Painting	**R**	NM Rehab Center
dB	de Bremond Training Site	**S**	S. Gutierrez Mid. School
DT	Department of Transportation	**SS**	Student Services
G	General Aviation Terminal	**U**	University High School
H	Hanger 84	**W**	Water Tower
I	ILEA	**Y**	Youth ChalleNGe
J	Job Corps		

New Mexico Rehabilitation Center (31 Gail Harris Avenue). Here patients from all over the state receive a wide range of rehabilitation services including physical and occupational therapy, speech and language therapy, social work, and psychological services. The Center, a major employer in the Roswell area, also operates an in-patient drug and alcohol treatment program.

Tourists are often told that military physicians autopsied alien creatures found with the crashed flying saucer in 1947 inside this facility. The RAAF Hospital in 1947 was actually a one-story frame building constructed on this site in 1942, however. This two-story brick building, completed in 1960, stands a little to the north and west of the original hospital but does have a unique claim to fame: the world's only "resident alien" ghost. Members of the Rehab Center night shift tell stories of unusual sightings in dimly lit corridors. One is of a military man in uniform who seems comforting as he walks the halls. A more interesting presence, only glimpsed occasionally at the end of a corridor, is about four feet tall, human-like, but very thin with a large head and dark, slanted eyes. Why would an alien ghost appear here? Several witnesses claimed that at least one alien was recovered alive from the saucer wreckage in 1947, only to die later in the RAAF hospital.

A new building for the Rehabilitation Center will be constructed on the ENMU-R campus some time in the next few years. The future of this current structure and its "residents" remains unknown. 347-3400.

International Law Enforcement Academy (ILEA). (47 Gail Harris Avenue). The United States Department of State established ILEA in 2001 to teach mid-level and senior-level law enforcement personnel, especially those from third-world or newly independent countries, how to carry out a system of justice in a democratic society. New Mexico Institute of Mining and Technology and Sam Houston University operate the program, but its students from around the world use ENMU-R facilities for food service and recreation. ILEA's new building was completed in 2006 on the site where the Walker Air Force Base Protestant Chapel once stood. 347-2289, www.ilearoswell.org

Youth ChalleNGe Academy (69 Gail Harris Avenue). The New Mexico National Guard established the New Mexico Youth ChalleNGe—the capital "NG" in the name stands for National Guard—boot camp program for 16- to 18-year-old "at risk" youth in 2001. Each group of approximately one hundred young men and women spends 22 weeks studying academics under military discipline. Participants often find ways to "turn their lives around." 347-2678, www.nmyca.com

de Bremond Training Site (71 Gail Harris Avenue). Youth ChalleNGe cadets live in three-story brick barracks here, as do National Guard troops when they come for training during the summer. Roswell's National Guard 200th Air Defense Artillery Unit used the green Duster Anti-Aircraft Tank at the south end of the obstacle course from the 1950s through the 1980s (p 111).

Old Fire Station (2 East Challenger Avenue). Now replaced by the new Fire Station to the east at 6 East Challenger Avenue, this station served Walker Air

Force Base and the RIAC until the 1990s. Its tower gave firefighters a good view of the runways that provided most of their business. There is talk of opening a museum in this building to tell the story of the Roswell Army Air Field and Walker Air Force Base.

Sidney Gutierrez Middle School (4 East Challenger Avenue). Roswell's only Charter School, this technology-oriented academy serving 60 sixth, seventh, and eighth graders selected by lottery from the applicant pool, is named in honor of New Mexico's second astronaut (after Harrison Schmitt), Air Force Colonel Sidney Gutierrez. A former test pilot and parachutist, he became a NASA astronaut in 1984 and flew on two shuttle missions: the first on the *Columbia* in 1991 and the second, during which he was Commander, on the *Endeavour* in 1994. Colonel Gutierrez retired from the space program later in 1994 and went to work for Sandia National Laboratories in Albuquerque.

Secret Cities (? ? ?). Rumors have circulated for years—and now appear on the Internet—about secret underground government installations in the Roswell vicinity. Most have some connection with the former Air Force base location. Some rumors claim that underground chambers interspersed among the runways still hide secret aircraft. Others describe a network of tunnels, including passageways that connect the former Base Commander's house on Walker Place with the airport control tower. Still others talk about entire underground cities dedicated to secret activities ranging from work on new weapons to breeding experiments on captured aliens. Whoever operates these facilities must be a tight-lipped, highly disciplined group. Nothing more than rumors has surfaced—so far.

New Mexico Department of Transportation Training Academy (132 West Earl Cummings Loop). This unusual school trains county, state, and tribal employees from all over New Mexico in management skills, truck driving, and the operation of 15 types of road equipment. Photographs of antique road equipment line the building's halls and lobby.

Parked in front of the Training Academy are two carefully restored antique road graders that trucks, tractors, and sometimes mules pulled in the 1920s. The smaller orange grader on the right of the entrance is a simple model with wheels and cranks to adjust the blade. The larger green model on the left is more sophisticated. Wheels, cranks, and gears control blade angle and elevation, the pitch of the wheels—so they can dig into the roadbed to keep the grader from being pushed sideways by the force of the dirt pushing against the blade—and the position of the wheels to the left or right of the blade. Why are the edges of the operator's platform angled up on each side? So the operator can always stand on a horizontal surface, even when working on the side of a mountain.

The large boulder under the tree by the orange grader came from blasting work on Highway 70 up toward Ruidoso. Pecos Bill would say that they used a dynamite charge so large that it blew the boulder clear to Roswell. How else could it have gotten here!?

The New Mexico Department of Transportation sponsors an annual Equipment Road-eo at the Eastern New Mexico State Fair in October: a unique and sometimes strange competition for heavy equipment operators. 624-6080.

Eastern New Mexico University—Roswell (ENMU-R) (52 University Boulevard). In 1958 Eastern New Mexico University, located 90 miles (145 km) northeast of Roswell in Portales, established a branch campus in Roswell: Roswell Community College. At first the community college held evening classes at Roswell High School but in 1963 classes moved to the old Federal Building on Richardson Avenue. When Walker Air Force Base closed in 1967, Roswell Community College took over some of the empty buildings and changed its name to Eastern New Mexico University—Roswell. Over the years as new structures have replaced old military buildings, the campus has acquired state-of-the-art facilities in many areas of study. Some of the few remaining Air Force buildings on campus are the Quonset huts housing the Physical Plant at the west end of Mathis Street including some in the back that look like they are made of . . . adobe?

Initially a two-year institution, ENMU-R now also offers access to four-year degrees in conjunction with ENMU and other universities. Academic classes and a large variety of career and technical classes, such as aviation maintenance, criminal justice, nursing, respiratory therapy, computer applications, air conditioning, and dental assisting, are available to its 4,000 mostly commuter students. On-line and satellite courses are also available from the main campus in Portales, and some master's level programs are even offered now. 624-7000, www.roswell.enmu.edu

The **Campus Union** houses the newly remodeled and expanded college cafeteria, which is open to the public. The building was originally completed as Walker Air Force Base Officer's Club in 1959. The grill makes good—and inexpensive—quesadillas, especially if you ask them to throw on some green chile. The original frame building on this site held the Roswell Army Air Field Officer's Club where Glenn Dennis and Nurse Selff met to discuss the alien autopsy—an interesting lunch stop on any UFO Crash tour.

An **outdoor pool** (originally part of the Officer's Club) open to the public for a small fee during summer months is just northwest of the Campus Union.

ENMU-R boasts an impressive art collection on display in its many public areas. Michael Orgel's 1998 bronze sculpture, *Departure*, representing a bird poised to take off from in front of the **Arts and Science Center**, celebrates diversity. The foremost piece in the art collection is a 4' by 16' (1.2 m by 5 m) painting by Roswell artist Peter Hurd, *Round Up at South Spring 1875*. In 1965 Hurd, the only civilian aboard a transatlantic Air Force flight, agreed to paint this mural for the Walker Air Force Base Officer's Club at the end of a rocky trip, later saying he would have promised anything to get off the airplane alive. He donated the tempera-on-masonite painting to what became the "Peter Hurd Dining Room" in the Officer's Club (now the Campus Union). The painting was later transferred to the college and is now on display in the **Student Services Center** two buildings south of its original location. A large untitled acrylic painting of a mountain by Roswell oil entrepreneur and artist Donald Anderson and a smaller oil painting by Roswell artist Bill Wiggins entitled *Green Apples* also brighten the lobby of the Student Services Center. Prospective students will find information about ENMU-R in this building.

At the height of the early 1980s oil boom ENMU-R developed a unique program to train technicians at its Oilfield Training Center. Over 500 students at a time learned the practical intricacies of finding and producing oil and gas through classroom instruction and work in an 18-acre simulated oilfield, directly behind the classroom building, that included a fully operational drilling rig. When the oil boom collapsed, so did the program. All that is left today is the building on Mathis Street—now called the **Lawrence C. Harris Occupational Technology Center**—with a display pump jack in front, cigarette butt receptacles made from oilfield drill bits along the sidewalk, and a lonely derrick frame out back.

University High School (25 West Martin Street). Roswell's third high school is currently an alternative school for students who benefit from instruction in a non-traditional setting. The New Mexico Legislature appropriated funds to turn University High into a technical-vocational high school and this process is currently under way.

Western Area

New Mexico Army National Guard Armory (1 West Earl Cummings Loop). This most recent National Guard Armory, built in 1988, is home to what is now the New Mexico National Guard 200th Infantry Unit recently returned from Iraq. This group traces its illustrious history back in various configurations to Teddy Roosevelt's Rough Riders. Battery A of the New Mexico 200th Air Defense Artillery guarded the border with Mexico after Pancho Villa's attack in 1916, fought in France during World War I, and served in an anti-tank battalion in North Africa and Italy during World War II. A small collection of Unit memorabilia is on display inside the Armory. Previous Armories stood at 108 West 5th Street (p 41) and 4203 West 2nd Street.

The green tank in front of the Armory is an M42A1 Duster, one of over 3,700 built between 1952 and 1957 to replace the World War II Twin 40 mm Anti-Aircraft Tank. During the Vietnam era they escorted tank columns and infantry units protecting them against attack from the air. Roswell's 200th Air Defense Artillery unit used this Duster and the one at de Bremond Training Site from the 1950s until the 1980s.

The sculpture on the Armory lawn represents the symbol of the New Mexico National Guard Air Defense Artillery: a Zia sun sign and a bolt of lightning. 347-3500.

Bus Plant (42 West Earl Cummings Loop). A bus manufacturing plant has operated on and off in the large blue building—originally built as a hangar for B-36 bombers—under different corporate logos since the 1970s. At one time when the plant manufactured buses for New York City, a Roswell wag wrote the Big Apple's mayor offering to organize groups of local Roswell youth to paint graffiti on the buses before shipping them out. The indignant mayoral aide who responded that "Graffiti no longer appear on New York City buses!" was clearly not amused.

Dean Baldwin Painting (82 West Earl Cummings Loop). This interesting business paints commercial airliners—one at a time. Crews strip away old paint, look for defects in the airplane "skin," then repaint the airliner with new color schemes and designs. They work around the clock because an airplane that is not in service is not bringing in revenues. Airlines send only one airplane at a time for the weeklong procedure so that passenger schedules are not disrupted. Sorry, no tours are available. 347-4168, www.deanbaldwinpainting.com

General Aviation Terminal—Great Southwest Aviation (100 Southwest Way). Small private and corporate planes use this area regularly. Flight instruction is also available. 347-2054, www.greatsouthwestaviation.com

President Reagan toured New Mexico in 1982, campaigning for the reelection of New Mexico's first astronaut, Senator Harrison Schmitt. The President incorporated Roswell's alien theme into his speech as he stood on an outdoor platform set up in this area by remarking about Senator Schmitt, "When he was first elected to the Senate, he probably thought that, like E.T., he had landed on another planet. He was one of the few among those alien big spenders, big taxers, who was working to bring economic order to our nation." In spite of Reagan's support, Schmitt lost the election. (How could you vote against an astronaut!?)

Vice-President Dick Cheney also spoke to a local crowd inside Hangar 32 in this area during a campaign stop in 2004. Supporters hoped he might reveal something interesting that day, as President Bush had made a campaign promise to put Cheney to work disclosing "the truth about UFOs" if he was elected. The Vice-President stuck strictly to politics, however. Some think the country would have been better off if Cheney had spent more of his time researching UFOs.

Eastern Area

Roswell Airport Terminal (1 Jerry Smith Circle). Roswell's spacious, attractive, and mostly empty passenger terminal was built in 1975. Large commercial and military jets often practice "touch and go's" on the 13,000' (4,000 m) airstrip, but actual airline service is extremely limited. American Eagle Airlines began daily jet service between here and Dallas-Fort Worth in 2007 while Mesa Airlines canceled service to Albuquerque the same year. The rows upon rows of airplanes visible from the terminal belong to companies that find Roswell's dry climate and abundant space good for airplane storage.

At times a snack bar—currently the **Frappucino Grill**—operates in the terminal lobby, but vending machines in the west corridor are always a reliable source of sustenance. Two car rental companies are the only other businesses in the terminal. The west corridor does house a small display of military aircraft models. A larger model of a B-29 bomber, *Dave's Dream*, hangs in the lobby. The original *Dave's Dream*—built in 1945 and decommissioned in 1960—served as camera plane when the atomic bomb was dropped on Nagasaki and participated in later atomic testing in the Pacific after the war. Some say this aircraft flew crashed saucer debris from Roswell to Wright-Patterson Air Force Base in 1947. 347-5703.

AAR Aircraft Services (511 East Challenger Avenue). One of Roswell's major employers, this aircraft storage and demolition company provides jobs for about 150 people. Occasionally, ominous crunching sounds echo from heavy equipment signaling the destruction of another airliner. 347-9903. www.aarcorp.com

Roswell Job Corps Center (57 G Street). This Federal training center (surrounded by the tan metal fence) has been educating disadvantaged youth, ages 16 to 25, since 1979. The 225 male and female students complete their high school diplomas or attend college while learning a vocation—culinary arts, electrical wiring, facilities maintenance, painting, health occupations, protective services, or automotive maintenance. Job Corps students in the building trades have donated their labor to construct many public facilities around Roswell. Like teens and young adults everywhere, students here perpetuate stories of ghoulish screams, moving shadows, and eerie presences in the former military barracks used as dorms but no supernatural happenings have been authenticated. 347-5414, www.roswell.jobcorps.gov

Water Tower (100 East Gillis Street). This red and white-checkered tower has supplied water to the RIAC area since 1940. Its bright pattern is meant to attract the attention of low-flying aircraft pilots so they will avoid hitting it. So far it has worked.

Hangar 84 (East Enterprise Avenue). It was here in this former B-29 hangar that the Air Force stored the 1947 UFO Crash debris and alien bodies until it shipped them off to Wright-Patterson Air Force Base in Ohio, so the story goes. The City occasionally uses Hanger 84 for events and activities, but most of the time it stands empty or is used for storage. At one time, tours were available but they are no longer conducted; the area is fenced and locked—no trespassing allowed. A small brown sign at the north end of this fourth of five large hangar-like buildings northeast of the Terminal identifies "R.I.A.C. Bldg. 84."

(Former Longhorn Manufacturing Company) (70 LeMay Drive). A fireworks manufacturing company was the first business to locate in the RIAC after Walker Air Force Base closed. Former ammunition storage bunkers were perfect for manufacturing fireworks. Longhorn went out of business in 2003, but for many years was a major contributor to Roswell's municipal fireworks show on the 4th of July.

Area 51 Dragway (LeMay Drive). The drag-racing season here lasts from March through October with racing on Friday and Saturday nights. This track has been in operation since 1995 when it moved here from a location at the old Municipal Airport in northwest Roswell. Here, unlike there, the noise bothers no one. www.area51dragway.com

Heading North along North Main Street (U.S. 285)

Roswell is generally growing to the north and northwest. This more recently developed part of town contains most chain store and chain restaurant locations, as well as new homes, businesses, and subdivisions.

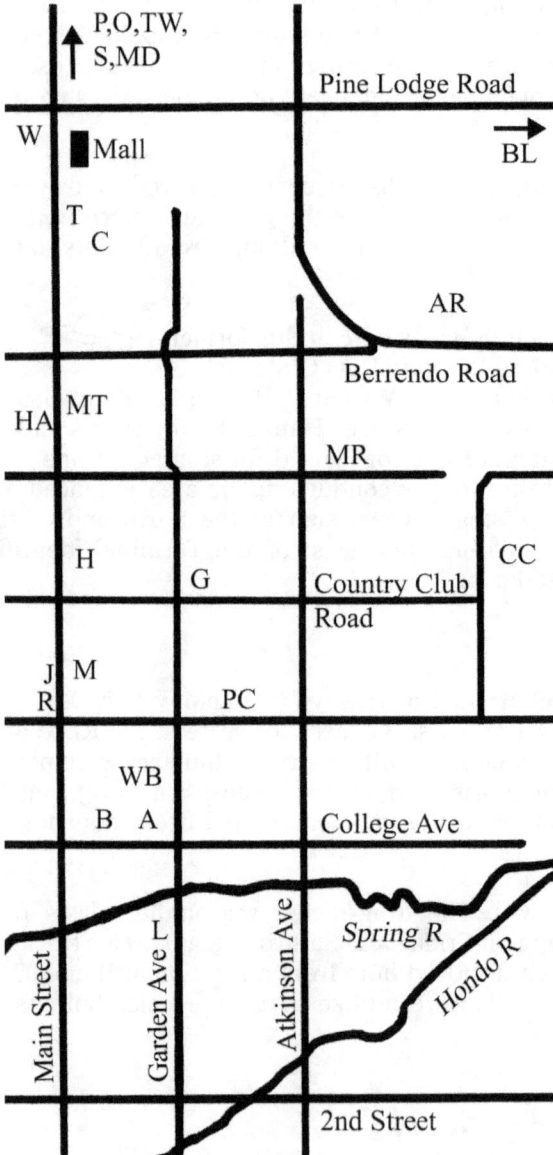

P,O,TW, S,MD

Pine Lodge Road

W

Mall

BL

T

C

AR

Berrendo Road

HA MT

MR

H

G   Country Club Road   CC

J M
R   PC

WB

B A   College Ave

Spring R

Hondo R

Main Street

Garden Ave

L

Atkinson Ave

2nd Street

KEY

A Anderson Museum
AR Artist-in Residence
    Compound
B Burrito Express
BL Bitter Lake National
    Wildlife Refuge
C Cecelio's Restaurant
CC Country Club
G Goddard High School
H Hunan Restaurant
HA Hungry American
    Restaurant
J J.D.'s Patio and Grill
L Livestock Auction
M Mi Cabana
MD Macho Draw
MR Mescalero Ranch
MT Mama Tucker's Donuts
O Overpass
P Price's Truck Stop Café
PC Poor Clare Monastery
R Rookies Sports Bar
S Salt Creek
T Tia Juana's Mexican Grill
TW Transwestern Pipeline
W Wal-Mart
WB Wool Bowl

Roswell—North and Northeast

J.D.'s Patio and Grille (2000 North Main Street, in the Best Western Sally Port Inn). 622-6430. Open for breakfast (a huge buffet plus menu selections) and dinner (sandwiches, steaks, and Mexican food) every day, holidays variable.

Rookies Sports Bar (2000 North Main Street, in the Best Western Sally Port Inn). This sports bar with lots of TV sets, drink specials, and tasty munchies has live rock music on Saturday nights and occasional pool tournaments and karaoke. 622-6430. Open every evening beginning at 4, Sun at 11:00 a.m., holidays variable.

Mi Cabana Restaurant (former Nothin' Fancy Café) (2103 North Main Street). After speaking to a select crowd at the Civic Center in January 2004 President George W. Bush and his entourage swooped into Nothin' Fancy Café unannounced for lunch. President Bush enjoyed ribs and buttermilk pie then promoted the food to the rest of his group. Unfortunately the restaurant closed soon afterward. Today, a branch of Mi Cabana on East McGaffey Street operates here (p 127).

Hunan Restaurant (2699 ½ North Main Street). Lunch specials at this small restaurant tucked away behind Peter Piper Pizza include soup, an egg roll, and a generous portion of rice in addition to the entrée. 623-8630. Open M-Sat for lunch and dinner, closed Sun, holidays variable.

China King Super Buffet (2810 North Main Street). The spread features sushi on the buffet. 625-9888. Open for lunch and dinner every day, holidays variable.

Hungry American (3012 North Main Street). Texas pit barbeque (beef, chicken, ribs, etc.) to eat here or "to go" draws in customers. 627-3908. Open for breakfast and lunch every day, holidays variable.

Mama Tucker's Donut and Cake Shop (3109 North Main Street). Delicious cupcakes—and regular cakes—plus all sorts of other baked goodies tempt patrons in this great place for a grandfather to bring a grandson. 625-1475. Open M-F 5 a.m.-5 p.m., Sat 5 a.m.-1 p.m., closed Sun, holidays variable.

Tia Juana's Mexican Grill and Cantina (3601 North Main Street). Owned by the same folks as the Cattle Baron and Farley's, this restaurant serves "Mexico" Mexican food in a cantina atmosphere. Favorites include Margaritas, Mexican pizza, pollo asado, potato casserole, flan, and watching their tortilla machine. 627-6113. Open for lunch and dinner every day, holidays variable.

Roswell Mall and Surrounding Area (4501 North Main Street). It's a mall—what else can you say? Stores come and go. Roswell's only movie theater—eight screens—is hidden behind the main structure.

    Wal-Mart Super Center west across Main Street from the Mall has a good selection of UFO and alien souvenirs and alien-themed window decorations—plus a selection of Roswell High School clothing. 623-2062. Open 24 hours a day, every day. **Pecos Trails**, the city bus service, makes its northernmost stop here.

Price's Truck Stop Café (5500 North Main Street). They've been serving up good ole American food like catfish and chicken-fried steak here for many years. 623-3443. Open for breakfast, lunch, and dinner every day.

Roswell City Limits (4.8 miles—8 km—north of 2nd Street). The sign reads "Welcome to Roswell, Dairy Capital of the Southwest"—why not "UFO Capital of the World"?

The Overpass (5.5 miles—9 km—north of 2nd Street). This is Roswell's only overpass—the next closest one is, who knows where? Maybe the Interstate at Clines Corners? There's even a sort of clover leaf. Who says we aren't up to date in Roswell!

The WIPP Road or the Roswell Bypass or, officially, the **Roswell Relief Route** branches off to the west from US 285 at The Overpass and circles the western edge of the city, reconnecting with US 285 (Southeast Main Street) south of town. It was completed in 1992 so that radioactive waste headed for the WIPP site (Waste Isolation Pilot Project) 100 miles (160 km) to the south near Carlsbad doesn't have to travel through downtown Roswell. Initially of course, the WIPP site was designated to receive only overalls, gloves, and similar materials lightly contaminated by radiation, but by now who knows what heavy-duty nuclear waste may be whizzing by. If you see a truck loaded with the characteristic round, squat Tru-Pak containers, keep your fingers crossed. In spite of what you might expect, the Relief Route is only a two-lane, non-limited-access road, so beware of two-way and cross-street traffic.

Transwestern Pipeline Company (6381 North Main Street). Including 2,400 miles (3,900 km) of bi-directional pipeline—meaning that the product can be pumped in either direction depending on the need—carrying natural gas to markets in the Midwest, Texas, New Mexico, Arizona, and California, this pipeline system is shaped like a "Y" lying on its side with the two arms pointed east. The upper arm collects gas from wells in the Anadarko Basin of Texas and Oklahoma while the lower arm collects gas from the Permian Basin of Southeastern New Mexico and West Texas. The two arms join here at Roswell, where one of two regional offices—the other is in Albuquerque—is located. From here the stem of the "Y" extends through New Mexico and Arizona into eastern California. An extra arm brings gas down from the San Juan Basin in Northern New Mexico and Southern Colorado to join the stem west of Albuquerque.

The pipe itself, 12 to 48 inches (30 to 120 cm) in diameter, is buried several feet below the surface for protection from the elements and animals, including man. Compressor stations every 100 miles (160 km) or so keep the gas flowing. Capsule-shaped mechanical devices called "pigs" travel through the pipeline periodically to clean or inspect it—and have figured in several James Bond movies (not in this particular pipeline) and in Tony Hillerman's New Mexico mystery novel, *The Sinister Pig*.

South Fork of Salt Creek (9 miles—15 km—north of 2nd Street). Dr. Robert Goddard conducted his experimental rocket launches west of the highway here from 1930 to 1942 on land leased from one of pioneer farmer Martin Corn's sons.

Goddard's wife Esther usually helped with the experiments. She had two jobs: the first was to film the launch; the second was to put out the prairie fire it caused. When Charles Lindbergh came to visit Dr. Goddard in 1934 and 1935 he flew his small plane here to circle the launch tower—now standing on the grounds of the Roswell Museum and Art Center—and inspect the proceedings.

Macho Draw (North Fork of Salt Creek) (14 miles—23 km—north of 2nd Street). While John Chisum was the original Pecos Valley cattleman, Martin Van Buren Corn (1841-1915) was the original Pecos Valley farmer. He arrived here from North Carolina, by way of Georgia and Texas, in 1878. With the help of Chisum, Corn and his growing family (he eventually fathered twenty children by two wives—no wonder there are still so many Corn descendents in the Pecos Valley today, although they no longer ride in the Eastern New Mexico State Fair Parade in the section called "Crops Raised in New Mexico") homesteaded land on the South Spring River—currently the location of Buena Suerte Ranch—a few miles southeast of Roswell. His corn, wheat, and alfalfa crops and his fruit orchards prospered, but in 1894 he sold his land to J.J. Hagerman and moved here looking for a healthier spot because of his asthma.

In an optimistic spirit, Corn named his new home "Eden Valley" (check the historic photo of Macho Draw in the Roswell Public Library lobby for any resemblance to the Garden of Eden) and tried to build an irrigation reservoir by damming Salt Creek, in one of Roswell's many failed irrigation schemes. He did manage to raise sheep, cattle, and prized vegetables for the Roswell market. Today this heavily irrigated area—the water now comes from wells—does present a spot of green in the otherwise brown prairie.

Farther upstream to the west, Macho Draw crosses today's Hub Corn Ranch near their UFO Crash Site. The sign and turnoff are about 25 miles (40 km) north of Roswell.

Northeast Roswell

Roswell Livestock Auction Company (900 North Garden Avenue). Have you ever been to a livestock auction? It's fun and exciting! But not for the squeamish or fastidious—even though the sign requests that you "Scrape stuff off your boots before you enter." Sales start every Monday morning at 9:00 a.m. and run until sometime in the afternoon or evening, or even the next day—depending on how much stock there is to sell. Don't worry about taking home a steer accidentally. You have to register as a buyer if you want to bid on the animals. 622-5580, www.roswelllivestockauction.com

A large parking lot—empty most days but crowded with pickups on Mondays—surrounds the sale barn. Pictures of outstanding livestock, a bulletin board for events and sale items, and a plaque, *The Code of the West* (they mean it!), hang in the lobby. Walk straight through to the sales arena, or turn right to the **Sale Barn Café** that serves hearty cowboy breakfasts till 11 a.m., then burgers and Mexican food. 622-1279. Open M 6 a.m. until the sale ends, Tu-Th for breakfast and lunch, F-Sun closed, holidays variable.

Burrito Express (211 East College Avenue). Roswell's largest and fanciest burrito place has lots of tables for "dining in" on their huge variety of flavorful burritos. 627-3863. Open M-Sat for breakfast, lunch, and dinner; closed Sun; holidays variable.

Anderson Museum of Contemporary Art (409 East College Avenue). This wonderful museum houses the stunning collection of contemporary art amassed by Roswell oilman and artist Donald Anderson, brother of former Atlantic Richfield Oil Company President Robert O. Anderson. Donald Anderson was instrumental in organizing the Roswell Artist-In-Residence Program that provides selected artists with a stipend, living space, and a studio in the artists' compound in northeast Roswell for one year. The works of over 100 former Artists-in-Residence, including Howard Cook, Elmer Schooley, and Stuart Arends, hang in this gallery and are available for purchase. Favorites include the school of golf bag fish and the fiberglass western sculptures of Luis Jimenez. Anderson's large stylized landscapes are also on display. 623-5600. Free admission. Open M-F 9-4, SS 1-5, closed holidays.

Wool Bowl (1701 North Grand Avenue). This stadium was completed in 1963 on land owned by New Mexico Military Institute. NMMI sponsored a post-season junior college football bowl game here, including a Wool Bowl Queen, from 1965 to 1971 and still plays occasional football games in the stadium. The Roswell Independent School District now leases and maintains the stadium so that Roswell and Goddard High Schools can reenact *Friday Night Lights* here nearly every fall weekend. They also use it for track events and hold their graduations here every May. The public is welcome to attend events. Some have an admission fee.

In building the field and stadium, a whole prairie dog town had to be relocated. The animals were flooded out of their holes, caught, and transported to a newly created Prairie Dog Town exhibit at the Spring River Zoo. They adapted well and their descendents are still content to remain in the prairie dog exhibit, for the most part. Occasional escapees have to be relocated back to Prairie Dog Town when they pop up in the bison or antelope enclosures.

Our Lady of Guadalupe Poor Clare Monastery (809 East 19th Street). Saint Clare founded her order of Catholic nuns in the Thirteenth Century under the guidance of Saint Francis of Assisi. In addition to the usual three vows of most orders—poverty, obedience, and chastity—Poor Clare nuns take a vow of enclosure. Cloistered from the world and maintaining silence much of the day, Poor Clares devote their lives to prayer, penance, study, and labor, hoping to surround the world with prayer. Today there are Poor Clare Monasteries in 25 states and 76 countries around the world.

Roswell's Poor Clare Monastery opened in a remodeled farmhouse in 1948. Former Abbess Mother Mary Francis (1921-2006) described its founding and her life in Roswell in her inspirational book entitled *The Right to be Merry*.

Roswell's Poor Clare Monastery welcomes the public to pray in their modern chapel any time during the day and to attend morning Mass at 7:30 or afternoon Rosary at 4:00 daily. Quiet voices of cloistered nuns singing on the other side of the grille inspire peaceful contemplation.

Goddard High School (701 East Country Club Road). Robert H. Goddard Senior High School, dedicated by Esther Goddard in a ceremony honoring her late husband, graduated its first class in 1965—"We came alive in '65!" In that Cold War era, an underground school seemed like a good idea. It certainly saves on heating and cooling costs and broken windows are never a problem. The gym, cafeteria, and some recent additions are all above ground, but students spend most of their day in subterranean classrooms, still safe from atomic blasts and the occasional tornado. An added bonus: no annoying cell phones ringing.

The sports teams of this school named for "The Father of Modern Rocketry" are the "Goddard Rockets." The two rockets out front, backed by a space mural, are not just decoration but are actual rockets donated by the United States Air Force. Inside, a sign in the cafeteria proclaims, "Nancy Lopez ate here," as this LPGA Champion is Goddard High School's most famous graduate.

Roswell Country Club (2601 Urton Road). In Roswell's early days this area was part of Judge Edmund T. Stone's large sheep ranch, the first major Anglo sheep operation in Southeastern New Mexico. Roswell Country Club was organized in 1905 and the clubhouse constructed in 1906 along with an 18-hole golf course. George Slaughter, who operated Slaughter's Hereford Home east of Roswell, brought his mules and scrapers over to excavate the artificial lake. Later when a swimming pool and tennis courts were added, the golf course was reduced to nine holes.

Use today is by members only, but the public can rent the facilities for wedding receptions, Quincineras, and Bar Mitzvahs. Noted Roswell artist Peter Hurd painted the large mural entitled *Picnic '08* behind the bar. It portrays a scenic view of Country Club Lake and the bluffs east of the Pecos River—identical to today's view through the wide bar windows, except for the 1908 picnickers and their antique autos. 622-3410.

Mescalero Ranch (1501 East Mescalero Road). Miss Effie Olds, of the Oldsmobile family, built this one-story Pueblo Revival style house in 1908. What a socialite heiress was doing in Roswell is hard to imagine—although some say it was mainly hobnobbing with the faculty and administration of NMMI. Later, Dr. Robert Goddard and his wife Esther lived here from 1930 to 1942 while he conducted his rocket experiments both here and on Salt Creek north of Roswell. The workshop that he set up to the west of the house has been recreated with its original equipment in the Roswell Museum and Art Center.

At the age of 17, four years before the Wright brothers first took to the air at Kitty Hawk, Robert H. Goddard (1882-1945), "The Father of Modern Rocketry," was inspired by H.G. Wells' science fiction novel *War of the Worlds* to devote his life to space flight. His experiments during World War I led to the development of a new weapon, the bazooka, but the military lost interest in rockets after the War.

By 1930 Dr. Goddard, then head of the Physics Department at Clark University in Massachusetts, was tired of difficulties with neighbors who objected to his backyard rocket launches. With the help of aviator Charles Lindbergh, Goddard obtained funding from the Guggenheim Foundation so that he, his wife, and his four assistants could set up shop in Roswell: a location with good weather "in the middle of nowhere," where his experimental rocket launches bothered no one.

Over his next 12 years in Roswell Goddard devised and perfected multi-stage rockets and their liquid rocket fuel, gyroscopic guidance systems, and fin-stabilized steering.

Esther and Robert Goddard enjoyed their time in Roswell. Both participated in civic and social activities and welcomed visitors to their Mescalero Ranch including the family of artist Peter Hurd and Charles Lindbergh with his wife, Ann Morrow Lindbergh.

Throughout the 1930s Dr. Goddard and Colonel Lindbergh tried unsuccessfully to interest the United States Government in military applications of Goddard's pioneer work with rocketry—with no success. The German government was much more interested however. Careful study of his publications and patents helped their rocketry expert, Wernher von Braun, develop the V-2 rockets that devastated London during World War II.

Dr. Goddard did finally receive recognition from the U.S. Government for his pioneering contributions to rocketry. When the U.S. space program began in earnest in the 1950s, the government realized (because of a series of patent infringement cases) that Goddard had already developed most of the necessary basic rocket technology. In 1959 the Roswell Museum and Art Center (p 35) dedicated a wing funded by the Guggenheim Foundation to him, and the U.S. Government awarded Goddard a Congressional Gold Medal. Exhibits, memorials, and institutions around the world such as NASA's Goddard Space Flight Center now honor Dr. Goddard's accomplishments. Roswell had already honored him in the 1950s with the name of its minor league professional baseball team, the Roswell Rockets, and then of course with Goddard High School and its teams, the Goddard Rockets.

Artist-in-Residence Compound (Howard Cook Road). Most tourists don't realize that Roswell is an important location in the international art scene. Roswell's prestigious Artist-In-Residence Program has been granting highly coveted year long fellowships to four artists each year since 1967: "The Gift of Time" which includes use of a small house and a studio in this Compound as well as a small stipend. Over 175 artists from North America, Europe, Asia, and Australia, such as the first Artist-in-Residence, Howard Cook, along with Barbara Latham, Stuart Arends, Luis Jimenez, Milton Resnick, Elmer Schooley, Gussie du Jardin, and Alison Soar have spent a year working in Roswell. Works of former Artists-in-Residence are on display in the Roswell Museum and Art Center and the Anderson Museum of Contemporary Art.

West of the Compound, the home of Roswell oilman and artist Donald Anderson, organizer of the Artist-in-Residence Program, is identifiable from East Berrendo Road by what looks like a Maine lighthouse and a portion of Stonehenge—actually a sculpture entitled *The Henge*—in a distant field. Reportedly, he keeps most of his large art collection in extensive underground chambers beneath the field.

Cecilio's Restaurant (107 Twin Diamond Road). This popular drive-thru with picnic tables for burgers and Mexican food is just northeast of the Comfort Inn. 622-6180. Open every day for breakfast and lunch, holidays variable.

Bitter Lake National Wildlife Refuge (4065 Bitter Lakes Road: North on Main Street to Pine Lodge Road just north of the Mall, then east on Pine Lodge Road 7 miles—11 km). Workers from the Civilian Conservation Corps—a government program providing work and training to young men during the Depression—who were living in the CCC camp located here from 1938 to 1940, completed this refuge in 1940. Water levels in the spring-fed lakes here, whose name comes from the high alkaline content that makes their water taste bitter, are managed seasonally to provide optimum habitats for the refuge's many inhabitants.

A wonderful spot for birding year-round, this refuge on the Central Flyway comes alive with Sandhill Cranes, Canada Geese, and Snow Geese in the fall and winter. Each morning airborne geese and cranes leave here in long straggling lines or V-shaped formations to feed in corn stubble fields around Roswell. In the late afternoon they return to spend the night on the water for protection from predators. Faint cries from above alert the earthbound to their presence in the skies. If the cries sound like geese honking, they are geese. If they sound like pterodactyls, they are Sandhill Cranes.

All sorts of ducks and a few White Pelicans also winter here. Certain areas are set aside for hunting and fishing in season. Endangered Least Terns and a variety of other shore birds nest around the lakes during the summer when dragonflies and damselflies are also abundant. Many visits to the refuge include a glimpse a Roadrunner zipping across the road, but always watch for rattlesnakes—three different species live here. Pecos Puzzle Sunflowers, which grow only in this area, turn the fields yellow in September. This threatened species is the only sunflower that grows in wet areas and marshlands: puzzling.

The recently completed Skeen Visitor Center, named for former New Mexico Congressman and Hondo Valley rancher Joe Skeen (1927-2003), provides information about animals and plants of the refuge. Early morning is the best time to see birds along the eight-mile (13 km) driving tour. The first Saturday morning of each month, staff members lead a two-hour tour of closed parts of the refuge to see sinkholes where tiny rare Pecos gambusia fish as well as two small snails and an amphipod—all three endangered and endemic to the refuge—live. The Dragonfly Festival takes place here in August, when over 200 species of dragonflies and damselflies are easily spotted. 622-6755. Free admission. The tour route is open every day during daylight hours.

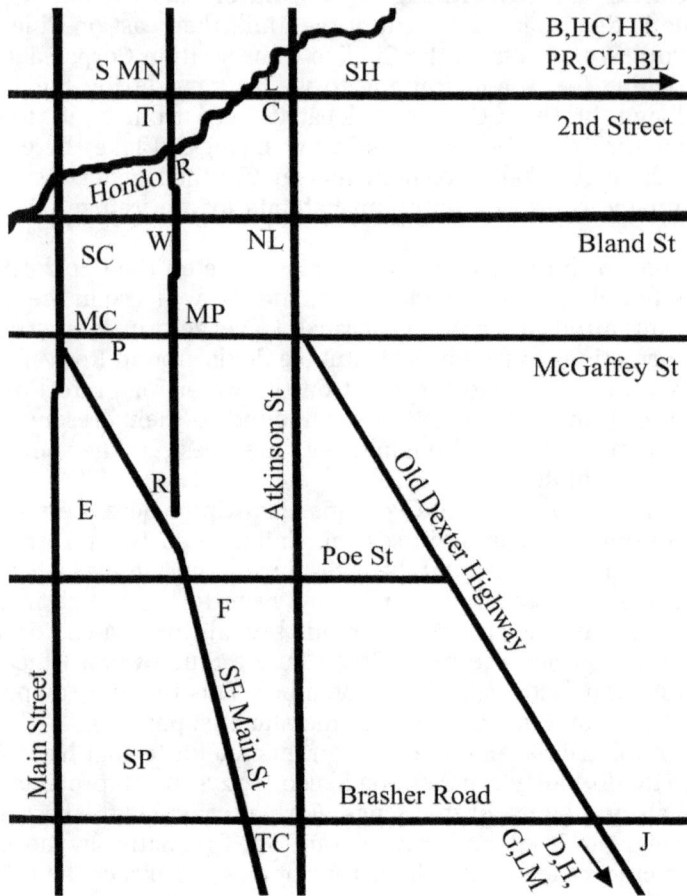

KEY

B	Buena Suerte Ranch	**MC**	Mi Cabana Restaurant
BL	Bottomless Lakes State Park	**MP**	Melendez Park
C	Cowboy Café	**N**	Nuthouse
CH	Comanche Hill	**NL**	N. Lopez Elem. School
D	Dairy farms	**P** Popo's Restaurant	
E	El Charro Mexican Foods	**PR**	Pecos River
F	Fairgrounds	**R**	Rosario's Restaurant
G	Graves Farm	**S**	Silver Dome
H	Hobson Gardens	**SC**	Saunders-Crosby house
HC	Hagerman Canal	**SH**	Slaughter-Hill farm
HR	Hondo River	**SP**	South Park Cemetery
J	Jinglebob Land and Livestock Co.	**T**	Thorne Park
L	Livestock and Farm Supply	**TC**	Town and C. Entertain.
LM	Leprino Mozzarella Plant	**W**	Work. Wom. Day Nurs.
M	Margarita's Restaurant		

Heading East along East 2nd Street (US 380)

"The Silver Dome" Bargain Barn (301 East 2nd Street). From 1939 to 1964 the Roswell Cotton Oil Company used this structure as part of a cottonseed processing operation located in several buildings in this area. Cottonseeds "ginned" from the cotton (separated from the white fibers) were stored in this huge space while waiting to be processed in the next building to the south where machines crushed the seeds, extracted the cottonseed oil, and compressed the remaining hulls into solid cakes to use for cattle feed. The imposing "Silver Dome" has served many purposes over the years. Today's owners use it as a second hand store for furniture, appliances, and miscellaneous "stuff." It's worth a visit just to step inside the cavernous dome—or to check out their selection of deer and elk antlers. 627-7411. Open M-Sat 10-6, closed Sun.

(Thorne Park site) (400 Block, East 2nd Street). After World War I Roswell built a stadium and ballpark here on the south side of 2nd Street and named it Thorne Park after its biggest promoter, Harry Thorne (1881-1956).

Jovial, long-legged 6' 4" (193 cm) Harry Thorne moved to Roswell in 1896 and became a rancher, a sheep and cattle inspector, a nearly permanent Chaves County Deputy Sheriff, and the actual Sheriff from 1929 to 1931, but his greatest love was sports. Thorne provided the land and much of the money to build a grandstand for the ballpark here, then organized and managed a semi-pro baseball team in the mid-1920s. By the 1930s the team was called the Roswell Giants, but had become amateur.

Baseball games, fairs, rodeos, and circuses took place in Thorne Park for many years. World Champion Cowboy Bob Crosby often performed here, and both Roswell High School and NMMI played their early football and baseball games on this field. In 1947 the last of the park structures was removed and commercial businesses took over.

Margarita's (409 East 2nd Street). This small Chinese and Mexican buffet is pretty tasty (but don't tell Lou Dobbs) and they serve great shredded beef tacos. 623-9603. Open W-M for lunch and dinner, closed Tu, holidays variable.

The Nuthouse (419 East 2nd Street). This pecan processor is the only place in town to buy locally grown nuts. Piñons (don't confuse them with Italian pine nuts) are available here some years when the crop is good. 622-4300. Open M-F 8-5, Sat 9-12, closed Sun and holidays.

Roswell Livestock and Farm Supply (1105 East 2nd Street). Roswell's real cowboys and ranchers shop here for shirts, hats, jeans, belts, livestock supplies, and everything else. The horse on top of the sign arrived a few years ago from Joe's Boot Shop in Muleshoe, Texas. 622-9164. Open M-F 7-5:30, Sat 7-5, closed Sun and holidays.

Cowboy Café (1120 East 2nd Street). Friendly folks, down-home cooking—they prepare their own green chile—and luscious chocolate pie make this place popular with those who shop at Roswell Livestock and Farm Supply across the street.

The building has housed a saddlery, a florist, and an appliance store since it was built in 1955. 622-6363. Open M-Sat for breakfast and lunch, closed Sun, holidays variable.

(Former Slaughter-Hill Farm) (1601 East 2nd Street). Texas cattleman and banker C.C. Slaughter bought this farm in 1898 where he and his son George (1862-1915) developed the stock farm they called "Slaughter's Hereford Home." George Slaughter managed the operation and raised some of the world's best Hereford cattle breeding stock, descendants of the prize bull Sir Bredwell, bought for the record sum of $5,000 at the 1898 Sotham's Annual Hereford Sale in Kansas City. Slaughter also established the American National Bank in 1906 and became its first President, but he died of a heart attack at the age of 53 after being struck by lightning. Slaughter's daughter Eloise and her husband Curtis Hill carried on the stock farm operation well into the Twentieth Century.

The only pioneer log house in the Roswell area is just visible from the road today, down a line of trees. Sam Cunningham, an early homesteader, built this one and one-half story log house in 1878 using pegs and dovetail joints but no nails. He brought the pine logs from the mountains 60 miles (100 km) to the west, undoubtedly at great effort.

Bluffs (East of the Pecos River but visible from this part of East 2nd Street). Non-eroded layers of Permian sedimentary rock that rise here extend eastward into Texas as the Llano Estacado. In the 1880s Sophie Alberding—later Sophie Poe—could gaze out the front windows of the Lea boarding house on Main Street, across the open prairie, to see these "crimson bluffs" that are especially striking in the late afternoon sun. Today the Courthouse and other buildings block the view from Pioneer Plaza, but even when the area was open Sophie had to have had pretty good eyesight to spot them at that distance.

Hagerman Canal (5 miles—8 km—east of Main Street). Lincoln County Sheriff Pat Garrett became famous after killing Billy the Kid in 1881—partly because of his own book, *The Authentic Life of Billy the Kid*—but many questioned the way he had shot Billy. Leaving law enforcement, Garrett moved his family from a ranch near the town of Lincoln back to his ranch (not currently accessible to the public) four miles (6 km) east of downtown Roswell that he had previously homesteaded in 1880. Here he and his wife reared their seven children.

In 1888 Pat Garrett joined Carlsbad wheeler-dealer Charles Eddy and several others to begin constructing the Northern Canal—now called the Hagerman Canal—as a part of a grandiose scheme to make a fortune by bringing irrigation water from the Hondo River to farmlands south of Roswell. They built a diversion dam on Garrett's ranch and began digging the canal using plows, graders, and scrapers pulled by horses and mules. The expense proved too great however, until wealthy Pecos Valley developer J.J. Hagerman finally invested in the company, but even he didn't finish the canal that eventually stretched southward thirty miles (50 km) until 1895. Although Pat Garrett had conceived the idea, Hagerman gradually took over the company and forced Garrett out, but Hagerman ended up losing much of his own fortune in the scheme. Today the canal endures, still providing irrigation water to Pecos Valley farmers south of Roswell.

When Chaves County split off from Lincoln County in 1889, Pat Garrett hoped to return to law enforcement by running for Sheriff of the new county. He lost the election so he continued to concentrate on ranching in Roswell and Texas for several years, with variable success. In 1896 he moved to Las Cruces and became Sheriff of Dona Ana County, then Teddy Roosevelt appointed him Customs Collector in El Paso in 1901. Garrett returned again to ranching when he lost that job. He died in a controversial incident in 1908; his alleged killer, Wayne Brazel—cousin of the man who would first report finding the 1947 UFO crash—was acquitted of the murder.

Currently, plans are underway to erect a statue of Pat Garrett by Texas sculptor Robert Summers in the area across Virginia Avenue from the Chaves County Courthouse.

Hondo River (5.5 miles—9 km—east of Main Street). The Hondo River, here carrying water from the Spring and Berrendo Rivers that join it a little upstream, flows into the Pecos River two miles (3 km) south of this point.

Pecos River (7 miles—12 km—east of Main Street). The 900-mile-long (1,450 km) Pecos River begins as a clear mountain stream in the Sangre de Cristo Mountains of Northern New Mexico. It flows due south, picking up silt as it travels through the High Plains down to Roswell. One small dam near Fort Sumner, 85 miles (137 km) north of Roswell, interrupts its flow and farmers divert much of its water for irrigation so that most of the year shallow channels of muddy water wind between banks and bars of red mud here near Roswell, but it can fill up during spring runoff.

Downstream from Roswell, the Pecos River flows nearly due south for 90 more miles (145 km) until it reaches Carlsbad, although irrigation canals divert even more water and Brantley Dam creates a large lake south of Artesia. At Carlsbad the river turns southeast and flows another 250 miles (400 km) to join the Rio Grande on the Mexican border in the Big Bend region near Langtry, Texas, home of the notorious Judge Roy Bean.

Although they brag about him much more in Texas than they do here (isn't that always the case?) the Southwest's "rootin-est, tootin-est cowboy," Pecos Bill, whose exploits rival those of Paul Bunyan in the North Woods, took his name from this muddy river. Some say his legend grew out of tales told by cowpunchers trying to outdo each other around evening campfires.

The first bridge over the Pecos River in the Roswell area was built in 1902 about one and one-half miles south of where the highway crosses the river here. Prior to that, the only nearby way across the river was on a ferry operated by Juan Chaves y Lopez (1826-?), or by fording the stream during low water—both dangerous undertakings because of currents and quicksand.

Double-ended quartz crystals called "Pecos Valley Diamonds" are found in the weathered Permian rocks just east of the Pecos River. They come in all sizes, from tiny single crystals to fist-sized clusters. Sandy areas along the river are the best places to hunt for them—watch out for both rattlesnakes and quicksand! The best places to *find* them are in the Historical Center Gift Shop or at the Chaparral Rockhound Society's Gem and Mineral show in June.

In frontier days the Pecos River defined the limits of Eastern civilization. In fact, "to Pecos" a person became a well-known phrase—and solution—around early Roswell. It meant to dump a formerly troublesome fellow, often a rustling varmint, into the river—as a way of disposing of the body. "Law West of the Pecos" in towns like Roswell was often non-existent, and when it appeared, Justice was swift and absolute. One example: In 1878 one of John Chisum's young cowboys shot and killed his crew boss near here for reasons unknown. Chisum assembled a jury of other cowhands on the spot and presided over the trial himself. The jury found the boy guilty of cold-blooded murder and Chisum pronounced sentence. There were no trees in the vicinity so the cowboys propped up a wagon tongue and tried a rope to it. They sat the boy on a horse, tied the rope around his neck, and led the horse out from under him.

Some of that frontier mentality remains today. Not *too* long ago a young Chaves County lawyer asked an experienced judge why he had sentenced a car thief to more time in prison than another man convicted of killing his neighbor in a water dispute. "Some men just need killing," the veteran judge replied, "but there are very few cars that just need stealing."

Comanche Hill (8 miles—13 km—east of Main Street). Roving bands of Comanches, the Shoshone group that gave this bluff its name, moved south from Wyoming and reached Texas and New Mexico by the 1700s where they quickly became fine horsemen after obtaining the animals from the Spanish. Known as fierce fighters, these nomadic bison hunters raided other native groups, especially Pueblos, Navajos, and Apaches, as well as Hispanic and Anglo settlers.

In the early days, the Pecos River formed a general dividing line here in Southeastern New Mexico between Apaches who usually stayed to the west and Comanches who roamed to the east. Before 1875 when the United States Army interned the last bands of Comanches at Ft. Sill, Indian Territory (later Oklahoma), Comanche Hill marked the beginning—or the end, depending on which way you were traveling—of fearful Comanche territory.

Bands of white gypsum, some of it grading into harder but easily sculpted alabaster, appear in the road cut here. This high point on the edge of the Permian limestone plateau east of Roswell provides a nice view of the Pecos Valley and the Roswell area, especially after dark when lights are twinkling.

Southeast Roswell

Working Woman's Day Nursery (former South Hill School) (502 East Bland Street). In 1885 a group of parents built the first school in Roswell proper, a two-room adobe structure on a stone foundation, called the Village School, on the corner of Tilden Street and Sherman Avenue on South Hill between here and the Hondo River. Ten pupils attended that school until 1891 when Roswell's first public school opened on Third Street. The building then became a residence until it was razed in the 1940s.

Two temporary 30' by 60' (9 m by 18 m) frame buildings were erected at Central School (that had replaced the Third Street School) in 1909. In 1918 the School Board moved one of these buildings to this site where it became South Hill School, a primary school for Roswell's Spanish-speaking children who had previously received instruction at the Salvation Army Mission School on the southwest corner of 2nd Street and Virginia Avenue.

In 1936 the Public Works Administration (a New Deal program) built a four-room, poured-concrete building on this site to replace the temporary building. From 1937 to 1954, Spanish-speaking children attended first through third grades here while learning English so they could enter Roswell's regular public schools by fourth grade. During the 1950s the need for this program declined and South Hill School became the Exceptional Child School—the beginning of Special Education in Roswell—whose programs were later integrated into neighborhood schools. Today this building houses a popular day care facility.

Nancy Lopez Elementary School (1208 East Bland Street). Nancy Lopez, the first Hispanic LPGA Champion, won a total of forty-eight Ladies' Professional Golf Association tournaments after becoming Rookie of the Year in 1978 and Player of the Year in 1978, '79, '85, and '88. She still plays occasionally in tournaments and exhibitions.

Born in California in 1957, Nancy Lopez was the daughter of Mexican immigrants Maria and Domingo Lopez. The family moved to Roswell when she was a child, where her father operated the East 2nd Street Body Shop (615 East 2nd Street, no longer standing) and the family lived at 1103 East 1st Street. Lopez played golf with her parents at the (then) rather primitive Roswell Municipal Golf Course, now the Spring River Golf Course adjacent to Cahoon Park. She later explained to sports writers that as Hispanics her family was not allowed to join the nicer Roswell Country Club. She managed to win the New Mexico Women's Amateur Championship in 1969 at the age of twelve anyway. It took an ACLU challenge to the School Board to gain her a spot on the Goddard High School golf team however—not because she was Hispanic but because she was female, as there was no girls' team at that time. When she was finally allowed to join the boys' team, they won two state championships.

In spite of these difficulties Lopez described growing up in Roswell as "wonderful." Attitudes have changed some since her childhood. A sign in the Goddard High School cafeteria now proudly proclaims, "Nancy Lopez ate here," and in 1991 the School Board changed the name of Flora Vista Elementary School that Lopez attended as a child to Nancy Lopez Elementary School.

Saunders-Crosby house (200 East Deming Street). Built in 1905 by Roswell banker C.C. Emerson, this is the finest example of Queen Anne style architecture in Roswell. Its interesting two-story hexagonal cupola is repeated in the smaller cupola on the porch. H.P. Saunders, of Roswell's American National Bank, purchased this house in 1907 and raised his family here. His son H.P. Saunders, Jr. attended NMMI, and then became its Commandant for thirty-one years. His daughter Sarah married Roswell attorney and businessman J. Penrod Toles whose name appears on the NMMI Learning Center. Saunders' daughter Ruby married Roswell businessman Stan Crosby. They lived in this house for many years, then in 1965 after her husband died, Ruby Saunders Crosby donated it to the American Red Cross. That organization used the house for offices until 2000, but now it sits boarded up, its future uncertain.

Mi Cabana Restaurant (109 East McGaffey Street). The Mexican buffet in this interesting eclectic Mexican log cabin (?) themed restaurant often includes posole or menudo. 623-8314. Open for breakfast, lunch, and dinner every day; holidays variable. **El Metate Tortillaria** next door makes flavorful and inexpensive corn and flour tortillas.

Popo's Mexican Restaurant (222 East McGaffey Street). Large helpings of delicious New Mexican food make it hard to find a parking spot here some days. 627-6436. Open M-Sat for lunch and dinner, Sun for lunch only, holidays variable.

Melendez Park (Corner of South Garden Avenue and East McGaffey Street). The City acquired this nine-acre (4 ha) park in 1960 and in 1971 named it in honor of community leader and social activist Urbana Juarez Melendez (1900-1970). Its play structures and open areas make this a popular neighborhood space. Melendez and her husband Eduardo raised a large family at their home in Chihuahuita where they founded the Iglesia Bautista del Calvario (Spanish Calvary Baptist Church), donating their land for the building site (p 104).

El Charro Mexican Food Industries (1711 South Virginia Avenue). Fresh tortillas and other Mexican food products, as well as a peek inside a tortilla factory, are available here at Southeastern New Mexico's oldest Mexican food company. 622-8590. Open M-F 8-5, Sat 9-2, closed Sun and holidays.

Antonio Trujillo (1910-1982) and his wife Aida (1915-2008) opened their first tortilla factory in the garage of their small house on Deming Street across from Missouri Avenue Elementary School in 1949. At that time tortillas were hardly known and rarely eaten by Anglos, while Hispanic families made their own at home. The Trujillos bought a machine that could produce 80 dozen tortillas an hour. Fortunately for their business, it also produced a whistling noise that attracted curious children on their way home from school. The Trujillos gave them free samples to taste and to take to their families, and before long Anglo as well as Hispanic families were buying El Charro tortillas to use in tasty dishes that Aida helped popularize. As the business expanded and they opened additional tortilla factories in Lovington and Amarillo, the Trujillos became active in civic affairs and won numerous awards over the years.

Today, grandson Michael Antonio Trujillo operates the company that now employs 18 workers and produces 4,000 dozen tortillas an hour from corn grown in Muleshoe, Texas. Carrying on his other family tradition of civic involvement, Trujillo serves as Chaves County Commissioner and even performed his duties long distance while serving with New Mexico National Guard's illustrious 200th Air Defense Artillery in Iraq throughout 2006.

Buena Suerte Ranch (former Corn farm) (1907 White Mill Road). Established in 1972 by Harriet Peaksham of Houston, Texas, on the site of Martin Corn's original farmland (p 117), this 326-acre (130 ha) quarter horse breeding ranch provides stud service and care for brood mares. Mrs. Peaksham's three-time World Champion Go Man Go (1953-1983) is buried here under a crown-shaped granite marker.

Bottomless Lakes State Park (East on 2nd Street 12 miles—20 km—then south on NM 409 3 miles—5 km). Ground water dissolved gypsum, salt, and even some of the limestone itself from the Permian limestone plateau east of Roswell over the centuries, creating passageways and caverns along fissures in the rock. When large underground cavities collapsed they formed sinkholes in the flat surface topography. Seven of these striking water-filled sinkholes make up Bottomless Lakes State Park—New Mexico's first state park—built here by Civilian Conservation Corps workers from the Bitter Lake CCC Camp (a New Deal program to provide work and training to young men during the Depression) during the late 1930s.

Cowboys called these small round lakes bordered by red bluffs "bottomless" because, as Billy the Kid once explained to a curious newcomer, he and some of his friends could not find the bottom, even when they tied their picket ropes together and put a weight on the end. Billy knew this area well. During the Lincoln County War he hid out in caves here, with help from John Chisum's nephew Will Chisum, while his wounds healed after Deputy Sheriff Matthews—later a Roswell Postmaster—shot him when Billy ambushed and killed Sheriff Brady.

The park provides hiking, camping, fishing and, in the summer, swimming and paddle-boating. Watch out for rattlesnakes! A small Visitor Center presents occasional evening nature programs during the summer, and the Bottomless Triathlon takes place here in July. Scuba classes use 90' (32 m) deep Lea Lake for training and certification dives. 624-6058.

Heading South along the Old Dexter Highway
(NM 2, US 285 Alternate)

Dairy Farms (East of the highway). Roswell calls itself "The Dairy Capital of the Southwest" with more than fifty dairies operating along the Old Dexter Highway between Roswell and the small town of Dexter 15 miles (24 km) to the south. Abundant cattle feed along with low operating costs brought dairy operations here, beginning in the 1980s. Now, wealthy dairy operators are rapidly joining ranchers and oilmen as the "aristocracy" of Roswell.

Throughout the Oil Patch, noxious fumes from oil wells and refineries have traditionally been described as "the smell of money." Today in Roswell, when the wind and humidity are right, a "dairy odor" wafts through town as the new "smell of money."

Roswell Vegetable Farms. When folks in Roswell want fresh local vegetables, fruits, and especially chile any time from July to November, they come to two farms not far off the Old Dexter Highway in this area. Both sell their corn, squash, zucchini, tomatoes, cantaloupes, watermelons, peppers, potatoes, garlic, pumpkins, onions, and all sorts of chiles—with roasting available in the fall—from enclosed sheds surrounded by vegetable fields. Watch for the signs. Both carry about the same produce, but a visit to each is worthwhile. They are only a mile (1.5 km) apart and some days one has just what you want while some days the other does.

Hobson Gardens, 366 East Hobson Road, 622-7289.
Graves Farm and Garden, 6265 Graves Road, 622-1889.

Jinglebob Land and Livestock Company (former South Spring River Ranch) (at Brasher Road). John Chisum, "Cattle King of the Pecos," (p 46) moved his vast cattle empire headquarters here to South Spring River Ranch along the South Spring River in 1875. He constructed a large adobe house, along with barns, bunkhouses, and other ranch buildings, then began breeding short-horned cattle and experimenting with growing alfalfa and various grains. The "Jinglebob Ranch," as it was nicknamed because of the distinctive earmark Chisum used to identify his cattle, was a social center for all of Southeastern New Mexico. Billy the Kid worked around the ranch for a time before the Lincoln County War and was rumored to have carried on a romance with Chisum's attractive niece, Sally Chisum, who served as ranch hostess.

After Chisum's death in 1884 other family members proved to be poor managers and his cattle empire dissipated. Mining and railroad millionaire J.J. Hagerman bought South Spring Ranch (he and subsequent owners dropped "River" from the name) in 1900 after ten years of developing irrigation and railroad projects in the Pecos Valley. Hagerman planted large fruit orchards on the land and shipped railroad cars of apples to markets "back east," as can be seen in photos hanging in the Roswell Public Library lobby. He also raised cattle but his cattle business was more of a costly hobby than a successful enterprise. Hagerman demolished most of the original Chisum buildings and constructed his own three-story red-brick mansion on the property, along with other ranch buildings. A barn and the mansion—with the top two stories removed—are just barely visible in a grove of trees about one-half mile east of the highway a little south of Brasher Road. The main entrance to the ranch is a little farther south.

After Hagerman's death in 1909 the ranch passed through several owners. In 1968 Roswell oilman Robert O. Anderson purchased South Spring Ranch and family members lived here for a time. The current owner, Tom Visser, continues to raise cattle that still carry the Jinglebob earmark, but like most everyone else, he is also planting pecan orchards. Irrigation wells have dried up the springs that fed the South Spring River, so that today all that remains are the two dry, shallow river beds (one for each of the two forks that joined between the highway and the ranch house) that cross the highway between Brasher Road and East Grand Plains Road. Peter Hurd's mural *Round Up at South Spring 1875* in the Student Services Center at ENMU-R gives a good idea of what the ranch must have looked like when the South Spring River was full and flowing. Tours charge a small fee to visit the ranch during Old Chisum Days in June.

Leprino Mozzarella Factory (5600 Omaha Road). Leprino's multi-story factory is visible to the west from where the highway crosses East Grand Plains Road. At night its brightly lit structure looms eerily in the dark countryside like a freighter arriving from some unknown galaxy.

The large number of dairy farms in the Pecos Valley brought Leprino Foods to Roswell in 1994. This world's largest Mozzarella factory—Roswell's largest private employer—produces 600,000 pounds of pre-shredded, quick-frozen cheese each day from six million pounds of milk. Nearly 500 workers keep the factory operating 24 hours a day, seven days a week, completing the entire process from pasteurizing the incoming milk to packaging and shipping the frozen shredded cheese to commercial buyers. Workers even process waste materials, separating out clean water to use for irrigation and solid waste to become fertilizer. No retail sales of its cheese are available but the Leprino Mozzarella Factory is open for tours for a small fee during the Chile-Cheese Festival in September. 347-9998.

Heading South along Southeast Main Street (US 285)

Rosario's Restaurant (1701 Southeast Main Street). Tasty toasted corn chips and spicy salsa prepare you for a variety of good Mexican dishes. 627-3408. Open M-F for lunch, SS closed, holidays variable.

Eastern New Mexico State Fairgrounds (Southeast Main Street at Poe Street). The first fairgrounds in Roswell were located just north of the Spring River in the area of today's Spring River Golf Course. Later fairs were held farther downstream, just east of Main Street where Wendy's, Arby's, and the Bus Station stand today. In 1920 the City purchased land here east of Southeast Main Street for the Eastern New Mexico State Fairgrounds.

The weeklong Eastern New Mexico State Fair, held here in early October since the 1920s, includes livestock and agricultural judging, arts and crafts entries, club and business exhibits, food booths, a commercial carnival, musical presentations, rodeos, and other entertainment. Monday of Fair Week is a school holiday for children to watch the parade along Main Street and make early visits to the fair.

Throughout the year, rodeos and musical performances take place in the Bob Crosby Arena, named for Roswell's own King of the Cowboys. Merle Haggard performed here for several recent summers—once bringing Willie Nelson along—until a dispute over ticket sales led him to take his show elsewhere.

Roswell High School plays its home baseball games at Coke Field on the northeast corner of the fairgrounds. Originally built in 1948 for Roswell's minor league team, the Roswell Rockets, it was named in 1977 for the Coca Cola Company that provided money to upgrade the field with new lights and a scoreboard. Joe Bauman Stadium (previously called Rocket Stadium) at Coke Field honors the Roswell Rockets' first baseman who held professional baseball's record for the most home runs in a season—72 in 1954—until 2001.

Varying fees are charged for fairground events and parking.

Town and Country Entertainment Center (3905 Southeast Main Street). Roswell's only bowling alley also includes a cocktail lounge with pool tables and video games. 623-8557. Open M-Th noon-9:30 p.m., F noon-1:00 a.m., Sat noon-11:30 p.m., Sun 1-9 p.m.

Next door, the same owners operate **Up Your Alley Bar** where crowds gather to dance on weekends. 623-727. Open F Sat, 9 p.m.-1:45 a.m.

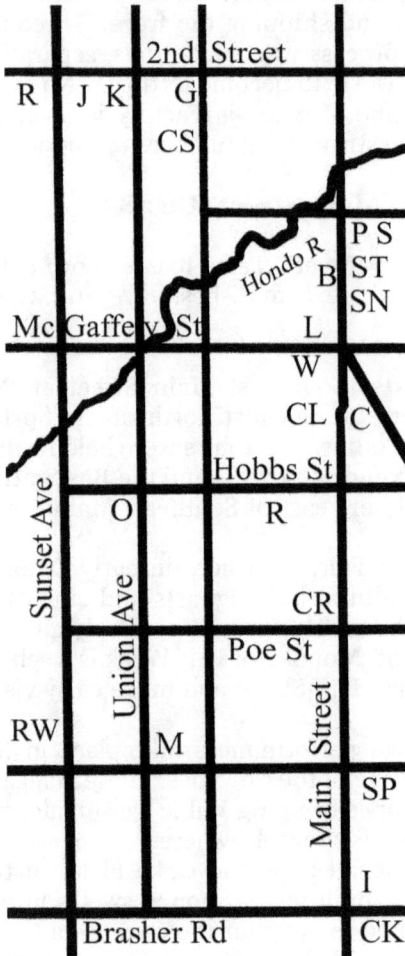

KEY

B	Ballard Funeral Home
C	Chaves County Administrative Offices
CL	Colored School site
CK	Christmas by Krebs
CL	Creative Learning Center
CR	Cattleman's Restaurant
G	Garcia Law Firm
I	Impact Confections
L	La Hacienda Restaurant
M	MLK, Jr. Park
O	Ooy's Express
P	Portofino Restaurant
R	Roswell High School
RW	Randy Willis Park
S	Savedra's Tienda
SN	Snazzy Pig BBQ
ST	St. Peter's Catholic Church
SP	South Park Cemetery
W	Whitmore house

Heading South along South Main Street

Portofino Italian Restaurant (701 South Main Street). Large portions of appetizing pasta, salads, pizza, subs, and desserts are served here. Beer and wine are finally available after a lengthy battle among City Commissioners who originally thought the restaurant was too close to St. Peter's Catholic Church to serve alcoholic beverages, although the church didn't mind. 622-2311. Open M-Sat for lunch and dinner, Sun for lunch, holidays variable.

Savedra's Tienda (114 East Bland Street). Ponchos, rugs, piñatas, pottery, and many more imports from Mexico are available in this jam-packed, fun-to-explore store. 623-5287. Open M-Sat 10-5:30, Sun 11-3, holidays variable.

St. Peter's Catholic Church (805 South Main Street). Franciscan priests organized this parish in 1903 for Roswell's Anglo Catholics. The congregation first met in an old soda-water bottling plant at either 911 South Main Street or 3rd Street and Virginia Avenue (accounts differ). In 1904 the congregation laid the foundation for the current building and met here in the enclosed basement until they completed the aboveground structure in 1917. St. Peter's opened a parochial school in 1905 with eight grades staffed by lay teachers and the Sisters of St. Cisinni from Chicago. It closed in the 1960s due to financial problems and difficulties getting teachers. Roswell's Community Kitchen serves a free lunch every weekday at St. Peter's Community Center, 111 East Deming Street.

The Snazzy Pig BBQ Joint (901 South Main Street). Originally opened in 2006 by owners of the Cattle Baron, this restaurant closed when the City Council—always on the lookout to protect Roswell's morals—denied it a beer and wine license because, like Portofino's, it was too close to St. Peter's Catholic Church. It eventually received its license and reopened in 2007, providing various styles of barbecued beef, pork, and chicken—as well as (be warned!) beer and wine. 622-2200. Open 11 a.m.-9 p.m. every day.

Ballard Funeral Home (910 South Main Street). Prosperous Roswell merchant Nathan Jaffa built this large house in 1903 and moved his family here from their home on South Richardson Avenue. In 1942 Bert Ballard, nephew of Sheriff Charles Ballard who led the Roswell area Rough Riders in 1898, purchased this house and transferred his undertaking business here from its previous location on Third Street. He later enlarged the building and added the white columns. Glenn Dennis was working here in 1947 when he received calls from the RAAF Mortuary Officer concerning small coffins and the preservation of bodies in the days following the UFO Crash.

Chaves County Administrative Offices: Joseph R. Skeen Building (St. Mary's Hospital site) (1 St. Mary's Place). The County Assessor and Appraiser, County Clerk, County Manager and Commissioners, Public Works Department, and Sheriff's Department occupy this newly constructed (2002) building named in honor of the long-time Congressman from southern New Mexico. Its green dome is reminiscent of the Chaves County Courthouse downtown. Genealogists and others interested in land records for Chaves County will find them here.

A Memorial commemorating military veterans of Chaves County killed in action stands in front of the building. Dedicated on Memorial Day 2002 to honor all veterans of all wars, it is inscribed with the names of local servicemen who died in combat, beginning with the Spanish-American War. A Blue Star Memorial By-Way Marker, placed at its base by the local Home Garden Club as part of a nationwide project originally begun to honor World War II veterans, now honors all veterans. Inside the building, a smaller 2004 bronze sculpture by Richard Rist, *All Gave Some—Some Gave All,* is "Dedicated to the memory of all who proudly served and protected their country." The dog tags name those killed in Iraq.

Previously, St. Mary's Hospital stood on this site. Four nuns of the nursing order Sisters of the Sorrowful Mother arrived in Roswell in 1904 and built the first portion of St. Mary's Hospital here in 1906 through contributions of land, labor, and money from the community. It originally functioned as a tuberculosis sanitarium for the many "lungers" who had come to the Pecos Valley seeking health in a warm, dry climate. The first patient was a Franciscan priest. Gradually the hospital took on general patients, eventually having the usual medical, surgical, pediatric, obstetrical, psychiatric, and emergency room areas.

Henry John Deutschendorf, Jr. was born in St. Mary's Hospital in 1943 while his father was stationed at Roswell Army Air Field as a pilot instructor. Deutschendorf died in an aircraft accident in 1997 after becoming famous as singer John Denver, who wrote the Colorado State Song, "Rocky Mountain High," as well as "Take Me Home, Country Roads" and many others. Demetria Gene Guynes, now actress Demi Moore, star of *A Few Good Men* and *Ghost*, was born here in 1962, attended El Capitan Elementary School (2807 West Bland Street) and Sierra Middle School (615 South Sycamore Avenue), and occasionally returns to Roswell to visit relatives. Jockey Mike E. Smith, who rode Giacomo to his win in the 2005 Kentucky Derby, was also born here in 1965.

Chaves County purchased St. Mary's Hospital in 1989, then combined it with Eastern New Mexico Medical Center, which the County had opened in 1955. St. Mary's Hospital buildings were demolished in 1999. Statues of the Virgin Mary and Bernadette, the shepherdess who saw her in a vision at Lourdes, were moved from a small stone grotto here on the grounds to a similar grotto at Assumption Catholic Church (2808 North Kentucky Avenue) at that time.

Cattleman's Steak House (2010 South Main Street). Friendly folks serve steak, ribs, burgers, and chicken. Just sniffing the aroma in the parking lot is a treat. 623-3500. Open Sun-F for late breakfast, lunch, and dinner; Sat for dinner; holidays variable.

Impact Confections (3701 South Main Street). This candy manufacturer, one of Roswell's largest private employers with nearly 200 workers, was organized in Roswell in 1981, although the corporate headquarters later moved to Colorado Springs. The largest manufacturer of 3-D lollipops in the United States, they make eight flavors of Alien Pops available in many of the souvenir shops around town and around the world—including at F.A.O. Schwartz Toy Company on New York's Fifth Avenue. Impact Confections has recently purchased War Heads, the top-selling brand of sour candy in the United States.

Christmas by Krebs (3911 South Main Street). Organized in Germany over fifty years ago, Christmas by Krebs is a leading manufacturer of hand-painted and machine-painted glass Christmas ornaments. The headquarters for their international organization is now here in Roswell, where they employ about 200 people. There is no retail store for their ornaments in Roswell but the company supplies Wal-Mart and Hobby Lobby nationally.

South Park Cemetery (3101 S. Main Street). Roswell's earliest cemetery was located in the Chihuahuita neighborhood just south of the Hondo River in the 1860s, although at that time family members often buried relatives in small private plots as well. The Anglo ladies of Roswell established a Cemetery Association in 1886 to care for the burying ground already established in this area by that time. The oldest marked grave here belongs to Captain Joseph Lea's niece, Sophie Pierce, who died in 1883. Chihuahuita's early graves were moved to this location in 1894 to make way for the Pecos Valley Railroad. Roswell ladies held fundraisers involving fortunetellers, flower stands, and plays at the (very short-lived) Opera House for the upkeep of this cemetery and continued to support it even after the City took over in 1915 and changed its name from South Side to South Park Cemetery.

Men and women prominent in Roswell's history buried here include Captain Joseph Lea, Elizabeth Garrett, E.A. Cahoon, Bob Crosby, John and Sophie Poe, J.P. and Amelia Church, Addison Jones, James Stockard, and Jim Hinkle. Kenny is not buried here.

During the cemetery's early years separate sections developed for Anglos, Hispanics, and African-Americans, as well as for Masons, indigents, and Sisters of the Sorrowful Mother, the nuns who operated St. Mary's Hospital. Today South Park Cemetery holds over 25,000 graves. Because Christian tradition says Christ will return from the east like the rising sun, most of the graves are arranged in an east-west orientation, with the dead ready to rise up and meet their Savior on that glorious day. Those in the Masonic Circle at the center of the cemetery, where headstones read like a list of the streets in Roswell—Richardson, McGaffey, Atkinson, Poe—are oriented in various directions however (make up your own explanation for this).

Before the City bought and planted the first trees here in 1900, the cemetery was just open prairie. Junipers now lining the west entrance road were shipped from Ohio and planted in 1941. Families were responsible for digging their own graves until the City hired gravediggers in the 1950s. Birding is good in the cemetery as its trees, bushes, and sprinklers attract wildlife. Renegade squirrels (?) from other parts of town are reportedly exiled here by Animal Control.

A large Garrison Flag flies at the cemetery office with several small veterans' monuments surrounding it. The American Legion erected flagpoles along the west entrance where flags fly every major holiday. A Memorial Day ceremony takes place here every year with Boy Scouts placing small American flags on the graves of all veterans, a practice that has continued since at least 1917 when Boy Scout Troops 1 and 2, including bugler and future artist Peter Hurd, came here to honor veterans.

In 2000 two English teachers from Mesa Middle School, Valarie Grant and Heidi Huckabee, organized their seventh- and eighth-grade classes to research and preserve information about Roswell's past. The resulting collection of short biographies of some of Roswell's citizens buried here, *South Park Cemetery: Exploring Roswell's Roots*, along with a free and quite interesting cemetery walking tour brochure, *Walking Through Roswell's Past*, are available at the Historical Center and the Roswell Visitor's Center.

A paved path called the **South Main Street Commuter Trail** that connects with the city sidewalk system begins here at the cemetery and parallels Main Street all the way to the RIAC, about two and one-half miles (4 km) farther south.

Southwest Roswell

Garcia Law Firm (former Amonett house) (106 North Washington Avenue). The Amonett family built this stucco New Mexico Vernacular style house in 1929 and E.T. (for Elijah Thomas, not Extra-Terrestrial) Amonett, by himself or with his son Edd (1892-1963), Edd's wife Nettie, and their daughter Jean, lived here off and on until 1945. E.T. Amonett had opened a boot shop and saddlery at 122 North Main Street in 1898 although it later moved to 210 North Main Street before Edd took over the successful business in 1913 when E.T. and his wife moved to El Paso. Items from this famous boot and saddle maker that remained in business until 1978—although Edd sold the business and retired in 1949—still appear on eBay.

This house remained a residence until 1983 when Roswell attorney Ramón Garcia took it over for his law offices. Over the years a dentist, a physician, a secretary, several military families, and the manager of the Dairy Queen just down the street lived here. At least one of the former residents doesn't seem to have left, as items in the former dining room, now one of the offices, are often mysteriously rearranged and noises sometimes come from the room when it is empty. One client asked about the odd lady wearing such old-fashioned clothes that she had seen standing in there, suggesting that the ghostly presence may be an early resident, perhaps even Nettie Lusk Amonett (1894-1982) who grew up on a ranch in the Sacramento Mountains west of Roswell with an unusually independent spirit: riding horses, breaking broncos, and herding cattle with her older brother Ewing Lusk, long-time principal of NMMI's High School Division. Does she still keep an eye on the place that was her home for so many years—and may still be?

(Colored School and Colored Masonic Hall site) (203 South Michigan Avenue). In the fall of 1907 Roswell opened its first public school for African-American students across the street in Smith Chapel CME but it soon moved to the Colored Masonic Hall on this site. One teacher, wife of the Smith Chapel minister, taught classes. In 1915 one of her students completed the eighth grade so she was paid an extra $5.00 a month to teach him high school courses. Frank Chisum, cattleman John Chisum's former slave, longtime employee and companion, and later a cattle rancher in his own right, worked here as a janitor in his later years. The school moved to its new building on East Hendricks Street in 1930, but the Colored Masonic Hall here did not close until 1960. The site is now an empty lot.

(Former Smith Chapel of the CME Church) (206 South Michigan Avenue). Benjamin Smith organized this Colored (later, "Christian") Methodist Episcopal Church early in the Twentieth Century when a number of African-American families lived here along South Michigan Avenue. Frank Chisum's first wife, "Aunt Jane" Chisum, was a "pillar" of the church, but died in 1945 before the current building was completed in 1949. The church closed shortly after the turn of this century but the building has recently been taken over by a construction company.

Sierra Blanca Peak (looking west on West McGaffey Street, or any of the east-west streets in this area). Violent volcanic eruptions 35 million years ago created this cone-shaped mountain 90 miles (145 km) west of Roswell, the tallest mountain in southern New Mexico. In winter, snow-covered Sierra Blanca certainly lives up to its name when the strikingly white peak stands out against blue sky and brown hills.

La Hacienda Restaurant (201 West McGaffey Street). Hearty American and Mexican breakfasts, daily specials including wonderful pollo verde, and huge platters of great food more than compensate for the cinderblock ambiance here. 625-2930. Open T-F for breakfast, lunch, and dinner; SS for breakfast and lunch; closed M; holidays variable.

Whitmore house (204 West McGaffey Street). In July 1947 Walt Whitmore, Sr., owner of Radio Station KGFL, brought Mack Brazel here to his Southwestern style house with Mission roof tile accents, built in 1930, to record an interview about the UFO Crash debris he had discovered. The recording was confiscated by the military before it could be aired (p 27).

RISD Creative Learning Center (200 West Chisum Street). Led by Roswell Independent School District Arts Coordinator Elaine Howe, daughter of Roswell artist Bill Wiggins, elementary school students completed a mosaic on the west side of the Creative Learning Center (formerly the Administrative Center for the school district) in 2005. This colorful mural depicts major fields of education.

Roswell High School (500 West Hobbs Street). Roswell's oldest high school began as a division of Central School on Kentucky Avenue and graduated its first class—of three students—in 1901. It became Roswell High School and moved to a separate building designed in the Rapp brothers' Military Gothic style at 500 South Richardson Avenue in 1911. All that remains of that first Roswell High School building are the gymnasiums and a few rooms at the Yucca Recreation Center. This current Roswell High School building, completed in 1954, bears little resemblance to the earlier building, or to the series of Roswell High School teen novels and the TV show of the last few years inspired by the UFO craze. Tourists and other aliens still like to have their photos taken in front of the RHS Coyotes sign out front though.

Ooy's Express (1000 West Hobbs Street). Huge portions of delicious Thai food—favorites include rice noodle soup, Phad Thai, and cashew chicken—are worth the wait. Fill the time by enjoying an order of pot stickers. 624-2040. Open M-F for lunch and dinner, closed SS, holidays variable.

Martin Luther King, Jr. Park (2701 South Union Avenue). Roswell's annual Juneteenth Celebration takes place in this park named for the famed Civil Rights leader. Juneteenth began as a celebration of Freedom when long-delayed news of the Emancipation Proclamation reached slaves in Galveston, Texas, on June 19, 1865. The first Juneteenth celebrations in the Roswell area took place in Black-dom, a town African-American homesteaders founded 16 miles (25 km) south of

Roswell in the early years of the Twentieth Century. The town died out in the 1920s due to lack of water for agriculture, but the mid-June commemoration continues. Lots of good food is still the main feature of Roswell's Juneteenth Celebration that today honors unity and multiculturalism in New Mexico, in addition to the end of slavery.

Randy Willis Park and Championship Field (2100 South Sunset Avenue). When the Roswell Lions Hondo baseball team won the Little League World Championship in Williamsport, Pennsylvania in 1956 they renamed their home field, just south of Roswell High School on Lea Avenue, "Championship Field." As the baseball program grew in size, it needed more space. In 1967 the Lions Hondo Little League moved to this park and brought along its bleachers and fencing as well as the "Championship Field" plaque. The entire park was later named in memory of Randy Willis, a member of that World Champion Little League team who died of leukemia in 1980, as a plaque at the base of the flagpole indicates. This remains the home field for the Lions Hondo Little League, one of three such organizations in Roswell. Photos and memorabilia from the 1956 World Championship Team are on display in the Historical Center.

Roswell Relief Route—Southwestern Sector (West 2nd Street to Southeast Main Street)

> **Irrigated Fields and Birding Areas** (Relief Route from West 2nd Street to South Sunset Avenue). East Coast children learn that if a piece of land is open, it is because a pioneer cut down the forest that used to grow there. In Roswell the opposite is true. If there is a tree growing on a piece of land, it is because someone planted it, watered it, and watered it some more. Here, as elsewhere around Roswell, clumps of trees springing up from the flat prairie mark water sources at scattered ranch houses, while dirt banks topped with bushes or small trees enclose irrigation ponds. Most of the time, if any field is green it is because someone is irrigating it.
>
> Water from small ditches or large mobile structures irrigates the fields along both sides of the Relief Route here during growing season. In September huge machines harvest corn—stalks and all—for silage. During the winter Sandhill Cranes and Canada Geese often feed in corn stubble fields along here. Occasionally, especially in the spring, huge flocks of seagulls scavenge at the landfill south of where Brasher Road crosses the Relief Route.
>
> **Fox Place** (Relief Route at Brasher Road). In the area just south of Brasher Road the Relief Route passes over Fox Place, an archeological site no longer visible as it is now buried underneath the roadbed. The Jornada Mogollon people occupied a pit house village here along the Hondo River continuously from 1250 AD to 1325 and then sporadically until 1425.
>
> The foundations of several small pit houses, along with pens for domesticated turkeys, were uncovered in constructing the Relief Route. During the subsequent archeological dig an underground kiva-like room also emerged with an amazing 15' (5m) long green clay painting of a Feathered Serpent covering two of the walls: most likely a religious shrine.

After archeologists finished studying Fox Place they covered the remains, and construction of the Relief Route continued on top of the site. Still, driving along this stretch of the road, one can imagine a Mogollon family gazing toward the same hills and mountain peaks we see today, or following the chants of their shaman-artist as he prays to the Feathered Serpent in their underground kiva.

Gravel Pit (3300 South Sunset Avenue). The gravel pit at the corner of the Relief Route and Sunset Avenue is clear evidence that Roswell rests on a flood plain. Although it is not much of a stream now, the Hondo River carried this sand, gravel, and rock down from the mountains over the centuries. This and similar sand and gravel operations produce Chaves County's second most valuable mineral product, after petroleum.

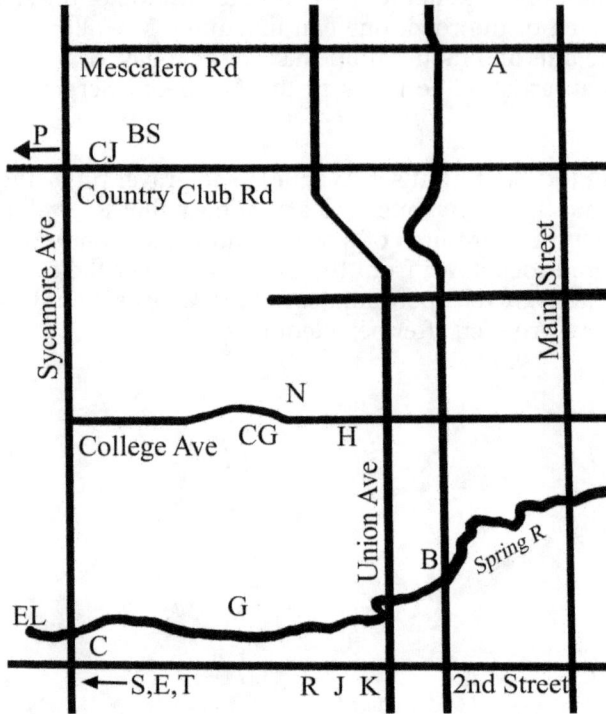

KEY

A	Grotto, Assumption Cath. Church	**H**	Howard house
B	Congregation B'nai Israel	**J**	Former Bauman Texaco
BS	Boy Scout Office	**K**	Kwan Den Restaurant
C	Chew's West Restaurant	**N**	Noon Optimist Park
CG	Cielo Grande Rec. Area	**P**	Pecan Orchards
CJ	Church of Jesus Christ of LDS	**R**	Red Onion Restaurant
E	Eight Mile Draw	**S**	Six Mile Hill
EL	Enchanted Lands Park	**T**	Two Rivers Dam

Heading West along West 2nd Street (US 70 and 380)

Kwan Den Chinese Restaurant (Wagon Yard site) (1000 West 2nd Street). In Roswell's early years this was the site of a popular wagon yard where cowboys could camp overnight while running cattle to Roswell and families could stay cheaply when they came to town to shop or sell produce. Women and children usually slept in rustic shelters while men slept in their wagons in the yard that continued to welcome travelers into the early 1920s. A favorite spot for club luncheon meetings today, this large Chinese buffet with lots of crowd-pleasing dishes also serves fried chicken and enchiladas. 622-4192. Open for lunch and dinner every day; closed 4th of July, Thanksgiving, and Christmas.

Car Tunes and Tint (former Joe Bauman Texaco Service Station) (1200 West 2nd Street). After playing first base for the Roswell Rockets Minor League Baseball Team in the 1950s—and setting the professional baseball record for most home runs in a season that stood until 2001 (72 in 1954)—Oklahoman Joe Bauman (1922-2005) lived the remainder of his life in Roswell (at 1700 N. Pontiac Drive) working for a beer distributor and operating his gas station, here in the building currently occupied a car stereo business, until his retirement in 1984. The City named the baseball stadium at Coke Field adjacent to the fairgrounds "Joe Bauman Stadium" in 2005. Bauman spoke at the dedication, but died later that year. Every year the Minor League Baseball Association still presents the Joe Bauman Trophy (and $2,000 for each home run) to the top Minor League home run hitter.

Red Onion Restaurant (1400 West 2nd Street). Patrons come here for hearty breakfasts, flavorsome Mexican plates, and juicy burgers. 622-3232. Open for breakfast and lunch every day, holidays variable.

Chew's West Restaurant (2513 West 2nd Street). Opened in 1990, the last of Jack Chew's four successive Chinese restaurants in Roswell offers a Chinese buffet with popular sweet and sour chicken and American selections. Jack Chew was born in China, came to the United States as a boy, graduated from Albuquerque High School in 1939, and served as a gunner on a B-17 during World War II. Shot down over Germany, Staff Sergeant Chew spent 21 months as a POW until General Patton's Third Army liberated him and his fellow Americans in 1945. His final station before discharge was Roswell Army Air Field. Chew's recipes and reminiscences are available locally in his cookbook *Cook and Chat With Jack Chew*. Although they no longer operate the restaurant, he and his wife still operate **Chew's Oriental Gifts** next door. Restaurant: 622-6484. Open for lunch and dinner every day. Gift Shop: 622-7239. Open 10-5 every day, holidays variable.

Six Mile Hill (Six miles—9 km—west of Main Street; guess how it got its name). Upthrusting of the eastern edge of a north-south fault created this ten-mile (16 km) ridge that forms Roswell's western horizon. Its layered sedimentary rock, called San Andres Limestone, is visible on the south side of the road cut at the crest of the hill, as is a little cave of the type common in this formation. The gray limestone here is honeycombed with fissures and small caves that are home to truly gigantic rattlers, or so the tall tales claim. What looks like a 10' wide plug interrupts the limestone layers in the road cut. Here a sinkhole dissolved in the limestone, then filled with dust and sand over the centuries forming the plug. Limestone for some of the houses in Roswell and all the rockwork in Cahoon Park, de Bremond Stadium, and the sloping sides of the Spring River came from an old quarry a little south of the highway.

It was over Six Mile Hill that Dan and Grace Wilmot watched a flying saucer disappear before the UFO Crash in 1947. Today Six Mile Hill is the location for some of the nicer homes in Roswell. Houses perched on the crest have a lovely view to the west of Capitan Mountain, Sierra Blanca Peak, and the Cloudcroft peaks silhouetted against brilliant sunsets in the evening, and of twinkling lights of "The Pearl of the Pecos" to the east after dark.

Eight Mile Draw (Eight miles—13 km—west of Main Street). This (usually) dry watercourse connects Blackwater Draw, coming off Capitan Maintain and crossing US 70 and 380 11 miles—18 km—west of Roswell, with the Berrendo River. Thunderstorms in the Capitan Mountains can turn Eight Mile Draw into a roaring torrent 30' (9 m) across, even though no cloud is visible over Roswell. The draw's fortified embankment on the south side of the highway hints at the force of raging water that descends with little warning.

During the first decade of the Twentieth Century, eight Anglo and six Hispanic families formed a close-knit community of homesteading farmers and ranchers north of the highway in this area. A small school served the forty or so pioneer children—an intermingling of the two ethnic groups that was unusual for this area at that time. The community did not last however, and only a few foundations and wagon tracks remain today in the uneven prairie. A deserted structure is visible about one-half mile (0.8 km) north of the highway, but new houses of "suburban Roswell" have begun to push into the area.

Two Rivers Dam and Reservoir (Turnoff to the south, fourteen miles—23 km—west of Main Street). From the founding of Roswell on into the mid-Twentieth Century, water from the Hondo River stood several feet deep along Main Street and throughout the business and residential sections of Roswell every few years—as pictured in a photo in the Roswell Public Library lobby and another in the Wells Fargo Bank lobby. In 1963 the U.S. Army Corps of Engineers finally completed the Two Rivers Dam and Reservoir project at a cost of five million dollars to protect Roswell from devastating Hondo River floods. Two separate earthen dams, one on the Hondo River and one on adjacent Rocky Arroyo, route occasional flood waters into the reservoir area. There some of the water disappears into the underlying porous limestone and the rest is released gradually downstream. In this instance, disappearing water is a good thing, unlike other occasions when Roswell developers have tried—unsuccessfully—to create reservoirs full of water. The large earthen dam does look a little strange if you are expecting to see a lake behind it, but then "strange" is a relative concept in Roswell. Picnic shelters are available at the dam and pronghorn often frequent the prairie along the seven-mile (11 km) entry road, especially in the fall. A little upstream of the dam—but on inaccessible private property—are the ruins of Plaza de Missouri, one of the earliest settlements in the Roswell area.

Northwest Roswell

Congregation B'nai Israel (712 North Washington Avenue). In 1903, even though there were only 36 Jews in Roswell and most of them belonged to his extended family, Roswell merchant and banker Nathan Jaffa organized Congregation B'nai Israel, today the oldest active Jewish congregation in New Mexico. Jaffa led the congregation in Friday services and Sabbath School in the home of his business partner, William Prager, which stood on the current site of the Petroleum Building. The tradition he began has continued for more than 100 years: a layperson has always led Congregation B'nai Israel with Rabbis coming to Roswell only rarely for special occasions.

Later, B'nai Israel held its services in the Masonic Temple, the Odd Fellows Hall, and other locations around town. Congregation membership grew when the RAAF and Walker Air Force Base brought more Jews to Roswell, and in 1949 members purchased this current building from the Church of the Nazarene. After Walker Air Force Base closed in 1967 the congregation dwindled. Today, even though the synagogue easily seats 100 people, regular attendance is only about twenty for of the twice monthly Sabbath services, although holiday celebrations and the occasional Bar or Bat Mitzvah draw more worshipers. Members come from Orthodox, Conservative, Reform, and Reconstruction branches of Judaism but B'nai Israel generally follows Reform practice, reading from a beautiful handwritten lambskin Torah. Plaques commemorating congregation leaders and deceased members, as well as artworks donated by WPA artist Joseph Vogel (1911-1995), hang in the sanctuary. The illuminated stained-glass window depicts the Ten Commandments and a seven-branched menorah, one of the oldest symbols of the Jewish faith.

Howard house (1006 West College Street). This architecturally unique house frequently draws interest from passers-by. Veteran stone and brick mason Thomas Howard began making brick here at his residence in 1900 but soon moved his brickyard to the corner of 7th Street and Virginia Avenue from where some say he furnished brick for the new Chaves County Courthouse in 1911. Previously he and a partner had opened Roswell's first brickyard in 1890, on Missouri Avenue just south of the Hondo River. This operation produced the brick to build the Third Street School (p 74) and probably his residence as well. Locally made brick was softer, and therefore less desirable, than brick made other places, so when "imported" brick became easily available by railroad (after 1899) it gradually put local brickyards out of business, although Howard continued to work as a building contractor and cement supplier until 1920.

Noon Optimist Park (1600 North Montana Avenue). One of Roswell's three Little League organizations uses this large, nicely manicured park as its home field. "Noon Op" has done well in state and regional tournaments in recent years.

Cielo Grande Recreation Area (former Roswell Municipal Airport) (1500 West College Street). Cielo Grande ("see-EL-o GRAHN-day," meaning "big sky") includes soccer fields, a walking track, a skateboard park, a UFO-themed play structure, and a marvelous view of Capitan Mountain. Roswell's annual 4th of July Celebration and fireworks display takes place here. The Unity Center for Teens in the old Terminal building provides a place to play pool and hosts concerts presented by local bands. Over the next few years the City plans to add additional recreational facilities here, eventually including a swimming pool. The current debate centers on whether it will be an indoor or outdoor pool.

Open spaces here give a magnificent view of 10,083' (3,073 m) Capitan Mountain, a volcanic laccolith formed by lava squeezing up through a crack in the rocks, that appears in the backgrounds of many Peter Hurd paintings. The birthplace and final resting place of Smokey Bear is in the Capitan Mountains just to the left of the peak, while one of the 1947 UFO Crash sites is on Boy Scout Mountain just to the right of the peak.

Roswell businessmen provided financing to build the Roswell Airport here in 1929—which mainly involved setting up a hangar and fencing a circular area of prairie 3,100' (945 m) in diameter to keep out pronghorn. There were no runways so private pilots who used the airport, including Charles Lindbergh who landed here in 1934 and 1935 on visits to Dr. Robert Goddard, could land and take off in any direction. By the time Lindbergh returned for his final visit in 1939 the City had bought the airport and built runways. Continental Airlines even initiated limited service to Roswell that same year.

Unfortunately, the only building present when Lindbergh landed here, a large corrugated metal hangar and airport office with "Roswell" painted on the roof, was demolished several years ago because of its deteriorated condition. The remaining tan brick Terminal, completed in 1948, with its large, glass-enclosed tower and outside observation decks represents buildings typical of regional airports during that era.

Roswell Municipal Airport moved to the RIAC after Walker Air Force Base closed in 1967. The Roswell Police Department was occupying the former Terminal in 1980 when the last airplane to use the airfield, a single engine Mooney, landed here during a snowstorm. Its disoriented and probably rather surprised pilot had to dodge barricades constructed on the runway for police training exercises.

Church of Jesus Christ of Latter Day Saints (2201 West Country Club Road). This lovely structure replaced the previous building in 1999 after the church organist's disgruntled gentleman friend burned it down at the end of an eight-year affair. A branch of the LDS Family History Library staffed by helpful volunteers is available here for genealogical research during limited hours. 624-1761. Library open T, Th 7 p.m.-9 p.m.; W, Th 9 a.m.-4 p.m.; Sat 12-4 p.m.

The open fields across Country Club Road from the church are one place where small groups of pronghorn occasionally gather. At times they create hazards by crossing the road to drink at the church and pecan orchard sprinklers.

Boy Scout Office: S. P. Yates Scout Service Center (2703 North Aspen Avenue). Roswell lawyer Harold Hurd, father of artist Peter Hurd, organized Boy Scout Troop 1 in Roswell in 1915 and the Scouting Program has been strong here ever since. Roswell Boy Scout offices were first located in the Courthouse, then the First National Bank building, a Clubhouse on North Pennsylvania Avenue, and the rock Boy's Hut by the swimming pool in Cahoon Park. In 1963 they moved into a previous building on this site. This current building, completed in 2002 with a time capsule buried in the entry area to be opened January 8, 2052, is named in honor of S.P. Yates, a Roswell oilman and longtime supporter of Scouting. Out front the Roswell Rotary Club placed the Minor Huffman Memorial Flag Pole honoring an early Roswell Scout, Scouting historian, and civic leader.

This building houses the offices of the Conquistador Council that covers all of Southeastern New Mexico. (The Apache Boy Scouts in Mescalero may have mixed feelings about being a part of the "Conquistador" Council but participate enthusiastically anyway.) Bricks in the Eagle Scout Patio on the north side of the building list the names of every Roswell Eagle Scout since 1920.

In the lobby, aficionados of Peter Hurd can view his original 1954 design for the Conquistador Council patch: the silhouette of a Conquistador with the silhouette of a Scout—actually his son Michael, now an artist himself—imposed over it. Beside it hangs a small Hurd watercolor entitled *Boy Scout Campfire* donated to the Conquistador Council in 1958 by the artist. His son Michael again served as the model for this painting of a Scout watching over a campfire as dinner cooks. Prints of other Peter Hurd paintings hang throughout the Center, in addition to a Michael Hurd print signed by the artist and inscribed "Once a Scout, always a Scout." 622-3461. Open M-F 8:30-5, closed SS and holidays.

Pecan Orchards (Country Club Road west of Montana Avenue). In 1963 oilman Olen Featherstone began planting pecan orchards in northwest Roswell, choosing mainly the thin-shelled "Schley" variety. The established pecan orchards in Roswell today are concentrated in the West Country Club Road area where new, heavily irrigated pecan trees cover more acres every season. Dairy farmers along the Old Dexter Highway southeast of Roswell have begun putting in similar orchards and pecans are rapidly becoming a major crop in the Roswell area.

Armies of workers prune, spray, and fertilize the orchards carefully throughout the year. Huge clouds of choking dust signal the harvest in December and January when large mechanical shakers grab the tree trunks and tumble the nuts to the ground. Giant brushes sweep them into bins, creating enough dust in the process to make the orchards appear to be on fire from a distance. The pecans are then sorted from the debris, packed, and shipped to processing plants out of state. It is no longer possible to purchase locally grown pecans in Roswell, except at the Nuthouse (429 East 2nd Street) where small producers still bring nuts for processing.

Some pecan growers run sheep through their orchards to keep down the weeds, and do a little fertilizing. Mule deer and pronghorn often take it upon themselves to serve the same function, and can become a serious hazard when they cross the road, especially at dawn and dusk. The New Mexico Game and Fish Department holds periodic roundups to remove them to other areas because they also chew on pecan bark and damage trees.

An interesting visual effect results from riding along West Country Club Road and staring down the rows. The patterns created at various angles by perfectly spaced trees change in an almost psychedelic array. Some people have also reported seeing a ghostly little boy who runs across the road between the pecan orchards crying, but only after midnight around Halloween.

In the 3600 block of West Country Club Road stands a local Field of Dreams. One middle school teacher enjoyed coaching youth baseball so much that he built a practice field for his team in his own back yard. Most of the year it stands empty but in spring it swarms with young players.

The Grotto at Assumption Catholic Church (2808 North Kentucky Avenue). Assumption Catholic Church was built in the 1960s to serve Catholics living in the northern part of Roswell. The parish opened All Saints Catholic School here in 2002 with 52 kindergarten and preschool students. It has recently grown to include students through 8th grade.

Franciscan Brothers built a grotto of native stone in 1924 on the grounds of St. Mary's Hospital in southern Roswell reminiscent of the cave at Lourdes where the Virgin Mary appeared to a young French shepherd girl in 1858. This Grotto served as a chapel for prayer and meditation and held two statues—one a replica of Joseph Fabisch's *Our Lady of Lourdes* at Lourdes, the other of the shepherd girl kneeling in adoration of the Virgin Mary. When the hospital was demolished in 1999, parishioners built this smaller grotto behind Assumption Church and moved the statues here. Other religious statues also grace this peaceful space behind the church.

Roswell Relief Route—Northwestern Sector (US 285 at The Overpass to West 2nd Street). Glimpses of cattle, horses, goats, sheep, chickens, and the occasional burro, ostrich, emu, or llama appear all along the Relief Route and in other fields around Roswell.

A few pronghorn graze in the large open areas on either side of the Relief Route between Country Club Road and West 2nd Street in most seasons of the year, but especially during the fall when bucks gather their harems. Six Mile Hill, topped by expensive houses with marvelous views in both directions, rises to the west of this area. This ridge figured in a potentially extraordinary happening as it became a refuge from possible cataclysm one summer night in 1936: a woman claiming to be a prophet had spent the day walking the streets proclaiming that Roswell was doomed to sink into the ground that very night. Many residents left town to camp overnight on Six Mile Hill—not that they believed the prediction, it just seemed like a lovely evening for an outing. Years later in 1947 this elevation figured in another extraordinary happening: Dan Wilmot reported that the flying saucer he and his wife watched on July 3rd had disappeared over Six Mile Hill.

Books

Fiction

Grady Lee Bryant. *Roswell One*. Hervey's Booklink, 1999. Mescalero Apaches and the UFO Crash—a mystery-adventure.

Don Burleson. *Flute Song* (1995), *Arroyo* (1999). Black Mesa Press. Science fiction that interweaves aliens, Indian legends, and government conspiracies in Southeastern New Mexico.

Emma Craig. Land of Enchantment series: *A Gentle Magic* (1998), *Enchanted Christmas* (1999), and *A Gambler's Magic* (2000). Dorchester Publishing. A series of historical romance novels set in Rio Hondo, NM, in the early 1870s.

———*Cooking Up Trouble*. Dorchester Publishing, 2001. An historical romance novel set in Roswell in 1895.

Alice Duncan. *Wild Dream*. Dell Publishing Corp., 1998. An historical romance set in Roswell in 1895.

———*Pecos Valley Diamond*. New Age Dimensions Publishing, 2005. A mystery set in 1923 Roswell.

———*Cactus Flower*. Five Star Books, 2006. An historical romance set in the fictional town of Rio Peñasco, based on Roswell.

Dewey Johnson. *Summer of Champions*. Texas Tech University Press, 2005. A coming-of-age story based on Roswell's 1956 Little League World Champions.

Glenn Marcel. *Chasing the Roswell Alien*. Invisible College Press, 2005. A tabloid journalist discovers frightening secrets when she digs into the mysteries of Roswell.

Melinda Metz. Roswell High series: *The Outsider, The Wild One, The Seeker, The Intruder, The Stowaway,* and *The Watchers*. Simon Spotlight Entertainment, 1998-2000. These and many more are alien teen stories set at a fictional Roswell High School.

Mary Moore and Stephen Moore. *Enchanted Lands—The Mission*. BookSurge Publishing, 2007. Young friends embark on a secret mission to help crashed aliens return home in this story for older children and early teens. Illustrated by Roswell artist Kim Wiggins.

Rachel Wilson. *Spirit of Love*. Berkley Publishing Co., 2000. An historical romance novel set in the fictional town of Pecos Wells, based on Roswell.

Non-Fiction

UFOs

Charles Berlitz and William L. Moore. *The Roswell Incident*. Grosset and Dunlap, 1980. This first book about the 1947 UFO crash reported information from numerous witnesses.

Stanton T. Friedman and Don Berliner. *Crash at Corona: The U.S. Military Retrieval and Cover Up of a UFO*. Marlow & Co., 1992. This third book on the topic focuses on a high-level government cover-up.

Kevin D. Randle and Donald R. Schmitt. *UFO Crash at Roswell*. Avon Books, 1991. This second book on the Crash adds information from additional witnesses.

Toby Smith. *Little Gray Men: Roswell and the Rise of a Popular Culture*. University of New Mexico Press, 2000. A fun sociological study of the UFO phenomenon.

Many, many more are available: Type "Roswell" or "UFO" into your online bookseller's search engine.

Wild West, Ranching, Cowboys, Lawmen, and Outlaws

Bob Alexander. *Fearless Dave Allison, Border Lawman*. High Lonesome Books, 2003. Includes stories from when Allison was Chief of Police in Roswell.

Walter Noble Burns. *The Saga of Billy the Kid*. Garden City Publishing Company, 1926 (reprint). The book that created Billy's mythical status and inspired a flurry of movies.

Thelma Crosby and Eve Ball. *Bob Crosby: World Champion Cowboy*. Wild Horse Press, 1961, 2006. A biography written by his wife, with help.

Elvis Fleming. *J.B. "Billy" Mathews: Biography of a Lincoln County Deputy*. Yucca Tree Press, 1999. He rode in the Lincoln County War, wounded Billy the Kid, then became Postmaster of Roswell.

Mark L. Gardner. *Songs of the Cowboys*. Museum of New Mexico Press, 2005. The early cowboy songs Jack Thorp collected in Southeastern New Mexico and West Texas and some he wrote including "Who's Old Cow" about Add Jones and "The Cowboys New Year's Dance," set in Roswell. Includes a CD of some of the songs.

Pat F. Garrett. *The Authentic Life of Billy the Kid*. Kessinger Publishing, 2004 (originally published 1882). Ghost-written by Roswell newspaperman

Ash Upton, this book's style may not appeal to modern tastes, but it certainly gives a flavor of the Old West, and it "made" Garrett's reputation.

Leon C. Metz. *Pat Garrett: The Story of a Western Lawman*. University of Oklahoma Press, 1983. Well researched, entertaining.

Barbara Patterson. *The Rock House Ranch: My Lazy-A-Bar Days*. Barbed Wire Publishing, 2002. Ranch life near Roswell during the 1930s and '40s.

Sophie Poe. *Buckboard Days*. University of New Mexico Press, 1981 (reprint of 1936 edition). Biography of her husband Sheriff John Poe and the early days of Lincoln and Chaves Counties.

Robert M. Utley. *Billy the Kid: A Short and Violent Life*. University of Nebraska Press, 1991. A scholarly account.

Michael Wallis. *Billy the Kid: The Endless Ride*. W.W. Norton, 2007. The most recent and one of the best of Billy's biographies.

Many other books have been written about Billy the Kid, Sheriff Pat Garrett, and the Lincoln County War.

Other Topics

Stephen Bogener. *Ditches Across the Desert: Irrigation in the Lower Pecos Valley*. Texas Tech University Press, 2003. More interesting than it sounds.

Dorothy Cave. *Beyond Courage: One Regiment Against Japan, 1941-1945*. Sunstone Press, 1996, 2006. The dramatic story of New Mexico National Guardsmen captured by the Japanese: the Bataan Death March, prison camps, and finally liberation.

David A. Clary. *Rocket Man: Robert H. Goddard and the Birth of the Space Age*. Hyperion, 2003. His life and work in Roswell.

Paul Horgan. *Peter Hurd: A Portrait Sketch From Life*. University of Texas Press, 1965. Biographical sketches by Hurd's Pulitzer Prize winning lifelong friend.

Carole Larson. *Forgotten Frontier: The Story of Southeastern New Mexico*. University of New Mexico Press, 1993. Well researched, scholarly but interesting.

Ann McGarrell and Sally Anderson. *The Roswell Artist-in-Residence Program, an Anecdotal History*. University of New Mexico Press, 2007. Stories from the artists.

Mother Mary Francis. *A Right to be Merry*. Ignatius Press, 1956, 2001. The Abbess describes the founding and inspirational daily life of Roswell's Poor Clare Monastery.

Roswell Symphony Guild. *Savoring the Southwest* (1994) and *Savoring the Southwest Again* (1998). Roswell Symphony Guild Publishing. Cookbooks interspersing images from local artists with Southwestern, gourmet, and UFO recipes.

Thomas Streissguth. *Rocket Man: The Story of Robert Goddard*. Carolhoda Books, 1995. For children grades 5-8.

Many books and DVDs featuring Pecos Bill are available.

Local Publications

Many of these are available at Cobean Stationery Company, 320 North Richardson Avenue (the best source because they have a wide selection and are open regular business hours), at the Historical Center Gift Shop, 200 North Lea Avenue, (a wide selection but they are only open 1-4 p.m. daily), and at Hastings Books, Music, and Videos, 1705 North Main Street (a limited selection but they are open regular business hours, plus evenings). Most of these are also in the Roswell Public Library collection, along with many out-of-print volumes.

Clarence S. Adam's. *Little Town West of the Pecos—1909*. Pioneer Printing, 1983. Articles from the Roswell newspaper in 1909.

Cecil Bonney. *Looking Over My Shoulder: Seventy-five Years in the Pecos Valley*. Hall-Poorbaugh Press, 1971. People and events, written by a Roswell pioneer.

Donald R. Burleson. *UFOs and the Murder of Marilyn Monroe*. Black Mesa Press, 2003. She knew too much about the government's Roswell UFO-cover-up.

Jack Chew. *Cook and Chat with Jack Chew*. Private printing, 2001. Memories and recipes of an Army Air Corps veteran and POW who became a Roswell restaurateur.

Elvis E. Fleming. *Captain Joseph C. Lea*. Yucca Tree Press, 2002. Biography of "The Father of Roswell."

———*Success Starts Here: A History of Eastern New Mexico University—Roswell, 1958-2000*. ENMU-R, 2003. A history of the junior college.

———*Treasures of History, II* (with Ernestine C. Williams, 1991), Chaves County Historical Society; *III* (with Ernestine C. Williams, 1995), Historical Society for Southeast New Mexico; *IV* (2003), iUniverse Press. Vignettes from the history of Roswell and Chaves County.

William E. Gibbs and Eugene T. Jackman. *New Mexico Military Institute: A Centennial History.* NMMI Centennial Commission, 1991. A well researched, detailed history.

A.B. Gwinn. *100 Years of Dreams and Realities: A History of the Roswell Parks System.* Roswell Printing Company, 1992. Details about Roswell parks.

James F. Hinkle. *Early Days of a Cowboy on the Pecos.* Hall-Poorbaugh Press, 1937. Personal reminiscences.

Heidi Huckabee and Valarie Grant, editors. *South Park Cemetery: Exploring Roswell's Roots.* Private printing. 2001. Biographies of some Roswell citizens buried in South Park Cemetery written by Mesa Middle School English students.

Lynn I. Petrigo. *Early Roswell, "Pearl of the Pecos."* Private printing, no date. Stories of the early days.

Edward J.D. Porter. *The Pictorial History of the New Mexico Military Institute 1891-1983.* NMMI Alumni Association, 1983. Historical photos (including the Harley-mounted machine gun) and commentary.

Joe Posz. *West Point of the West: A Family Odyssey.* Private printing, 2003. A NMMI family over the years.

Treasures of History: Historic Buildings in Chaves County, 1870-1935. Chaves County Historical Society, 1985. Photos and descriptions of historic buildings.

Linda Stockley Weiler. *Relocated Houses of Roswell* (2003), *Lost Landmarks of Roswell* (2004), *Old Places with New Faces (Changing Facades of Roswell)* (2005), *Historic Outbuildings in and around Roswell (Barns, Carriage Houses, Sheds and Silos)* (2007). Wonderful photos and histories of Roswell buildings.

DVDs

Roswell—The Complete First, Second, Third Season. TV series about alien teens.

Unsolved Mysteries: UFOs. TV series in which facts about unsolved mysteries (including the 1947 Roswell UFO Crash) are presented through interviews and reenactments.

History Channel:
  Roswell: Final Declassification
  Roswell Secrets Unveiled
  (and many more)

Sons of New Mexico. A 1948 Gene Autry movie full of rugged action and cowboy songs. Filmed at NMMI.

Chisum. A 1970 John Wayne movie about the Cattle King of the Pecos and the Lincoln County War. Not filmed here.

Pat Garrett and Billy the Kid. Sam Peckinpah's classic 1973 movie, with Bob Dylan's score. Not filmed here.

Lords of Discipline. A 1983 movie of Pat Conroy's story about racism in a southern military academy. Filmed at NMMI.

Silent Tongue. Sam Shepard's 1994 ghost story of the Old West, filmed in the Roswell area. River Phoenix's last released movie.

Six Days in Roswell. A comedy-documentary about the 1997 (50th Anniversary) UFO Festival.

Over 60 movies about Billy the Kid have been filmed. Many are available on DVD.

CDs

Jack Thorp's Songs of the Cowboys, 2005 (comes with Mark Gardner's book).

Jon Shannon Webster. *Heart and Hat in Hand.* 1996. Includes "UFO Breakdown." Available from *www.texasartgallery.com* or Feral Word Music, 5212 7th Avenue South, Birmingham, AL 35212

Our Website

Please visit the Roswell section of **www.cleananpress.com** where you will find travel updates, along with more information about Roswell and . . .
  ➢ The 1947 UFO Crash
  ➢ Historical figures and events
  ➢ Rocket science—Robert Goddard to moon rocks
  ➢ Art, art, art—and artists
  ➢ Billy the Kid and other Wild West characters
  ➢ Much, much more
          from this outpost in the Land of Enchantment!

INDEX

About the Creators of This Guidebook

Lynn Michelsohn, Author

Although she has lived (enjoyably), worked (as a psychologist), and written (books including an award-winning self-help bestseller and a delightful children's travel guide) in Roswell for 28 years, she still feels like an Alien.

Larry Michelsohn, Researcher

Of course he's an Alien, he's from Brooklyn.

Moses Michelsohn, Illustrator

Actually, he's a Native, and a graduate of Goddard—not Roswell—High.

Aaron Michelsohn, Photographer

At 6' 6" with that red beard he's simply Out of This World.

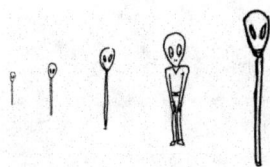